THE NEW GUIDE
Michael's

NORTHERN CALIFORNIA

THE NEW GUIDE
Michael's

NORTHERN
CALIFORNIA

Managing Editor
Michael Shichor

Series Editor
Amir Shichor

INBAL TRAVEL INFORMATION LTD.

Inbal Travel Information Ltd.
P.O.Box 1870 Ramat Gan 52117
Israel

Intl. ISBN 965-288-123-6

Text: Allan Rabinowitz
Graphic design: Michel Opatowski
Cover design: Bill Stone
Photography: Shahar Azran
            Amir Shichor, Avi Maromi, Hadas Niv, California Offic
            Tourism, EMA Samm International, The Californias
Editorial: Sharona Johan, Ofer Wasserman
D.T.P.: Irit Bahalul
Printed by Havatzelet Press Ltd.

**Sales in the UK
and Europe:**
Kuperard (London) Ltd.
9 Hampstead West
224 Iverson Road
London NW6 2HL

**Distribution in the UK
and Europe:**
Bailey Distribution Ltd.
Learoyd Road
New Romney
Kent TN28 8X

U.K. ISBN 1-85733-100-1

CONTENTS

TABLE OF MAPS

Preface

California, the "Golden State", is the legendary land of promise where anything is possible, attracting gold-hunters, nature lovers, loners and revolutionaries, radical reformers, refugees, immigrants, and a perennial stream of tourists wanting to taste the good life.

California's extraordinary beauty and mild climate are no doubt part of the attraction. California, once the edge of the Western frontier, today functions as the jumping-off point for connections extending beyond the Pacific to the Far East. California has a population of more than 30 million, most of whom live in the metropolitan centers, but this state is rich in other resources as well; it has some of the most fertile land in the U.S.A and it also has the most productive economy. The clear skies, sunny climate and wide open spaces make it an ideal location for the aerospace industry, and the "Silicon Valley" area is a leading center for high technology. Hollywood, the cradle of the film industry, still attracts thousands of actors, scriptwriters, directors and producers, and the music industry also thrives here.

For the millions of tourists that visit California every year, the big attractions are the inspiring natural wonders of the national parks, spectacular coastlines, golden beaches, haunting desert landscapes and misty cool forests, plus the excitement of Los Angeles and San Francisco, and the magic of Disneyland.

We aim to give you a deeper understanding of California, to help you plan your trip to the best and most exciting attractions, ensuring you maximum pleasure from your trip. We are sure that the effort invested in the compiling of this guide will be justified by your enhanced enjoyment.

Michael Shichor

Using this Guide

In order to reap maximum benefit from the information in this guide, we advise the traveler to carefully read the following passage. The facts contained in this book were compiled to help the tourist find his or her way around and to ensure that he enjoys his stay to the upmost.

The Introduction provides details which will help you make the early decisions and arrangements for your trip. We suggest that you carefully review the material, so that you will be more organized and set for your visit. Upon arrival in California, you will feel more familiar and comfortable with the country.

The suggested routes are arranged according to geographical areas, a system that allows for an efficient division of time and ensures a thorough knowledge of each region. More so, this guide will direct you to unexpected places that you may not have heard of and did not plan to visit.

The chapters on main cities include maps and indexes of sites that will help you find your way. On reaching each city, the guide will direct you to recommended accommodation and restaurants.

The rich collection of maps covers the tour routes and special attractions in great detail. Especially prepared for this book, they will certainly add to the efficiency and pleasure of your exploration of California.

To further facilitate the use of this guide, we have included a detailed index. It includes all the major sites mentioned throughout the book. Consult the index to find something by name and it will refer you to the place where it is mentioned in greatest detail.

Because times and cities are dynamic, an important rule of thumb when traveling, and especially when visiting a place like California, should be to consult local sources of information. Tourists are liable to encounter certain inaccuracies in this guide, and for this we apologize.

In this guide we have tried to present updated information in a way which allows for an easy, safe and economical visit. For this purpose, we have included a short questionnaire and will be most grateful for those who will take the time to complete it and send it to us.

Have a pleasant and exciting trip – Bon Voyage!

PART ONE –
A FIRST TASTE OF WHAT'S TO COME

California is a multi-faceted gem, each facet contributing to creating a strange, yet enticing and unique gleam. This is a state of great physical contrasts, but the physical extremes are mild compared to the social, cultural and political ones. It is a land where the life-style of some verges on the hedonistic, while others choose to join religious sects with strict codes of behaviour. It is a society generally tolerant of ethnic diversity, yet marred by a history of vicious racial outbursts. Here the agricultural heart of the nation is just an hour away from the nerve center of the microelectronics industry. The birthplace of the modern environmental conservation movement, California suffers from untempered greed and rampant exploitation which have been driving forces behind its growth. The land of bean sprouts and tofu, it also serves the most gimmicky, greasy fast-food stands. The cauldron of the 1960s radicalism, California also gave the nation two deeply conservative presidents, Richard Nixon and Ronald Reagan. A land that has attracted dreamers, outcasts, desperate hopefuls, fugitives, artists, rebels and ambitious achievers, California has nonetheless nurtured more than its share of swindlers and con-men; somehow they all manage to find a place in the cultural milieu of California.

History and Population

For thousands of years, Indian tribes considered every niche of California's diverse environment their territory. In 1542, Juan Rodriguez Cabrillo, a Portuguese seaman in the service of Spain, set forth to explore the completely unknown coast north of Mexico, with the goal of claiming land for Spain, motivated by the Spanish empire's desire for expansion in the New World. It really was a new world, promising endless riches, as well as vastness and mystery. Only 50 years had passed since Columbus discovered America, and less than 25 since Cortez vanquished the Aztecs in Mexico; Cabrillo himself had marched with the famed *conquistador*. Mexico brimmed with rumors of vast fortunes piled in the northern hinterland. Antonio de Mendoza, Viceroy of Mexico and Cortez' rival, had dispatched Francisco Coronado to seek the fabled Seven Cities of Cibola in the region of New Mexico, and two years later he sent out Cabrillo, a skilled navigator, determined to break through the known limits of the earth.

INTRODUCTION

Cabrillo's quest was inspired by the legend of an island kingdom whose huge warriors carried swords of gold, as well as by hopes of discovering a secret passage to the Orient.

Cabrillo set sail in June with two small ships from the Mexican port of Navidad, reaching San Diego Bay in late September. He then pushed northward along the coast, toward the island of **Santa Catalina**, observing the plains and mountains of the interior. The landmarks he passed and named (most of the names have been lost) were claimed for the King of Spain. His ships hugged the coast, trailed by Indians in canoes eager to barter.

In November, Cabrillo landed in the Channel Island archipelago, probably on **San Miguel Island**. As he rushed ashore to help some soldiers who were scuffling with Indians, he fell and broke a leg. Infection set in, and Cabrillo's condition deteriorated over the next six weeks. Amazingly, he retained command and steered his ships north through battering storms off the coast of **Big Sur**.

Cabrillo sailed northward as far as present-day **Fort Ross**; then he returned to what was probably San Miguel Island where he died and was buried, though his grave has not been found. Under the chief pilot, the expedition continued as far north as southern Oregon before finally returning south.

The expedition reached Navidad in April, 1543, ten months after its departure, bringing back a wealth of information about the bays, inlets, natives and rich potential of the northern coast; the land claimed for Spain went unchallenged for almost three hundred years. Neither a golden sword nor a passage to China were found, but the intrepid explorer did leave his imprint.

Cabrillo's exploration of the Pacific Coast opened California up to the European world, but there was little settlement by the Spanish or anyone else. The **San Francisco** area was claimed in 1579 for the Queen of England by Sir Francis Drake. Various other explorers made forays along the coast, but it was only when the Russians began moving down from Alaska and establishing hunting and trading outposts as far south as the Sonoma coast, that the Spanish began to initiate settlement.

The first settlement, established in 1769 in **San Diego**, was a joint

military-religious enterprise, with Father Junipero Serra overseeing the construction of a mission intended for the conversion of the local Indians. San Diego became the first of a chain of missions built by Serra, an effort which was continued by others after his death.

A mission was often first established with just a *presidio* (a military post), and only later did a *pueblo* – a secular civilian settlement – grow near it. For example, the San Gabriel Mission, established in 1771, provided the impetus for the construction of a small village nine miles away, called **Los Angeles**.

The missions were all built along the coast, about a day's journey apart. The paths and dirt roads connecting the missions were eventually turned into a main coastal road, called El Camino Real, still marked by road signs today.

The *padres* of these far-flung Franciscan missions immersed themselves, as well as being padres, in both physical and spiritual labor; they were pioneers and settlers, for whom everything was new, untouched and deeply beautiful.

The missions prospered. The padres tilled the fertile valleys. They planted crops such as grains, fruits and vegetables, including olives, figs and grapes from Spain and Mexico. They raised large herds of livestock grazed on the virgin grasslands. In some missions the padres built extensive sophisticated irrigation systems. The tracts under Franciscan ownership and tillage were immense. By the time the last mission was completed in 1823, one sixth of the total land in California was under the control of the missions.

But much of this progress was on at the expense of the local Indians. Many Indians were drawn to the missions, which represented a new way of life, while others were pressed into service against their will. There were many forced conversions, which led to rebellion and consequent repression and punishment. The urge to hasten the Indians' acceptance of Christ was particularly strong if the natives happened to dwell upon a fertile stretch of land; in one case, about 2,000 Chumash Indians were removed en masse from Santa Cruz Island to the Santa Barbara mission.

Written testimony from the early 19th century details regular whippings of Indians in some missions. Even the much-praised Father Serra was reprimanded by the Spanish governor for exerting excessively heavy punishments. The changing of age-old life-styles, sexual molestation by local soldiers, and exposure to the white man's epidemics, brought the Indian population in those areas, in the years of the Spanish control, down from about 130 thousand to 83 thousand, with a much higher death rate among the mission Indians.

The 1820s witnessed a subsequent rebellion that was anti-clerical as well as anti-Spanish. Having won independence in 1821, Mexico wrested the missions from Franciscan control. The missions, secularized and divested of their vast tracts of land, went into decline, and some into deep decay. Various parties found ways to claim title to land parcels. Later, some of the missions were restored to the Franciscans.

The legacy of the missions in Mexico and America is legendary. They were the first to take advan-

Old books on display at Mission San Luis Rey

tage of California's tremendous agricultural potential. They bequeathed a style of architecture harmonious with the landscape, and bestowed their names on today's major cities. The local Indians were taught skills for life in the new world that was fast approaching.

When Mexico won independence from Spain in 1821 and the missions were secularized, efforts were redoubled to settle California with Spanish/Mexicans, though even then, the "*Californios*" felt different from the regime to the south. There were several attempts by the Spanish/Mexican settlers to split off from the newly independent nation. Meanwhile, an increasing number of American settlers and sailors were moving into California. By the mid-1840s there was a call in the east for the annexation of California, as part of the American "Manifest Destiny" which pushed for the establishment of a republic from coast to coast. In 1846, a group of American settlers seized control of **Sonoma** and declared the independence of "The Bear Flag Republic", only to relinquish control of it to the American government which seized California (1848) after declaring war on Mexico. That same year, gold was discovered in California in the Sierra foothills of **Sutter's Mill**. Within a few years, the population

escalated by about 1,000%. California became a magnet for American settlers who dreamed of striking it rich.

Gold-hungry Americans used the local Indian population to work the mines, and the Indians were enormously abused. California historian Josian Royce describes how some miners used Indian villages as "targets for rifle-practice, or to destroy wholesale with fire, outrage and murder, as if they had been so many wasps' nests in our gardens at home". The 100,000 Indians in California in 1846 were reduced to 31,000 by 1852. Those left were humiliated, uprooted and exposed to epidemic diseases and alcohol. A treaty signed in 1850 left over 7 million acres to the Indians of California, but this was subsequently whittled down to a pitiful 500,000 acres. It was only in 1963 that the Indians of California were awarded $27 million by the federal government as long overdue compensation for the lands they lost.

Following the Civil War (1861-65), the national economy and industry boomed, and in 1869 California was linked to the east by the first trans-continental railroad.

California's history has been a series of booms and depressions; of land sales, land grabs and land frauds; of the discovery of new resources and the sudden influx of people to exploit them. The discovery of oil in **Los Angeles** and **Long Beach** at the end of the 19th century created an economic boom in Los Angeles.

With the evolution of the movie industry in Hollywood, a new kind of wealth emerged in California, evidenced by the large number of self-made millionaires who suddenly sprouted. The glamour surrounding movie stars was created, and in its wake thousands of hopefuls flocked to Los Angeles seeking glory in celluloid; instead of glory they found jobs as cooks, waitresses and cops.

During the Great Depression, more hordes crossed the continent into California's valleys, seeking not fame and fortune but work, bread or a little land. An ideological clash between radicalism and conservative, land-holding interests developed with this influx of "Oakies". Labor protests burst forth everywhere and were violently supressed.

In the 1940s, during World War II, fear of the Japanese replaced fear of the "Reds". In anticipation of the Japanese invasion that never came, thousands of American citizens of Japanese descent were interned in isolated camps, and much of their property was confiscated or looted.

In the post-war prosperity of the 1950s, the pull of California became even stronger. The aeronautics industry attracted thousands of workers to become the state's industrial and technological mainstay, which it remained until the recent surge in microelectronics took hold in the **Silicon Valley** (at **San Jose**) and revolutionized technology. The steady stream of immigrants to California made it into the country's most populous state, surpassing N.Y. in 1964.

Many people, including foreign immigrants, are attracted to the "sunbelt" of the west and southwest. California has always attracted a variety of ethnic groups with its multitudinous economic opportunities. Today's immigrants do not come from European countries, but from the Pacific areas and Latin America.

From the moment of statehood California has been in flux. For over a hundred years, the population has doubled every twenty years. Although that rate has slowed slightly, the change in the ethnic fabric of the state has accelerated. In the last 20 years, the percentage of Hispanics has almost doubled and the percentage of Asians has almost tripled, while the percentage of the Caucasian population has dropped considerably. Immigration is one of the key issues of California's future just as, in a sense, it has been for over 150 years. The number of children growing up speaking a mother tongue other than English is rapidly growing, yet English has been voted as the single official language of the state.

Meanwhile California's breakneck development and technological advancement continues, causing its population to swell, taking over rich farmland and exploiting natural resources. The population today exceeds 30 million, and whatever the future holds, there is no doubt that California will face it in its typically dynamic, experimental and completely individual way.

Mission Bay Park, San Diego

Geography

The coast of California is about 900 miles (1440 km) long, from **Crescent City** at the Oregon border to **San Diego** at the Mexican border. Endless acres of tall pines and redwoods cover the northern end of the coastal area. The coast itself is rocky and studded with cliffs; just beyond the beach the coastal mountain ranges rise.

The mountain ranges stretch east, reaching towering Mt. Shasta at the southern tip of the Cascade Mountains. In the northeastern corner of the state, the terrain turns into a strange, weathered and pockmarked world of ancient lava. South of the Cascades, which span the width of California, the topographical features run in a north-south direction, parallel to the coast.

Along the northern border, down past the Golden Gate and **San Francisco**, past **Monterey Bay** to the cliffs of **Big Sur**, the coast is stark, and the weather is foggy due to cold currents. Further south, near **Santa Barbara**, the ocean currents become warm, the weather gentler and the sand on the beaches softer.

Towards the Los Angeles basin, surrounded by mountains, the land becomes drier and scrubbier. South of this point, the climate is governed by a hot, constant, semi-tropical sun.

A range of hills runs south along the coast, almost all the way down to Mexico. They also extend towards the east and into the rich San Joaquin Valley, a 400-mile (640 km) long fertile furrow running through the heart of the state. The valley stretches from the foot of the Cascades in the north, past **Sacramento** to **Bakersfield**, stopping before the thin barrier of the Tehachapi mountain range that separates the valley from Los Angeles. Parallel to this great valley is the long granite massif of the **Sierra Nevada** in the eastern part of the state, with mountain slopes that rise gently from the west, in round compact hills where the discovery of gold launched the mad rush of the 1850s. Higher up on the slopes of these hills grow sequoia trees, the largest living things on earth.

Yosemite National Park, Lake Tahoe, and Kings Canyon/Sequoia National Parks are the main sights

Wind is well exploited in California

of the Sierras. The cliffs, domes and cascades of the Yosemite Valley and other canyons were carved out by numerous westward-flowing rivers and ancient glaciers. Through the whole range runs a majestic spine of craggy snow-covered peaks.

The eastern slope of the Sierras drops like a sheer granite wall, into a high semi arid plateau. This is the Great Basin, characterized by isolated mountain peaks, alkaline flats and ancient bristlecone pines 4,000 years old.

At the edge of the Basin, begins the desert, the state's largest geographical entity. East of the Sierras, it extends south towards Mexico and stretches across the border. In the east, it extends to the Colorado River, into Nevada and Arizona, and in the west towards Los Angeles.

Climate

The climate in California varies greatly according to the region. In the south, the summers are hot and dry and the sun shines most of the year. The rains usually come in winter, though interspersed with sunshine. Near the beaches especially, summer may be tempered by refreshing breezes, but in the L.A. metropolitan area it can also bring on smog alerts, when the sky becomes hazy not from fog but from the brown clouds of pollution; venturing forth in such conditions can actually be hazardous. Winter temperatures of 40°F (4.5°C) are considered cold enough here to wear minks and down jackets.

The deserts can be comfortable during most of the year but broiling in the summer. The dry heat of summer, however, is more bearable than humidity in other places. Desert summer nights are warm and comfortable, but temperatures can sometimes drop sharply at sunset. An occasional summer rain in the desert is a welcome relief. The clouds swirl and gleam, and the rain churns up delicious fresh smells from the desert floor. In winter the desert can be quite windy and cold.

Seasons in the California mountains are more sharply demarcated than along the coast. Summers can be hot, punctuated by rains, and summer evenings can turn breezy and cool. In the immense areas of conifers, autumn can barely be distinguished, but in some areas where deciduous trees follow the course of stream, the autumnal mountains are etched with rivers of blazing gold.

The first snows can fall as early as late September, and they fall not only in soft white flutterings but in full-fledged blizzards. Snow can pile up to 20 feet (7 m) or more, lasting well into spring. In the mountains in late spring streams become turbulent and swollen with melted snow.

In the San Joaquin Valley, the summer heat is humid, and extremely unpleasant.

Northern California, along the coast, is characterised by wet winters, often with very heavy rainfall. Nevertheless, there are plenty of fresh blue-skied winter days as well. The summers can be cool, foggy and overcast, but generally not for long. Inland, the winters are a bit drier.

California Literature

California, as a physical reality and state of mind, has attracted both American and foreign writers since before the Gold Rush days. A number of books will give you a feel for the unique texture of California.

Raymond Chandler's mysteries: Corruption and murder in a young Los Angeles, as seen through the eyes of private eye Philip Marlowe.

Richard Henry Dana, *Two Years Before the Mast*: A vivid and detailed travelogue in the 19th-century tradition. He describes with tremendous accuracy the coast of what was then a new and wide-open world.

Joan Didion, *Slouching Towards Bethlehem*: Well-known essays on the life and manners of modern California.

Allen Ginsberg, *Howl*: Ginsberg's

The desert – California's largest geographical entity

unleashing of this powerful poem became a literary turning point in San Francisco. Together with Jack Kerouac, he helped create a new literary movement.

Dashiell Hammett's mysteries: The San Francisco bars frequented by the hardened detective Sam Spade still hold their own today. Hammett's tough laconic style greatly influenced many other mystery writers, particularly Raymond Chandler.

Bret Hart, *The Outcast of Poker Flat*: An American story writer and journalist, Hart was the first to depict life in the gold-mining days.

Robinson Jeffers' poetry: Jeffers spent many years on the Big Sur coast, and uses the cliffs and waves as powerful metaphors.

Jack Kerouac, *On the Road*: This, the most sincere of Kerouac's writing, preached a "spontaneous" way of life. This work helped launch the beatnik generation.

Henry Miller, *Big Sur and the Oranges of Hieronymous Bosch*: After exploring the alleys and brothels of Paris, Miller stumbled into the wild coast where he found a sense of peace and a focus for his prose.

John Muir, various writings: Elegant descriptions of nature and the wilderness.

John Steinbeck, *The Grapes of Wrath, Of Mice and Men, East of Eden, Cannery Row, Tortilla Flat, In Dubious Battle*: *The Grapes of Wrath* is Steinbeck's masterpiece about the odyssey of a migrant family to the farmlands of California. Virtually all of his best writing concerns California. No one writes of the state and its less fortunate

characters with more wisdom, warmth and compassion.

Mark Twain, *Roughing It*: A hilarious, shrewdly observant portrait of the frontier and the Gold Rush.

Evelyn Waugh, *The Loved One*: A biting satire on the American funeral industry, based on a gaudy and pretentious Los Angeles cemetery.

Pop Architecture

Weird and wonderful architectural forms are as much a part of California's heritage as the rambling Victorian buildings and stucco cottages with red tile roofs. Giant donuts, ice cream cones, owls and hearts, big hats and tractors, towering cowboys, lumberjacks and dinosaurs decorate the California landscape.

Imaginative architecture, which served as advertising, sprang up in the 1920s, with the advent of the automobile, a growing highway system and a newly-mobile middle class. Even during the Depression years, such building continued. It became the expression of hundreds of small private dreams and fantasies.

INTRODUCTION

California seemed a fertile place for such imaginative advertising. Space was wide open, land was available, and the state was already becoming based on the automobile. There was relatively little existing architectural tradition, and the commercial and imaginative climate was right for a bit of profitable whimsy. Any commercial gimmick that might turn a buck had a chance in California. You might say that scattered along the highways of southern California were the precursors of Disneyland. Igloos and castles, southern manors and quaint thatched-roof villages became landmarks. The *Tail o' the Pup*, on the 300 block of La Cienega in Los Angeles, was clever play on the word "hot dog". An L. A. institution, it has appeared in many movies including the relatively recent *Ruthless People*. In Castroville, during a public-relations effort to get the local artichokes on the map, a 16-foot (5 m) artichoke, complete with spikes, was planted in the ground.

The king of pop art architecture in California is surely *Dinny the Dinosaur*, at the Cabazon exit off I-10 on the way to Palm Springs. It is the creation of Claude Bell, who was inspired as a boy by a giant elephant-shaped hotel in the New Jersey resort of Margate. He designed many sculptures and buildings for fairs and parks.

When he moved to California and bought a desert plot on which he opened a restaurant, Bell's dream evolved in the shape of a brontosaurus three times the size of a real one. Dinny was a labor of love that took ten years to build. His belly houses a museum and small apartment, reached by a stairway through the tail. It surpasses other roadside models not only in size but through the graceful proportions and meticulous detail, down to the wrinkles and lumps in his hide. Bell was still busy working on his primeval pets into his nineties, having added a tyrannosaurus (with a viewing platform on its head and a slide down its back) to keep Dinny company. The two prehistoric reptiles are clearly visible from the highway and look poised to gobble up the trucks lined up outside the restaurant.

Dinny the Dinosaur, a representative of pop art architecture in California

PART TWO – SETTING OUT

Getting There

By air: The two major airports in California are **Los Angeles International Airport (LAX)** and the **San Francisco Airport (SFO)**. Both airports are served by major international and domestic airlines. San Diego airport also serves an increasing amount of national and international air traffic. Special deals offered by airlines are worth investigating.

By land: Main train routes to California run from Seattle to San Francisco, Chicago to San Francisco and Chicago to Los Angeles. The major bus company is *Greyhound*, which has special offers and varied travel options. The best way of getting around California is probably by car.

Documents and Customs Regulations

VISAS
Foreign visitors must enter the United States with a valid passport and visa. Most B-2 tourist visas are valid for 6 months. A lost visa can be replaced through the embassy of the visitor's country. To apply for a visa extension, or to replace the arrival/departure form received on arrival, a foreign citizen must go to the nearest U.S. Immigration and Naturalization Service office.

If you have any problems, it is advisable to contact the nearest consulate of your country. Many countries have consular offices in Los Angeles and/or San Francisco.

A foreign visitor may bring in $400 worth of gifts into the U.S. duty-free for personal use only (be sure to keep receipts), up to 200 cigarettes, and a liter of alcohol. Some fruits and vegetables are not permitted in the United States. There is no limit on foreign currency. Prescription drugs should be clearly labeled, accompanied by a copy of the doctor's prescription.

INTERNATIONAL DRIVER'S LICENSE
A driver's license valid for the U.S. should be obtained in the country of origin. It will not be issued in the U.S.

Crossing the border – from Mexico to the U.S.

STUDENT CARDS
Students with proper identification can often receive considerable discount on transportation, hotel rates and admission prices. Proper identification includes either a valid university i.d. card, or an **International Student Identity Card (ISIC)**. The latter can be obtained with proof of full-time student status. This could be a university identification card, a stamped letter from the registrar, a current grade report, etc. Students enrolled for the previous fall semester are eligible for the card.

The Council of International Educational Exchange (CIEE) sponsors a special discount plan which, for a small sum, entitles the holder to a 25% savings on room rates at various lodgings as well as advice on travel. To use these services, an ISIC is required, obtainable from the CIEE.

INSURANCE
Medical Insurance is essential, even though most major centers do have crisis centers or public clinics that will offer immediate care to the uninsured. University hospitals often do the same. In case of emergency, call the local emergency number or the crisis center mentioned in this book.

The insuring of valuable objects, such as cameras, is obviously a personal choice. In the big cities especially, professional thieves abound and are very smooth. This is not meant to frighten you, but it is best to be realistic. A moment's carelessness and a camera can disappear.

Safety Precautions
It is best to avoid bus terminals and train stations late at night, and do not walk in deserted downtown neighborhoods at night. Avoid public restrooms in the cities.

It is advisable to keep some money separate from your wallet and to keep a list of traveler's checks separate as well. Make a note of important numbers – driver's license, credit card, passport – in case your wallet is stolen, and keep it somewhere safe.

Many travelers choose to carry money and important documents in a money belt that fits around the waist inside the shirt or hangs around the neck. Some carry a "decoy" wallet in a pocket, to draw attention away from the money belt. All this is a matter of personal choice. The most important thing is to take the precautions necessary for your own peace of mind and maximum enjoyment.

When to Come

California is a vacationland for all seasons. During every season of the year, there is at least one part of the state where the weather is just perfect.

Most people flock to California in the summer, and prices tend to rise accordingly in most tourist areas. The exception to this is the desert

resort of Palm Springs where prices actually go down in summer due to the intense heat. Winters in southern California are delightfully sunny and warm; summers in northern California are refreshingly cool. In the Sierra Nevada and the other mountain ranges, each season has its own beauty and activities. Some mountain passes are closed in winter, but the mountain ski resorts are popular.

Planning a time for your visit may be not so much a matter of weather but rather of crowds. There is no doubt that most tourist facilities are far more crowded in summer, with a commensurate rise in prices. If possible, try to avoid traveling on the following days:

Memorial Day weekend, around May 31st.
Independence Day weekend, around July 4th.
Labor Day weekend, at the beginning of September.

From Memorial Day onwards, there is a great increase in the number of vacationers on the roads, with a sharp decline following Labor Day. In fact, in terms of numbers, prices, and the accessibility of facilities, early fall is an ideal time to travel; children are back at school and students are back at college.

The weeks surrounding Christmas and New Year's Day are also crowded with visitors. However, the rest of the winter is considered off-season, except at ski resorts.

American public holidays include:

New Year's Day, January 1st.
Presidents' Day, the third Monday in February.
Memorial Day, the last Monday in May.

Independence Day, July 4th (businesses close on the nearest Monday or Friday).
Labor Day, first Monday in September.
Columbus Day, second Monday in October.
Veteran's Day, November 11th.
Thanksgiving, last Thursday in November.
Christmas, December 25th.

What to Wear

Dress in California tends to be casual. For southern California, be sure to pack a heavy sweater and light waterproof coat for the winter. You will need these in summer in northern California.

Ties are usually worn by businessmen, but this is not as strictly enforced as in the east. Colors for both men's and women's fashions are brighter in California than in some other regions, and are also brighter in the south than in the north. Californian casual dress has become a style in its own right, blending a bright, tailored tapered look with comfort. A good pair of walking shoes are appropriate in a variety of situations. For women, slacks are acceptable for most occasions, and are worn by many. There always seems to be a sale at one or another of the numerous clothing stores, so it is easy to pick up anything you need.

California is also the place for down-to-earth second-hand funk. "Contemporary Salvation Army" has become so popular that charity and second-hand stores raised their prices.

If planning to enjoy California's natural wonders, be sure to include

Catching some sun

durable clothes and sturdy shoes. In southern California especially, a hat, preferably broad-brimmed, is advisable during the summer. Sandals are increasingly accepted as everyday summer footwear. Birkenstocks, though more expensive than other brands, are sturdy, long-lasting, comfortable and popular. For hiking shoes, the new models made of light water resistant material, have gained in popularity. These are suitable for California's diverse terrains.

How Much will It Cost

The amount of money a visitor spends is, of course, very subjective, depending on the individual's needs, tastes and style. The point to remember is that there is enough variety in resources and alternatives in California, more than other places, to enable most people to relax and enjoy themselves within their means.

The main expense, besides transportation to California, is naturally accommodation. The prices of average lodging has sky-rocketed in recent years. For a standard basic motel room, expect to pay a minimum of $40 per day. Most cost considerably more. For an average motel room or a room in a B&B a visitor could easily pay $90-$110 per day. Of course there are plenty of better hotels that charge up to $250 per day; spending more is never a problem.

Nevertheless, a person on a strict budget can definitely find cheap, relatively comfortable accommodation; hostels, for example, though not the last word in luxury or privacy, rarely cost more than $15 per day, and provide a unique traveling experience. YMCAs offer another inexpensive solution. Private and public campgrounds for those traveling by car or camper are numerous, ranging between $8-$20 per night, depending on the location, facilities, etc.

Transportation costs can also vary greatly. Car rental can range from $30-$90 per day; insurance is added on a daily basis (see "Car Rental"). Transportation between major cities is by private bus companies. Bus fares vary, depending on route, distance and operating company, and local bus rides may cost between $1 to $3. Usually discounts for seniors and the disabled are available.

Those preferring to work on a fixed budget for transportation may want to base costs on monthly car rentals ($500 and up, plus insurance), or monthly bus or train passes. These can be combined with local public transportation, daily car or bicycle rental (see "Transportation").

As for **food**, there is a wide range of budget possibilities, especially in the two major urban areas where the choice and variety is enormous. Cheapest of all is to buy food in grocery stores, delis and at fast-food stands, but a good filling meal in certain restaurants can be had for as little as $6-$10. Many places, especially simple Chinese restaurants, offer cheap lunch specials. Mexican restaurants cost slightly more. Salad bars start at about $7 and up.

Steak or fish meals in good restaurants start at about $20, but the same meal served earlier in the day as an "Early Bird Special" will cost about $14. Though there is almost no upper limit in restaurant prices, the lower limit, even the most inexpensive special will cost at least $10, including beverage and tip.

California, especially southern California, is a shopper's and bargain-seeker's paradise. Discount houses proliferate and large drug-store chains sell merchandise at cut-rate prices.

Entertainment – night clubs, concerts and shows – can be expensive. Many clubs demand a cover charge and a one or two-drink minimum. First run movies cost about $7-$9. Attractions such as amusement parks are especially expensive. Admission for some of these private tourist attractions is over $25 per person, with a parking fee for cars slapped on top.

On the other hand, some of the top museums in the country are found in California and are open to the public at nominal prices. Many museums set aside special hours or days when admission is free.

Los Angeles' modern architecture

PART THREE – EASING THE SHOCK: WHERE HAVE WE LANDED?

Transportation

Airports

The two major airports in California are the **Los Angeles (LAX)** and the **San Francisco (SFO)** airports. LAX is one of the busiest in the world. All major domestic and just about all major international and foreign lines serve the two airports. There is also an extremely busy commuter lane between SFO and LAX, in addition to numerous flights taking off to and from smaller airports within the same corridor.

The **San Diego** airport (SAN) also services flights along the coast and handles an increasing amount of national and international traffic.

There are several airlines that operate mainly in the West, and others that operate solely within California. It is possible to fly all around the state with small airlines such as Pacific Coast or Sky West, as well as on larger regional airlines such as Western. A number of smaller metropolitan airports handle major national carriers, not only reducing the strain on the major airports, but allowing the visitor greater flexibility. During high-season or on busy holiday weekends, it might be wise to avoid major airports such as LAX and to rather land in a less frequented local airport. The possibilities for direct air connections to the outlying areas of California are often greater than visitors realize.

The following airports handle national airlines:

Arcata/Eureka: Tel.707-839-5401.
Bakersfield (Meadows Field): Tel. 805-393-7990.
Burbank-Glendale-Pasadena: Tel. 818-840-8847.
Fresno: Tel. 209-251-7554.

Los Angeles International Airport, one of the world's busiest airports

Long Beach: Tel. 310-421-8295.
Los Angeles: Tel. 310-646-5252
  (also for international flights).
Monterey Peninsula: Tel.
  408-373-3731.
Oakland: Tel. 415-577-4000
  (also international flights).
Ontario: Tel. 909-988-2700
  (also international flights).
Palm Springs: Tel. 619-323-8163.
Reno: Tel. 702-785-2575.
Sacramento: Tel. 916-929-5411.
San Francisco: Tel. 415-761-0800
  (also international flights).
San Diego: Tel. 619-231-5220
  (also international flights).
San Jose: Tel. 408-277-5366.
Santa Barbara: Tel. 805-967-7111
  or 805-967-7111.

Since the deregulation of the airline industry a few years ago, the air traveler has benefitted from the new companies that spring up and the growing competition. If you shop around and are a bit flexible with your flying schedule, you can find some amazing deals (especially compared with what passengers paid some years back). Of course this is subject to change; the airline industry, at least in America, is in great flux, but right now it is a flier's market.

When booking a flight, do not settle for the first price you get from either an airline or a travel agent. Try other airlines and other agents, until you have a good idea of the price range.

It is up to you to ask the pertinent questions and sometimes you must ferret out the details: they are not always volunteered. Are there student fares? Stand-by fares? Midnight fares? Does a round-trip bought in advance cost less? Would the price be lower during another season? With some special flight bargains, however, the deal comes with restrictions which airline officials will make clear to you.

If you have purchased a round-trip ticket to the United States abroad (some companies may require foreign residency), you should look into purchasing a **VUSA** (Visit USA) ticket. This allows you to fly literally all over the United States for one set price which is usually less than one standard cross-country flight. There are several similar types of VUSA tickets, which, for a set price, allow unlimited number of flights with the airline issuing the ticket, to be used within a specific time limit. The only restriction is that you cannot leave from or enter the same terminal more than twice.

Even if you plan to stay in one region, such as California or the West Coast, a VUSA might still be worthwhile, as it may cost the same as one standard flight from the East Coast. Furthermore, some regional airlines have arrangements which honor the VUSA ticket of certain major airlines. If, for example, you buy a VUSA from Northwest Airlines, you can use it on Western all through California and the West with no extra charge. Check this out, because the arrangements may change periodically.

Many airlines have introduced, to

the travelers' delight, a variety of **Frequent-Flyers** programs, in which the miles you fly can be used as credit toward free future flights; business persons who travel frequently clock up enormous amounts of free mileage. Check these schemes carefully, as some companies give you points only according to the number of flights, regardless of the mileage of each flight.

Keep in mind also the new, unofficial "bumping game" that has been adopted by the airlines, which now make a practice of overbooking certain, generally crowded, flights, to compensate for the number of people who make reservations and who do not turn up. If most or all passengers show up, however, the airlines have more people than seats. Thanks to the efforts of consumer advocate Ralph Nader (after he himself was ignominiously "bumped" from an overbooked plane), government regulations require that passengers bumped involuntarily must be given cash payments, sometimes double the cost of the ticket; and they can still sue.

Financially ailing airlines, to avoid having to fork out cash, have come up with another solution. They ask for volunteers to give up their seat, and offer free tickets to various destinations in addition to a guaranteed seat on the next flight. This has become so commonplace that people make a sport of it. They've learned the angles and purposely book themselves on busy flights, their hands ready to shoot up the moment volunteers are requested. In other words, if your schedule is flexible, the wrong flight may turn into the right flight, resulting in a voucher for a free trip somewhere else.

Trains

Train travel is a throwback to a bygone era. The conductor rattles off the names of exotic-sounding frontier towns; the train pulls into an elegant Spanish-style station, or past a small smudged brick depot bordered by decrepit hotels and bars; people chat casually in the lounge car while the countryside glides by at eye-level. The traveling becomes as rich an experience as arriving in a new place.

Amtrak, the national passenger rail carrier, made a big push recently to encourage train travel by introducing extended routes, lower rates, package-tour deals, streamlined equipment and so forth. All this is geared to fill their trains, which were, for a while, pitifully empty.

The main train routes leading into California include:

Seattle to San Francisco (*The Coast Starlight*).
Chicago to San Francisco (*The California Zephyr*).
Chicago to Los Angeles, either directly through San Antonio, or through New Orleans (*The Desert Wind*).

An intricate system of buses and local commuter trains connects with *Amtrak* rail lines, greatly extending access by rail.

There are several main train routes within the state. The *Coast Starlight* takes ten-and-a-half hours between Los Angeles and San Francisco. This route affords a slow but pleasant way to travel between the major cities without the hassle of driving. Although it does not follow the rugged Big Sur Coast, the train passes some gorgeous shoreline.

In the San Francisco area, the actual departure station is in industrial Oakland. A special *Amtrak* bus connects to the San Francisco station, the Trans-Bay terminal, at 1st and Mission.

The California section of the **Zephyr** follows the route of the early transcontinental railroad, with access to the Truckee-Lake Tahoe area, as well as to Reno just across the Sierra Nevada.

The San Joaquin route runs through the main cities of the Central Valley. From Bakersfield in the south, a special *Amtrak* bus brings passengers to the *Amtrak* station in the Los Angeles area. In the north, the train connects with the main east-west line and with the train going north to Seattle. At various points along this route, there are connections with local and regional bus lines. At the **Merced** station, a private bus runs to Yosemite Park.

In California, the *Amtrak* network includes the following lines:

The Capitols – 4 daily trains link San Jose, Oakland and Sacramento/Roseville.

The San Joaquins – 3 daily trains link Bakersfield and Oakland.

The San Diegans – 9 daily trains link San Diego, Los Angeles and 2 run to Santa Barbara.

Amtrak has a special scheme whereby for any regular ticket purchase of a certain sum or more, the return fare is significantly smaller. You need to return by the same route, and there are no stopovers. The special fare is good for 45 days after the original trip. There are certain peak traveling seasons when the ticket is not valid, so check this out carefully. The company also has special fares for traveling within or between various regions of the country. As with the airlines, *Amtrak's* offers change quite often, so it is important to call for updated information.

The San Diego Trolley

Amtrak also offers total travel packages with hotels, tours, etc. There are such tours for Hearst Castle, the wine country, San Francisco and Disneyland. Trains have sleeping accommodation, ranging from a pillow for the seat to separate bedrooms, complete with bathroom. Some trains – or specific types of cars – require reservations, while others do not. If you buy your ticket on the train, when the station booth is open, you will be required to pay an additional sum. It is possible to bring bicycles aboard certain trains, without dismantling the bikes. For general *Amtrak* information and reservations call: Tel. 800-USA-RAIL. This number will provide you with local *Amtrak* numbers, if needed.

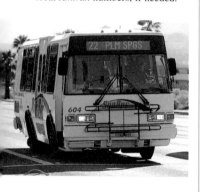

Buses

The major private bus company is *Greyhound*. The company offers special excursion fares, summer-travel fares and so forth. As with *Amtrak*, these rates and schedules change often, so it is always worth double-checking. *Greyhound* with its *Ameripass* offers unlimited travel for a fixed price, within a fixed number of days. Although most buses are stream-lined and comfortable, there is a limit to how long you can remain seated. Compare prices with *Amtrak*. Surprisingly, in some cases the train's

bargain pass may actually be cheaper. The bus company offers a 15-day one-way fare for traveling in one direction for up to 15 days – a cheap way to reach California. For information call Tel. 800-321-2222.

Children between 12-16 travel by bus for half-fare, and children aged 11 and under ride free. Seniors receive a 10% discount except on special fares. Bicycles can be stowed in the baggage compartment, making it possible to combine an itinerary of bus rides and bike rides.

Bus stations almost always seem to be located in the worst part of town. If possible, avoid arriving late at night or having to wait around a dingy and depressing bus station in the wee hours of the night.

Green Tortoise buses offer alternative tours which are adventurous (slightly), eccentric and cheap. The company once had a reputation as the "freak" bus line, but now it attracts a wide variety of people, from hippies to foreigners to professionals and spunky seniors seeking an unusual travel experience. The buses have bunks (bring your own sleeping bag or bedding), and two drivers to enable nighttime traveling and daytime excursions and diversions. For the lone traveler with a budget one notch above hitching, *Green Tortoise* provides a chance to meet similar travelers, make contacts, pick up traveling tips and enjoy the company of others.

Green Tortoise main office: P.O.Box 24459, San Francisco, 94124. Tel. 415-956-7500, with offices on the East Coast and along the West Coast, and a toll-free number; Tel. 800-TORTOISE.

Car Rental

Renting a car can be the most convenient, though most expensive, means of travel in California. It is worth checking with several rental agencies because rates and conditions vary widely. Daily rental rates could cost between $30-$90, and monthly rates between $450-$550. The larger agencies – *Hertz, Avis* and *National* – have desks at airports and major tourist centers, but do not necessarily offer the best deals; the small agencies sometimes boast the best prices. Most major cities in California have the equivalent of "rent-a-wreck" car rentals, supplying just what the name applies, at commensurate prices, along with a certain distance limitation.

The average mileage included in car rentals – 3,000 miles (4,800 km) a month – may seem sufficient, but this breaks down to just over one hundred miles per day, which, if you are a hard-pushing traveler, is not really very much. Los Angeles commuters easily cover that distance daily.

The real drawback to renting a car can be the insurance, which may cost $6-$12 per day. Some agencies might advise you to attach yourself to the insurance of a relative, but be very wary of this as it is legally a bit shaky. When inquiring about the insurance, find out exactly what is covered. Agents have been known to quote insurance prices, only to subsequently reveal that the coverage is only "partial", and pressing you to take on "extra" protection ("Perhaps you'd like your left tires covered as well?").

The larger agencies sometimes offer special weekend rates. These can start as early as Thursday, with a package deal for rental through Sunday.

Having access to a car makes all the difference in the world, especially in southern Califonia. For both the business traveler on a strict schedule, and the tourist, it may be best to fly between destinations and rent cars locally. California's excellent in-state and inter-region air connections allows this to be done with flexibility and ease.

A **drive-away** company offers a slightly uncertain but inexpensive way to travel, both to California and within the state. These companies find drivers to transport cars from one destination to another. It is usually easy to find cars being transported from coast to coast. Sometimes you may need to be a bit flexible and accept a car to Bakersfield even if you want to end up in Los Angeles. You may need to leave a credit card print. Occasionally a cash deposit will be sufficient. The time and mileage allowed is limited, but it is sometimes possible to squeeze in a short excursion to a nearby site. Such transport is available within the state of California as well, but cars between Los Angeles and San Francisco are not easily found and are snapped up quickly. Major cities in the country have such offices. Check in the phonebook under *car transport*, *auto transport* or *drive-away*.

Roads

California has an excellent road system. Interstate and in-state freeways criss-cross the state. What they provide in directness, speed and convenience, however, is made up for in monotony. Nothing can be more dangerously mesmerizing to a night driver than an endlessly flat straight road with one white stripe after another zooming past you. Taking a backroad, on occasion,

use the same caution as you would at a stop sign. At a marked cross-walk, drivers must yield to pedestrians. This may sometimes be annoying, but as a pedestrian you will appreciate the regulation.

The maximum speed limit on highways and freeways is 55 miles per hour (90 kph). In residential areas the speed limit is 25 mph (40 kph). On main thoroughfares the speed limit may vary.

California has one of the strictest drunk-driving laws in the country, requiring the immediate arrest of anyone found to be driving under the influence of alcohol.

that passes through tiny towns will enrich your visit.

Rest stops are interspersed along the interstate highways. These usually include rest rooms, drinking water, a patch of green, some picnic tables, and perhaps a map and additional information about the area. It is perfectly okay to park here overnight and sleep in the car, and it's usually safe, especially if several large trailer trucks are parked nearby. People even sometimes flop their sleeping bags down on the grass. They are usually not disturbed, but officially this is not permitted. For information on road conditions within California call: Tel. 800-427-7623.

Auto Clubs

The *American Automobile Association* is the best known of the auto clubs. Membership fees vary from state to state. Services include trip planning, maps, travelers' checks (American Express) and, especially important, 24-hour emergency road service anywhere. Also worthwhile is the club's auto insurance.

In northern California, the AAA is listed as the California State Automobile Association. In southern California it is listed as the Automobile Club of Southern California (ACSC); Tel. 800-765-4222.

Some Driving Tips

In both San Francisco and Los Angeles, parking can be a problem. Parking is not allowed alongside red or white curbs; green curbs mean limited-time parking only and even at unpainted curbs parking may not be allowed during rush hours, street-cleaning hours, etc.

Right turns are allowed at red lights, unless otherwise indicated;

Accidents

Call the police immediately in the event of an accident. On municipal streets, call the local police. On freeways, even within cities, and on highways and roads between cities, call the California Highway Patrol (CHP) or dial 911. On city freeways, the phones in the emergency callboxes link automatically to a CHP office. Otherwise, ask the operator for Zenith 1-2000, the CHP emergency number.

Rides and Hitchhiking

To find a fellow traveller to share expenses and provide company, or to find a ride, check the nearest college or university. Most such centers have some sort of "ride board". Alternative radio stations and newspapers also provide a service like this.

Hitchhiking has declined a bit in California. There have been a few gruesome incidents, with both drivers and passengers as the victims, though obviously, the vast majority of hitchhikers and drivers are perfectly safe.

Whether you are the driver or the rider, ask a few questions first, while trying to size up the person the best you can. In the region of a national park, a hitchhiker with a backpack standing in the middle of nowhere has probably just emerged from a trail and is trying to reach the nearest bank, shower and burger stand.

Sometimes, though not always, approaching a driver near a restaurant or gas station is likely to elicit a positive response.

Backpacking

For the backpacker California offers a whole world to explore. Information about backpacking is easily obtainable, and trails in parks around the state are well-maintained.

Army-Navy surplus stores, often found in the downtown sections of larger cities, can supply many of the smaller items. Today, camping has become a gigantic business, and new and improved equipment is produced annually. Everything but a jet-propelled backpack is on the market.

The *Sierra Club* is an excellent source of information about camping in California. The club, a national conservation organization, originated in California. In addition to organizing hiking trips for members, the various branches will be able to provide printed guides and maps on specific regions in the state.

Accommodation

The range of accommodation in California is almost unlimited. Luxurious hotels styled after old Roman villas, quaint beach lodges perched above the beach, sleazy downtown rattraps, sterile stucco motels, homey inns, and trailer campgrounds resembling suburbs on wheels – they are all to be found here.

Overnight accommodation is not particularly cheap, and real bargains are hard to find. Even in a standard motel rates begin around $40.

Many local Chambers of Commerce distribute lists of local accommodation, as do visitor centers; policies vary at these agencies about listing prices or making recommendations. All those listed are members of the local chamber.

A list of suggested accommodation is available from the California Hotel and Motel Association, P.O. Box 160405, Sacramento, CA 95816-0405; Tel. 916-444-5848.

Remember when considering price, that hotels in California tag on a hotel tax. This rate differs from area to area, ranging usually from 6%, to as high as 10%.

The major hotel chains are well represented in the cities and

outlying areas of California. In resorts, prices tend to rise on weekends. In major cities, hotels which cater to a business population and conventions, often change things around: they offer discounts on weekends, sometimes very sizeable ones, determined on the booking situation in a given hotel that weekend, or as part of a regular weekend special. Often these rates will only be quoted on request, so be sure to inquire about weekend discounts or special packages. Below is a sampling of some of the specials available. The toll-free numbers listed are generally for reservations and information about weekend specials, or may refer you to particular hotels. Even within a single hotel chain, the discount may vary from hotel to hotel, city to city or season to season.

Best Western International: Tel. 800-528-1234. Discounts of 20-50% off regular rates.

Hilton Hotels: Tel. 800-445-8667. Various areas have their own 800 numbers. Ask specifically about the "Rainbow Weekend".

Hyatt Hotels: Tel. 800-233-1234. Various weekend programs may include reductions of up to 50% on deluxe rooms.

Marriott Hotels: Tel. 800-228-9290. Ask about "Super Saver" and "Escape" packages for weekenders.

Ramada Hotel Group: Tel. 800-228-2828. "R and R" weekend specials.

Sheraton Hotels: Tel. 800-325-3535. Ask about "Time of your Life" weekends.

Westin Hotels: Tel. 800-228-3000. Most have lower weekend rates.

Motel 6 is a safe, standard, reliable and inexpensive motel chain. Most have pools but television is extra. There are about 400 motels in the chain nation-wide, and almost 100 in California alone. For a directory, write: *Motel 6*, Inc., 51 Hitchcock Way, Santa Barbara, CA 93105.

For an annual membership fee, the *Quest International hotel* marketing organization, arranges a 50% discount off regular rates at more than 500 hotels in the United States, British Columbia and San Juan. The half-price reduction is offered in regardless of seasonal price fluctuations. Quest International, Chinook Tower, Box 4041, Yakima, WA 98901, Tel. 509-248-7512.

Bed-Breakfast (B&B) Inns have increased in number and popularity in recent years. There are several hundred scattered throughout California, but they are found predominantly in the north. They tend to be rustic and old. Some may be refurbished farmhouses, others old family-run hotels or Victorian houses. Many are small, family-run operations, perhaps even in a wing of a private home. The rooms vary in style and furnishings and often there is an emphasis on old-time decor. Such inns may be located in the center of town, in completely residential areas, or in the country side where they offer an inside glimpse of country life that hotel guests may not otherwise see. Staying at a B&B inn is a little more adventurous than staying in a conventional hotel. The atmosphere is often warm and casual, and it is easy to meet the other guests or the owners. The breakfasts may include such touches as freshly-squeezed juice and home-baked muffins, as opposed to the standard coffee-shop fare. Often there are complimentary afternoon beverages, or use of the library or a bicycle, or other touches that make the experience more home-like.

There was a time when B&Bs were generally less expensive than hotels. The prices are now on a par, and sometimes over-priced, even outrageous. Nevertheless, there are plenty around which, while costing no more than the average motel, offer an experience which no motel can provide. Because each inn is run according to the whim of its owner, features you would expect at a motel must be double-checked in a B&B. Be sure to ask questions such as: How big is the bed? Is the room furnished? Is the bathroom private? Is there a bath or only a shower? Are there any extras? Is breakfast full or continental (beverage, juice and rolls)? Are there weekday or off-season rates?

Various organizations who represent B&Bs in different regions have appeared, making it easier for the visitor to find a special one. These organizations know the characteristics of the different inns, and can also make suggestions and sometimes handle bookings.

Besides the B&Bs, there is also the possibility of a "homestay", in which guests actually rent a room in a private residence. This can be less expensive and more homey than a B&B. Information is often available through the B&B associations and publications, some of which are listed below.

Bed and Breakfast International: P.O. Box 282910 San Francisco, CA 94128-2910, Tel. 415-696-1690, fax 415-696-1699.

Bed and Breakfast Directory of San Diego: P.O. Box 3292, San Diego 92163, Tel. 619-297-3130 or 800-619-ROOM.

Santa Barbara Bed and Breakfast Innkeepers Guild: Tel. 800-776-9176.

Bed and Breakfast Innkeepers of Northern California: 2030 Union St., Suite 310, San Francisco 74123, Tel. 415-921-7150.

Association of Bed and Breakfast Innkeepers of San Francisco: 737 Buena Vista W., San Francisco 94117, Tel. 415-921-7150.

A brochure listing B&Bs throughout the state is published by the *Californian Association of Bed & Breakfast Inns*: 2715 Porter St., Soquel, California, Tel. 408-464-8159.

Youth Hostels provide another lodging alternative. A national network of Youth Hostels is operated by *American Youth Hostels* (AYH). The AYH is part of the *International Youth Hostel Federation* and its membership card is valid for International Youth Hostel facilities. Conversely, a card from abroad is valid in the United States.

Hostel facilities are often found in schools, old hotels, and YMCAs, but sometimes they have their own buildings. Some hostels have smaller private rooms as well as dorm-like rooms, and most have kitchen facilities.

Youth hostels are by no means only for youth. Many others, such as professionals and seniors, use hostels in order to spice up their vacation. Hostels are ideal places for the lone traveler to strike up acquaintances and pick up travel tips.

Overnight fees are usually around $12 for members, and $3 more for non-members. AYH offices can be found in most major cities in the country.

Information regarding youth hostels can be obtained from your local AYH office. For further information and a membership application write or call the following offices:

Los Angeles Council: 1434 2nd St., Santa Monica, CA 90401, Tel. 310-393-3413.

San Diego Council: 335 West Beach St., San Diego, CA 92101, Tel. 619-338-9981 or 619-239-2644.

YMCAs have traditionally provided wayfarers with decent and simple lodgings, often in dormitories. Today, they may range from the very inexpensive to the price of an average motel room. Usually, the price includes use of some or all of the sports facilities. The lodgings may range from shabby to sleek. Reservations are often recommended. For a listing of YMCAs and general information, contact: *The Y's Way*, 333 7 Ave. New York, Tel. 212-308-2899. If you want a catalogue, send a self-addressed stamped envelope.

The Young Women's Christian Association (YWCA) offers the same type of lodging and facilities, but generally for women only. Contact: *The Young Women's Christian Association*, 726 Broadway, New York, N.Y. 10003; Tel. 212-614-2700.

Food

As with almost everything else in California, the world of food is rich, colorful and diverse. Eating out is a regular pastime. Restaurants range from the elegant, elite and outrageously expensive to the incredibly cheap. In addition to American steak restaurants, Chinese and Mexican restaurants are extremely popular, widespread and fit any budget. More varieties of both Asian and Latin American food are becoming available. Italian restaurants are very popular as well.

Fish and meats grilled on mesquite coal is served in many California restaurants. There is an emphasis on fresh produce of excellent quality, mixed together in myriad ways. In recent years, with the increased emphasis on health, vegetarian cooking has developed into an art. Vegetarian restaurants are common and serve a surprising variety of dishes, some tremendously imaginative. In conjunction with this is the increasingly common appearance of the salad bar, available as part of a larger meal or by itself. These salad bars are creations in themselves; gone are the old days of tomatoes and shredded lettuce. An average salad bar may include an array of cheeses and dressings, several kinds of nuts, potatoes, bread, fish, noodles and fruit – in other words, a salad can be a delicious and filling meal in itself. One of the best and most reliable salad bars can be found in the *Sizzler* chain of restaurants. The emphasis in this buffet type restaurant is on steak, but the salad bar is a welcome sight to those who prefer not to eat red meats.

Fast-food stands line the highways of California, having expanded from the old simple burger stands; they now include pizza, tacos, roast beef, chicken and ice cream. Prices are generally uniform at different branches of the same company. Occasionally, a chain will run some sort of advertised special, but a typical burger-fries-milkshake meal at a fast-food stand, besides containing dubious nutritional value, can sometimes cost as much as a sit-down meal at, for example, a small Chinese lunch counter.

The 24-hour coffee-shop chains are another characteristic California institution. Each chain has standardized designs, prices, menus, quality and employee uniforms. One can imagine the same soft music playing simultaneously at hundreds of different coffee shops.

However, there is something comfortable about these places, especially when it is 2am and the bright sign of a *Denny's*, *Sambo's*, *Norm's* or *Bob's* shines invitingly

up ahead at the next highway exit. The soft lights, familiar booths, smiling waitresses, bottomless pot of coffee and precisely sliced pie is somehow reliable and reassuring, even if rather bland.

It is possible to get a taste of California's superb produce directly from the farm. As mentioned throughout this book, many regions publish maps showing which local farms accept visitors, what the farm produces, etc. This is a good way not only to obtain fresh produce, but to break out of the tourist mold and meet the locals in an unusual setting. The produce you can sample ranges from vegetables and fruits to nuts, wines and cheeses. The regional directories can be obtained through local chamber of commerce offices, or through one central office: The Dept. of Food and Agriculture, 1220 N St., room 427, Sacramento 95814.

"Dive!" – a S. Spielberg restaurant

Parks and Reserves

National Park Service (NPS)

An extraordinary diversity of preserved land is under the jurisdiction of the *National Park Service* including Yosemite, Death Valley, the Channel Islands and Redwood.

The park service enforces strict rules about the protection of natural areas. Entrance fees are charged and camping fees are extra. Fees for primitive campsites are nominal, and for backcountry free, but permits are required.

The *Golden Eagle Passport* allows unlimited entry into national parks for the holder and accompanying passengers in a single car. The pass can be purchased at a national park or NPS regional office.

The *Golden Age Passport* is free to seniors from age 62. It provides free life-time entry to all park lands, and 50% discounts on various fees, such as camping. Available at most national parks, it must be obtained in person. A similar pass, the *Golden Access Passport*, is available for blind and disabled individuals. This too must be obtained in person.

For information contact the *National Park Service Information*, Fort Mason, Bldg. 201, San Francisco, CA 94123; Tel. 415-556-0560.

National Park Campground Reservations (through MISTIX): Tel. 1-800-365-0560.

National Forest Service

National Forest Service lands differ from National Parks in that they are multi-purpose. Logging and grazing, for example, is permitted under carefully controlled conditions. Few specific sites or regions are preserved for public visits, and there is not the same system of guided tours and activities as in National Parks. National forest land can, however, be stunning and certain areas have been designated as protected wilderness. There may be extensive trail networks throughout national forests. Camping is usually less expensive than in national or state parks, and in many areas it is free. For reservations contact the *National Reservation System* at 800-280-2267, open Mon.-Fri. 8am-5pm, Sat. and Sun. 9am-2pm. You can also contact the *U.S. Forest Campground Reservations* (through MISTIX): Tel. 1-800-283-2267.

Campers can buy camp stamps at designated retail outlets or forest

At the Anza-Borrego Desert State Park

mail from *California Travel Parks Association*, ESG Mail Services, P.O. Box 5578, Auburn, CA 95604, Tel. 916-823-1076.

Fishing and hunting permits can be obtained at the *California Dept. of Fish and Game* 3211 S St., Sacramento, CA 95816. Tel. 916-227-2244; 916-227-2266 (24-hour Info.)

Practical Tips

Mail
Mail can be forwarded to your hotel. It can also be sent to the General Delivery of the post office of any city or town; in the large cities, this is usually found in the main post office downtown. Users of *American Express* travelers' checks can use that company's offices to receive mail, but only by prior request.

TELEPHONES
Telephone numbers are preceded by a 3-digit area code. There are 9 area codes within California. In some areas the boundary for area codes may fall within a populated area. Dialing from one area code to another, the prefix "1" must sometimes be added. By no means is it assured that within one area code all calls are local calls. In the Los Angeles area, additional charges may be added to calls within the same area code. Public phones take nickels (5 cents), dimes (10 cents), and quarters (25 cents). The operator is not needed to make a long-distance call from a pay phone. Just dial "1", the area code and the number, and an operator or a recording will tell you how much money is needed, so keep a pile of change handy. If an additional

service offices, equal to the necessary camping fee. The user pays only 85% of the amount listed, thereby saving 15%. For further information contact *USDA Forest Service*, 630 Sansome St., San Francisco, open Mon.-Fri. 8am-4:30pm, Tel. 415-705-2874.

State Parks
California runs a huge state park system, with some land as stunningly beautiful as that protected in the state's national parks. There are extensive camping and hiking possibilities within the park system. With its mobile and recreation-oriented population, California's state parks can often be crowded. Admission to campsites is charged. Backcountry sites are generally free but permits may be required. Reservations are accepted at most parks. They may be made through called MISTIX. Call toll-free, Tel. 800-444-PARK.

State Park Publications: 916-653-4000.

State Park Information: 916-653-6995.

Private Campgrounds
A directory which includes lists of facilities and locations of private campgrounds can be ordered by

charge is owed at the end of the call, the phone will ring when you hang up.

Long-distance rates are substantially lower between 6pm and 8am, and on weekends from 11pm Friday to 5pm Sunday. For international calls, the lowest rates are between 3pm and 9pm.

Many companies now use toll-free numbers, recognizable by the 800 prefix to the number. No area code is necessary to call this number, but sometimes a "1" must precede the 800. An 800 number good for in-state calls may not be applicable for calls from outside the state, and some companies have both in-state and out-of-state toll-free numbers. Local Yellow Pages list a company's toll-free numbers.

Currency and Exchange

Foreign currency can be exchanged in international airports and certain banks. If possible buy traveler's checks in American dollars, at the correct exchange rate. Foreign currency is not honored in the United States.

To send money to the United States it is best to give the name and address of an American bank correspondent to your bank at home. Money can be cabled, usually within 48 hours, for a certain charge. A draft check, sent by mail, is a little cheaper but much slower.

BANKING

Banking hours in California are from Mon.-Thurs. 10am-5pm, and 10am-5:30pm on Fridays. Most major banks are open on Saturday. Electronic tellers are now common and widespread among all major banks.

TRAVELER'S CHECKS

Traveler's checks are a must. They are available at banks or through organizations such as *American Automobile Association*, at a reduced price or at no charge.

American Express traveler's checks are the most widely recognized, and the company provides a measure of assistance and reassurance to those whose checks have been lost or stolen. *American Express Travel Service* offices will help arrange temporary identification, cash personal checks, arrange for new traveler's checks immediately, report and cancel credit card numbers and, in general, provide assistance. In addition, if arranged by mail beforehand, check holders may use the local *American Express* office as a mailing address.

CREDIT CARDS

A credit card is worth taking as an emergency source of cash or to pay for large items. Recognized credit cards will allow the holder to withdraw in cash the sum remaining in his credit. Make sure you know where to report a lost or stolen credit card, and do so immediately. Major credit cards such as *Visa*, *Mastercard* and *American Express* are recognized throughout California. If coming from another country, check whether your credit card is affiliated with an American company. When using a credit card, always check the amount before signing, and be sure to get the receipt. In addition, ask for the black carbon and destroy it immediately. Occasionally, a business will want to keep the carbon, but refuse stubbornly. Carbons have been used to produce counterfeit credit cards and should never leave the owner's possession. Likewise, never give your credit card number for identification purposes; use a passport or driver's license instead. Credit cards can also be used for long-distance calls in specially equipped public telephones.

Smoking, Alcohol, Drugs

Smoking is no longer "cool" in health-conscious California. It is prohibited by law in elevators, city buses and many public rooms, and is permitted only in restricted areas in restaurants and inter-city buses. Californians have become increasingly bold and persistent in requesting others not to smoke in their proximity.

The drinking age in California is 21. It is against the law to drive with an open container of alcohol in the car. Drunk-driving laws in California are strict and strictly enforced.

California is viewed by many as the land with a free-and-easy attitude towards drugs, especially marijuana. Possession of marijuana is no longer a felony, though one sometimes has to pay a fine. Marijuana is, frankly, very common, but it is not something to brag about; foreigners especially should be careful.

Photography

If you are a photography buff, you will find ample subjects in California, among the stunning and diverse natural scenery, and the tremendous mixture of people and lifestyles.

If you want to buy a camera, you might wait until you reach California, where competition is fierce, and many discount houses and department stores have camera departments which undercut the prices of regular camera shops. The camera shops, however, give expert

advice, which a clerk in a discount store is unlikely to have.

In the urban areas, one-hour and one-day developing services can easily be found. The large chain drugstores will often handle developing, and periodically run specials, such as two rolls for the price of one.

Disabled Travelers

New hotels and other public buildings must, according to California law, be accessible by wheelchairs. Businesses and communities are becoming more aware of the needs of the disabled. Car rental companies can supply special cars for the disabled. *Greyhound*, *Amtrak* and the airlines are now equipped to accommodate the disabled. Some companies give special rates to the disabled as well as to the elderly. Special parking spaces are reserved for the disabled.

For information on travel for the disabled, contact: The Society for the Advancement of Travel for the Handicapped, 26 Court St., Brooklyn, N.Y. 11242; Tel. 212-4477-284.

Senior Citizens

Many seniors are taking advantage of travel discounts and programs oriented towards them. Discounts are available in theaters, museums, on public and private buses and in many other places. The American Association of Retired Persons (AARP) offers information on traveling for seniors, as well as considerable discounts on lodging and other travel expenses. For information, contact: AARP Membership Communications, 1909 K St. NW, Washington, DC 20049; Tel. 202-434-2277.

Important Phone Numbers

California is a very tourist-oriented state. Material written to assist visitors is voluminous and available from public and commercial sources. The **California Division of Tourism** in Sacramento, will, for the price of postage, send its booklets to those interested. This office can provide a directory of Chambers of Commerce and Visitors' Bureaus throughout the state, a map and small pocket guide, a calendar of events, and a listing of Bed & Breakfast Inns. Write to: California Division of Tourism, 801 K St., Suit 1600, Sacramento, CA 95814; Tel. 916-322-5639 or (toll-free) 800-GO-CALIF, fax 916-322-3402.

Some other useful addresses and numbers:

Department of Parks and Recreation: Publications, P.O. Box 942896, Sacramento, CA 94296-0001. A guide to California's state parks is available.

U.S. Forest Campground Reservations (through MISTIX): Tel. 800-283-2267.

California Travel Parks Association: ESG Mail Services, P.O. Box 5578, Auburn, CA 95604, Tel. 916-823-1076.

Department of Fish and Game: 3211 "S" Street, Sacramento, CA 95815; Tel. (916) 227-2266. For fishing and hunting information and regulations.

U.S. Bureau of Land Management: 2800 Cottage Way, Sacramento, CA 95825. For a list of BLM campgrounds.

Sierra Club: 530 Bush St., San Francisco, CA 94108. For information on California's ecological resources, as well as the clubs organized trips.

Nature Conservancy: Western Regional Office, 425 Bush St., San Francisco CA 94108. Information on educational trips designed to teach about the environment.

Wine Institute: 425 Market St., Suite 1000, San Francisco, CA 94105, Tel. 415-512-0151.

Road Conditions: dial 800-427-7623 to receive information on highways throughout the state, accessed by touch-tone commands; Southern California: 213-628-7623; Northern California: 916-445-7623.

House Call Physicians Service: Tel. 800-DOCS-911, nation-wide free telephone consultation.

The local **Chamber of Commerce** of any city or small town is a resource worth consulting with throughout your travels in California. These offices can tell you about small, obscure attractions that you might otherwise miss. The people in these offices are proud of their hometowns – sometimes inordinately so – and share unusual stories. In the popular resort areas, many Chambers of Commerce give out brochures with various discount coupons for sites in the area. Most interesting of all is the opportunity to meet people.If you express curiosity and interest in someone's hometown, you may be surprised at the open response.

Electricity, Measurements, Time

Electric current is 110-115 volts 60Hz. For those planning to buy American appliances, note that American plugs are two flat pins which will require adapters for foreign usage. Foreign appliances brought to the United States, generally require a transformer as well as an adapter.

Measurements: The U.S. measurement system is not a decimal one. Following are several conversion tables and "instant" tricks:

WEIGHT
31.103 grams – 1 ounce
0.453 kilograms – 1 pound

VOLUME
0.473 liters – 1 pint
3.785 liters – 1 gallon

DISTANCE
2.540 cm – 1 inch
30.480 cm – 1 foot
0.914 meter – 1 yard
1.609 km – 1 mile

TEMPERATURE
To convert Fahrenheit to Centigrade (Celsius) subtract 32 from the Fahrenheit temperature, multiply by 5 and divide the total by 9.

TIME
All of California is within the Pacific Time Zone, which is GMT-8. This is three hours behind the East Coast. Daylight Saving Time begins on the last Sunday in April, and ends the last Saturday in October.

Watching a whale show at Sea World in San Diego

CALIFORNIA

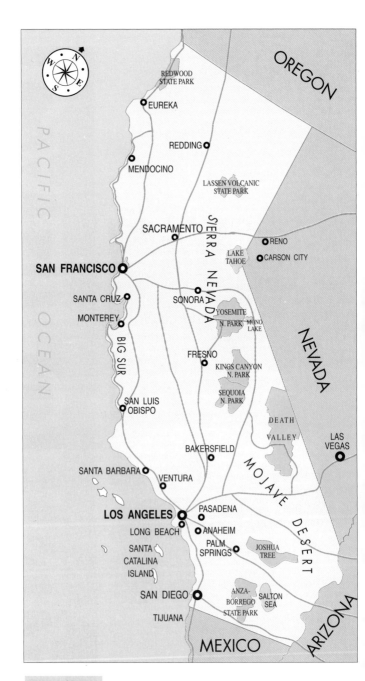

BIG SUR

On rising I would go to the cabin door and, casting my eyes over the velvety, rolling hills, such a feeling of contentment, such a feeling of gratitude was mine that instinctively my hand went up in benediction.

Henry Miller: *Big Sur and the Oranges of Hieronymus Bosch.*

Big Sur's mountains are not the highest, nor its forests the richest, nor its canyons the deepest; nevertheless, there is something inexpressibly wild and beautiful in the rugged, foggy coastline between Carmel and San Simeon.

Big Sur lies in the middle of the central coast of California, an area defined roughly as extending from the San Louis Obispo region in the south to the Monterey Bay and Santa Cruz in the north. Big Sur looms up as a border between the two.

From the days of the earliest settlers, Big Sur has held a strange attraction. Some came to cut down the redwoods or to build a navigable port; others drifted in, looking for a simple back-to-nature lifestyle and lived as small farmers, carpenters and the like. A few artists discovered the area and moved in. The American poet Robinson Jeffers worked as a stonecutter in these hills while steeping himself in images of "the prehuman dignity of night".

With the completion of Highway 1 (much of it by convict labor) along what was once a rutted wagon trail, Big Sur was opened up to the rest of California and the world; as could be predicted, this was accompanied by encroachments, developments and plans for profit-making resorts. Today, the cliff is dotted with expensive homes here and there. The area became a magnet for people who, during and after the 1960s, sought quieter, simpler lives based on crafts and independent physical labor. It has attracted many people seeking alternative lifestyles, therapy, cults, etc.

Today there are even fewer people living in the area – between 700 and 800 in all – than there were in the beginning of the century when great efforts were made to exploit the local resources. The "urban" area runs through the valley paralleling the Big Sur River, set back a mile or so from the coast. It extends from the **Jules Pfeiffer State Park** and the

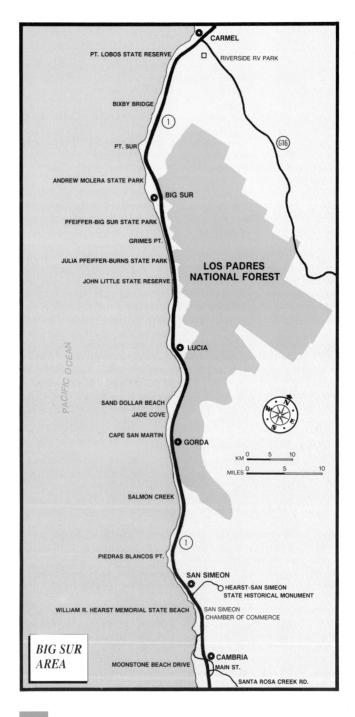

BIG SUR AREA

Big Sur Lodge, to the north for about six miles (4 km). There are a few lodges, hotels and restaurants in the area, plus an occasional gift shop, a few mailboxes and no-trespassing signs on dirt roads.

How to Get There

By car: The drive between San Francisco and Los Angeles, along the gorgeous coast highway, takes about 12 hours. If you need to get to the cities quicker, Freeway 101 can be picked up at either end of this stretch – at San Louis Obispo in the south and Monterey in the north. It is very difficult to reach Big Sur other than by car, organized tour, or bicycle (hitching not recommended).

By bus: From the south, the nearest public bus that runs to Big Sur is the *San Louis Obispo System* bus between San Simeon and Morrow Bay.

In spring, the hills are covered with flowers all the way down to the ocean. Autumn has a burnished beauty all its own. The winter brings damp, chilly mists and heavy rainfall, but rarely snow; and the greyness of winter is often broken by gleaming blue skies. The bank of fog seldom crosses the coastal ridge into the interior, so inland hikers may find the weather broiling hot even though the weather on the coast is cool. Avoid Big Sur on the Labor Day and July 4th weekends.

Facilities vary between the very elegant and expensive cliffside or hilltop restaurants and inns, to off-trail campsites. There is little in between. Everything from gasoline to beer to a cup of coffee could cost up to double the price here, so fill up the tank, cooler, and thermos. Camp out if you can, and try, whenever possible, to park your car and go hiking. There are pull-offs along the road, as well as extensive trails in the parks. Groves of

redwood trees fill the deep ravines that go right down to the cliffs, making for beautiful walks. Some paths lead down to the beach, others along the edges of sheer cliffs (the sign that warns of danger should be heeded!). In Big Sur you escape the hordes of motorists the moment you pull off the highway into a hiking area.

ACCOMMODATION AND FOOD

Lodging in the Big Sur area is generally outrageously overpriced, but do not allow this to deter you from enjoying a vacation in this special place.

Fernwood: Lodge, campground and motel units. Restaurant. More reasonable than others. Tel. 667-2422.

Big Sur Lodge: In Pfeiffer Big Sur State Park. Swimming pool, sauna. Guests have park privileges. Fireplace, kitchen, additional. Starting from $70 for a double. Tel. 667-3100.

The Ventana Inn and Restaurant: Just south of Pfeiffer Big Sur State Park. The epitome of Big Sur luxury and inflated prices. The cottages are quaint, the views stupendous. The Ventana is raved about for everything, from its latticework to its chocolate torte. Rooms start at $180 for a double. Reservations for dinner only. Private campground. Tel. 667-2331, Res. 800-628-6500.

The Nepenthe: A well-known local spot with a spectacular view, where the artists supposedly hang out. There's dancing around the fire in the summer. Open year round, until midnight in summer. Tel. 667-2345.

IMPORTANT PHONE NUMBERS
Area Code: 408 (south-805).
Emergency: Tel. 911.
Big Sur Chamber of Commerce: Tel. 667-2100.
Gas Stations: River Inn; Ripple wood; Fernwood; Loma Vista; Lucia Lodge; Pacific Valley; Gorda; Ragged Point. Opening hours vary, so it's advisable to keep your tank full.

Public Parks and Campgrounds

Big Sur has an excellent system of parks, enabling visitors – from the casual stroller and photographer to the serious hiker – to get a taste of the varied beauty of the area. There are enough campgrounds

and enough variety to please every kind of camper. Cyclists can stay in any state parkground and cannot, by law, be turned away. The different parks are listed here in geographical order, from north to south.

At the northern end of Big Sur, south of the *Rocky Point Restaurant* and a few miles north of the **Point Sur Lighthouse**, Paolo Colorado Road turns to the east, toward **Botcher Campground** (Forest Service) in the hills. There is also an unnamed Forest Service campground off a dirt spur to the left, through a gate which is not always open. A drive through the lower part of the canyon is in itself beautiful, with quaint little houses nestled between the trees.

Situated near the mouth of Big Sur River, the entrance to **Andrew Molera State Park** is on the west side of the highway, but vehicles cannot pass beyond the unpaved parking lot. From there a quarter-mile long path leads to (about 50) campsites in an open meadow. The path continues through a pretty wood, and then to the flood plain formed by the river. The park faces both the shallow river and the rough ocean. It is pleasant to be away from all the trailers and highway noise. There are ten miles (16 km) of hiking trails. Campsites have a three-night limit. For information:

Pfeiffer Big Sur State Park, Tel. 667-2315. Adjacent to the park, **Big Sur Trail Rides** offers short guided horse rides, as well as pack trips, into the Ventana wilderness area.

The **Pfeiffer Big Sur State Park** (not to be confused with the Julia Pfeiffer Burns State Park further south) is a highly developed park, with a lodge, cabins, a store, a restaurant and campfire programs and nature walks in summer. It is a great park for hiking, as there are many short, interlocking trails. There is a very short nature trail, as well as longer, tougher trails throughout the park, and trails leading into the Ventana Wilderness. Within this one park there are redwood forests, waterfalls, oak forest, high chaparral, and stunning views of the mountains and the rocky coast stretching in both directions. There is a beautiful hike to **Pfeiffer Falls** through a fern-lined canyon. The park has both campsites and trailer slots available by reservation, with a seven-day limit. For reservations call *Mistix Camping Reservations*, Tel. 800-444-7275. For specific information call the park itself, Tel. 408-667-2315, or the Department of Park and Recreation in Sacramento, Tel. 916-653-6995.

Just south of the Big Sur State Park entrance is the National Forest Service information booth. The **Ventana Wilderness**, which is part of the Los Padres National Forest, covers a large area of forest and chaparral behind the Big Sur State Park. This area is isolated and filled with wildlife. Wilderness permits (free) are required, and are available from 8am to 4:30pm at the station or in advance by calling or writing: P.O. Box 64, Big Sur, CA 93920 (Tel. 667-2331). Maps of Ventana Wilderness trails are available at the station.

Also administered by the Forest Service is **Pfeiffer Beach**. Turn west onto **Sycamore Canyon Road**, just a hundred yards or so south of the forest service information station, down a short steep incline that leads after about one-and-a-half miles (2.5 km) to a parking lot. This is where you begin walking. The first thing

No sound but the water's – at Julia Pfeiffer Burns State Park

you will notice is the monolithic rock looming from the water like the prow of a huge ship. The beach is unusually flat and wide for the Big Sur coast, and uncrowded as well. The beach which is for day use only has spur-like cliffs at either end, merging in the north with the beach and hills of Andrew Molera State Park, providing quite a large area for beach combing and exploration.

A little less than 10 miles (16 km) further south is the **Julia Pfeiffer Burns State Park**, a shady and peaceful day-use area situated right off the road. There's a fee for entering by car, but there is space to park outside alongside the road, which is what lots of people do. Trails lead up through a narrow, dark and peaceful redwood grove, or under the highway to a waterfall that drops right into the ocean. Although camping is not officially allowed, and fires are absolutely forbidden, there seems to be an understanding that camping is permitted in a certain area. Just outside the park entrance, only 30 yards or so to the south, look for a gate on the ocean side of the road. Beyond this gate, a path curves around the cove from which the waterfall plunges. The path goes down through an open field and doubles back into a shaded grove just above a rocky promontory where the waves surge and blast as if through a tunnel. In this peaceful grove which seems to be a locally known spot there is enough space for four or five tents. The rocky shore is a haunt for sea otters, and the area is, in fact, an underwater refuge as well. Threatened with extinction not long ago, the otters now survive among the thick offshore kelp beds.

Further to the south are two forest service camp-grounds, the *Kirk Creek Campground*, Tel. 805-927-4211, located at the Mill Creek picnic area, and the *Plasket Creek Campground*, Tel. 805-927-4556, near **Sand Dollar Beach** and **Jade Cove**. It is sometimes possible to find jade washed up at **Jade Beach**, which is also a nude sun-bathing spot. For reservations, call *Mistix* (Tel. 800-283-2267).

Several other sites are of interest: the **Esalen Institute**, named after the local Indians, has crystallized into an institute of all the various disciplines and forms of the "human potential movement" which is as uniquely Californian as the redwoods. You can choose courses in self-realization, meditation, yoga, centering, gestalt therapy, massage, holistic healing, Reichian work, etc., or you can just come between 1-5pm to relax in the natural baths. Except for these bathing hours, entry is by pre-arranged appointment only. The gate guards can be strict and unspiritually obnoxious. The Institute is situated a few miles south of Julia Pfeiffer Burns State Park. Look for the wooden sign on the west side of the road, and park in the lot at the top (Tel. 667-3000).

The writer Henry Miller lived in these hills for 17 years and wrote lovingly both of the landscape and his neighbors. One of his closest friends was Emile White, a bohemian wanderer from Europe, whom Miller encouraged to paint. After Miller's death, White turned his home into the **Henry Miller Memorial Library**, crammed with White's paint-

ings and Miller memorabilia, as well as copies of all sorts of obscure private publications of Miller's. Located across the road from Nepenthe hotel. Open every day, flexible hours. Tel. 667-2574. Sales of books and posters help keep the non-profit foundation going.

The Henry Miller Memorial Library amid the lush greenery

MONTEREY PENINSULA

North of Big Sur, the Monterey Peninsula juts forth into the ocean. From the northern end of the peninsula Monterey Bay curves inland towards Santa Cruz and the mountains. The bay is studded with small fishing towns and state beaches, and inland toward the coastal mountains there are small farm towns. The towns of Carmel, Monterey and Pacific Grove are located on the peninsula, where the weather is fair, sunny and breezy, with rain in winter and beautiful coastal fog which drifts in and condenses on trees and shrubbery.

The beauty and charm of this area attract over six million visitors each year who come for the old hotels, quaint countryside inns, excellent seafood restaurants, numerous golf courses and tennis courts, as well as places to walk, wade and watch crabs and seals.

HOW TO GET THERE

By air: Monterey Airport is served by *United Airlines*, as well as by regional and in-state carriers.

By land: The Monterey Peninsula is located just off the Pacific Coastal Highway. Just north of Monterey, this highway meets up with U.S. 101, the fast route to Monterey. Highway 1 is more scenic. Buses are available to and from L.A., San Francisco and other places. The coastal *Amtrak* route stops in Salinas, with free bus links to Monterey. For those traveling to or from Santa Cruz, transfer is at the Watsonville terminal. This is generally a cheap but time-consuming way to travel. *Greyhound* is more expensive but much faster; the Monterey depot is at 351 Del Monte Ave.

The *Monterey-Salinas Transit* (MST) system is convenient, and the routes are clearly shown on the schedule, available at the Visitors Center. There are three main terminals; at Monterey, Salinas, and Watsonville. The terminal in Monterey is really just a small plaza right in the middle of downtown, where Munras, Pearl, Folk, Alvarado and Tyler converge. From here the bus lines, including

those to Carmel radiate. Buses 4 and 5 run to the center of Carmel, and 1 and 2 to Pacific Grove. The main stop in Carmel is near Ocean and Mission. During the summer, two buses a day serve the Pt. Lobos State Reserve and Big Sur, reaching as far as Nepenthe (bus no. 22). If you plan to take more than 2-3 rides a day get the Day Pass. After Labor Day this bus schedule changes.

ACCOMMODATION
Lodgings on the Monterey Peninsula fill up very quickly and reservations are recommended year-round. During the summer, especially around the time of the Monterey Jazz Festival, reservations are essential. Fremont Ave., towards the fairgrounds, is Monterey's approximation of a motel and hotel row. Here a wide range of mostly conventional accommodation can be found.

It is important to remember that during the tourist season, the hotels in the Monterey area fill up to full capacity; you must find a place for the night by 4pm. Otherwise, you might find yourself spending the night in your car. On the weekends, the problem worsens and you must reserve a place in advance.

The Chamber of Commerce will supply a list of local lodgings. For last-minute help in finding a room, call Tel. 800-822-822 for Monterey and Pacific Grove; Tel. 624-1711 for Carmel.

Luxury Hotels ($230 and up)
Carmel Highlands Inn: Highway 1, 4 miles south of Carmel, Tel. 624-3801, Res. 800-682-4811. Condominium-style units at a superb site, offering a view of the Pacific Ocean. Plenty of facilities, as well as privacy.

Moderate Hotels ($100-$220)
Carmel Mission Inn: Highway 1 and Rio Rd., Carmel, Tel. 624-1841, Res. 800-348-9090. Modern hotel with jacuzzi and pool etc. Close to fashionable shopping centers. Big but convenient.

Holiday Inn Resort: 1000 Aguajito Rd., Monterey, Tel. 373-6141, Res. 800-234-5697. Pool, spa, restaurant, lounge, tennis.

Monterey Marriott: 350 Calle Principal, Monterey, Tel. 649-4234, Res. 800-228-9690. Pool, restaurant, lounge.

Inexpensive Hotels (less than $100)
Sand Dollar Inn: 755 Abrego St., Monterey, Tel. 372-7551, Res. 800-982-1986. Pool, spa, restaurant.

Cotton Inn: 707 Pacific St., Monterey, Tel. 649-6500, Res. 800-848-7007. Spa, kitchenettes, tennis.

Monterey Peninsula Youth Hostel – Summer hostel in one of the public schools around town. Location changes yearly, so call Tel. 649-0375 for information.

FOOD
Along Cannery Row are a number of restaurants, some known for their early bird specials and good seafood.

Bullwacker's: 653 Cannery Row, Tel. 373-1353. Attractive prices, with a choice of several house specialities that include red snapper and calamari.

Captain's Cove: 643 Cannery Row, Tel. 372-4000. The early bird specials include salad or soup, pasta or fries, fresh vegetables, beverage and a seafood entree, with sparkling wine.

Steinbeck Lobster Grotto: 720 Cannery Row, Tel. 373-1884. A fine location over the water, and a wide variety of seafood entrees. Special price for early bird specials.

Rosine's: 80 Bonifacio on Alvarado St. near Old Monterey, Tel. 375-1400. An elegant but relaxed setting and a wide range of entrees, with trimmings.

Sancho Panza Restaurant: 590 Calle Principal, Tel. 375-0095. Set in the Casa Gutierrez, an adobe which dates back to 1841 and is part of old Monterey. The interior is dark and cosy, and the patio is beautiful. The Mexican food is good, the prices reasonable and the service friendly.

Adobe Inn: Dolores and 8th St., Carmel, Tel. 625-1750. Excellent early bird dinner specials which include prime ribs, the day's fish catch, freshly baked bread and salad bar, between 5-6pm.

Hogs Breath Inn: San Carlos St. and 5th Ave. A local hang-out, with a delightful courtyard; Clint Eastwood is the owner.

The Whole Enchilada: At Route 1 near the turnoff for Moss Landing. An unbeatable combination of fine Mexican food and fine jazz every Saturday and Sunday night.

The Covey at Quail Lodge – 8205 Valley Greens Dr. Carmel, Tel. 408-624-1581. One of the best restaurants in the area. Continental cuisine. Elegant and expensive. Reservations needed.

Restaurant Hotline: Tel. 372-DINE. A free service which makes recommendations and reservations for restaurants in the Monterey area.

IMPORTANT PHONE NUMBERS

Area code: 408.

Monterey County Visitors and Convention Bureau: 380 Alvarado St., P.O. Box 1770, Monterey, CA 93942, Tel. 649-1770.

Pacific Grove Chamber of Commerce: 584 Central Ave., Pacific Grove, 93950, Tel. 373-3304.

Carmel Business Association: San Carlos and 6th, Carmel-by-the-Sea, 93921, Tel. 624-2522.

Amtrak: 40 Railroad Ave., Salinas, Tel. 422-7458.

Greyhound: 351 Del Monte Ave., near Fisherman's Wharf, Tel. 373-4735 (They run a tour to Hearst Castle that includes entry fee).

Monterey-Salinas Transit (*MST*), Tel. 899-2555. Main stop is Transit Plaza in downtown Monterey.

Sierra Club, Ventana Chapter: Box 5667, Carmel 93921, Tel. 624-8032. An ongoing schedule of trips and brochures available, to members and non-members.

Carmel

Carmel is a combination of a quaint country village, artists' colony and well-guarded enclave of the wealthy. There are strict controls on everything including street signs, billboards, cutting down trees (it's forbidden), house numbers (there aren't any), and the selling of ice cream cones. Tourists are welcome here; the restaurants and lodgings tend to be more expensive than in Monterey, although some good deals can be found. Numerous galleries sell the usual renditions of luminous crashing waves, but there are many good artists in the area too, as well as further down the coast toward Big Sur.

Since the late 1920s, Carmel has been a center for the art of photography. Edward Weston, who experimented with the limits of photography and influenced a whole generation of photographers, lived in Carmel for about 30 years, and got to know the area intimately. Some of his last photographs were of the Pt. Lobos coast. Carmel has many fine photographers carrying on Weston's tradition.

Examples of local photographic art can be seen at the **Photography West** Gallery, Ocean Ave. and Dolores (open daily 11am-5pm, Tel. 625-1587); and at the **Weston Gallery**, 6th and Dolores, Tues.-Fri. 11am-5pm, Sat. 10am-5pm.

Just south of the town's center, off Highway 1, is the Mission San Carlos Borromeo del Rio Carmelo – the **Carmel Mission** for short. The mission and its three museums are worth a visit. 3080 Rio Rd. Open daily 9:30am-4:15pm; June-Aug. 9:30am-7:15pm. Donation requested, Tel. 624-3600.

Built in 1771, this mission succeeded the one built in Monterey a year earlier. The graceful structure is one of the finest surviving examples of California mission architecture. Father Junipero Serra, the founder of the chain of California missions, is buried inside. About 2,000 local Indians are buried in the Mission cemetery, where some of the graves are marked by abalone shells.

The Carmel Mission is also the site for the highlight of the **Carmel Bach Festival**. This renowned and popular festival is held in July. For tickets and details contact: The Carmel Bach Festival, P.O. Box 575, Carmel, 93921, Tel. 624-1521.

Ocean Ave. leads down to the ocean at Carmel City Beach. From here the gorgeous beaches of central California stretch southwards. Parking can be a problem on weekends, but if you head south just a few blocks on Scenic parking is easier and there are fewer people on the beach. Still further south, reachable by foot or by car along Scenic drive, is

River Beach. Around Carmel Point is the **Carmel River State Park**, a great place (and legal) for a driftwood fire.

The peninsula of Point Lobos juts out into the Pacific

At the corner of Ocean View and Scenic drives stands **Tor House**, which the poet Robinson Jeffers built himself using boulders from the beach. Tours Fri.-Sat. from 10am-3pm. Reservations required, admission required, Tel. 624-1813.

The shopping centers of Carmel have become very popular with tourists. Particularly attractive are **Carmel Plaza** in the eastern part of the village, and **The Crossroad**, which has over 100 shops and is situated south-east of Highway 1, at the entrance to town.

About three miles (5km) south of Carmel, the smaller peninsula of **Point Lobos State Reserve** juts out into the Pacific. A protected area, this mosaic of rugged headlands, coves, meadows, tidepools and rocky promontories has retained its pristine character. There are natural stands of Monterey pine and gnarled Monterey cypresses. Deer graze in the meadows. The reserve has a network of easy trails heading from several parking lots, making the stunning views available

*Along the Seventeen
Mile Drive*

to virtually anyone. One can observe at close view sea lions, sea otters, seals, elephant seals, grey whales and an occasional killer whale off the coast during the migration season.

The adjoining tide area and the submerged rocks of Carmel Bay, just to the north of the Pt. Lobos headlands, comprise the **Carmel Bay Ecological Reserve**, including the underwater canyon 1,000 ft. (340m) deep just beyond Monterey Beach. The surf is dangerous; children must be carefully watched, and the water approached with caution.

Even though it is not large in size, the Point Lobos State Reserve is a beautiful spot in which lovely trekking routes have been forged for the convenience of visitors. It is particularly recommended to leave the car and proceed on foot. A good time for a visit is before sunset, when the reserve is quieter and its fauna more alert. It is important to remember that the speed limit within the reserve is 15 mph (24kph).

Point Lobos can be crowded on weekends, even during the winter. The main ranger station is off Highway 1. No camping is allowed. Open from 7am-11pm in summer, but the parking lot closes at sunset. During the rest of the year, open 7am-5pm. On a crowded weekend, the parking lot fills up by noon. Divers interested in exploring the underwater reserve must show proof of certification and must register at the ranger station. Guided walks are led by rangers or docents, as staffing permits, usually every day in the summer, and on weekends during the off-season. Admission charge, Tel. 624-4909.

Monterey and Carmel are separated by the **Del Monte Forest**, a 5,600 acre chunk of beauty turned into a barony. A fee is charged for entry to the famous **Seventeen Mile Drive**. There is no charge for cyclists between 8-11am, and no charge for pedestrians at any time. There are numerous turnoffs with each view more stunning than the previous one. Stop to photograph the lone cypress; you won't be the only one. The forest includes a game preserve, where deer are allowed to nibble at the gardens. Behind the walls stand some modest mansions built between the world wars. There are four famous golf courses, including the one at Pebble Beach. The beautiful Lodge at Pebble Beach has sea views, several restaurants and free hors d'œuvres during the happy hour. However, why pay good money to visit a rich man's estate when incomparable Pt. Lobos and Big Sur are just down the road?

Pacific Grove is a small quiet town which is virtually contiguous with Monterey, and separated from Carmel by the Del Monte Forest. Tide pools are scooped out of its rocky shore. Old Victorian buildings and small cottages are common. John Steinbeck did much of his early writing in a cottage here. Every October waves of monarch butterflies are welcomed by the town with a festival as they migrate thousands of miles, from the autumn chills of the north. The monarch literally "hang" around for months on foliage; when warm weather comes, they seek food; When spring comes they fly north again.

Pacific Grove

The **Pacific Grove Museum of Natural History** houses displays on the monarch butterflies as well as on sea birds and sea mammals. A relief map depicts the deep oceanic canyon off the peninsula, explaining how the nutrient-rich cold water supports such great diversity of marine life. Forest Ave. and Central Ave. Open Tues.-Sun. 10am-5pm. Admission free, Tel. 648-3116.

At **Lovers Point** there is a small rocky beach, and glass-bottomed boats are available in summer. Further on, the **Point Pinos Lighthouse**, the oldest on the west coast, built in 1855, overlooks both the ocean and golf course. There is a small U.S. Coast Guard Maritime Museum upstairs. Located at Seventeen-Mile Drive, Tel. 373-2469. Open on summer weekends, 1-4pm. Admission free.

Monterey

Monterey played an important role in early Californian history. Discovered by Juan Rodriguez Cabrillo in 1542, it was only in the 1770s that Spanish settlers, soldiers and priests began to settle the area. Eventually, it became the capital of Spanish, and later Mexican, California. From the 1820s onward, a trickle of American sailors, whalers, trappers and traders based themselves in Monterey. A sea trading line was established between Monterey and Boston. After California fell into American hands in the Mexican War in 1846, Monterey became the capital of the new American territory; when California became a state, the constitution was drawn up in Monterey. However, with the discovery of gold in the Sierra foothills in 1849, the focus of business and trade shifted to the new port of San Francisco and to Sacramento inland. The graceful capital of the Old California became something of a backwater.

The center of Monterey with its fisherman's wharf has undergone a great deal of tourist development, so that little remains of the charm and innocence of yesteryear. During the hectic tourist seasons the restaurants and boutiques are full of tourists and it is difficult to find parking space. The beach towns north of Monterey offer a quieter retreat.

Monterey today has the greatest concentration of tourist attractions on the peninsula, the main ones being **Fisherman's Wharf**, **Cannery Row** and

historic **Old Monterey**. It has some excellent seafood restaurants – many with great early bird specials – and a wide variety of others as well. Monterey also sustains an extremely active and lively cultural life. Literature available from the visitors center or free newspapers around town keep the visitor informed of what's happening. The **Monterey Jazz Festival** in September is perhaps the biggest event in Monterey and in the world of jazz. Centered at the fairgrounds, it features some of the greatest names in jazz. Tickets should be purchased months in advance; by the time the festival begins, the hotels and motels are packed.

OLD MONTEREY

Over 40 original adobe buildings in Old Monterey remain from the pre-1850 era, about 13 of which are open to the public, housing museums, restaurants and a theater. A copy of Monterey's "Path of History", a self-guided tour of about two miles (3km) through Old Monterey, is available at the visitors' center. A small fee per adult buys entry to all the state historical buildings for one day (some are more interesting than others). The stroll through the area is easy and pleasant. The transit plaza is a convenient place to begin and nearby Alvarado St. has plenty of reasonable eating spots. Some of the buildings on the tour are:

Old Monterey – yesterday's architecture

The Customs House: 1 Customs House Plaza, 115 Alvarado St. The first U.S. government building on the Pacific Coast, restored and filled with piles of cargo from the era: casks of liquor, cases of coffee, and an old harpoon gun.

Pacific House: 8 Customs House Plaza. Used as a tavern, newspaper office, court, church and ballroom over the years, and now a museum featuring the life and artifacts of the local Indians, Spanish explorers and early American settlers.

Colton Hall: Pacific and Jefferson streets. The first constitutional Congress of the new State of California was convened here in 1849. A "Path of History" map is obtainable here. Open daily 10am-4pm, Tel. 646-5640.

The **Monterey Peninsula Museum of Art** focuses on Western and local art, and the Charlie Russel bronze statues will make the West come alive. 559 Pacific Ave. across from Colton House. Open Tues.-Sat. 10am-4pm, Sun. 1-4pm. Admission charge, Tel. 372-5477.

Stevenson House: 530 Houston St. Robert Louis Stevenson lived in a rooming-house here in 1879, having come to visit the woman he later married. Much of *Treasure Island*'s vivid Pacific scenery was inspired by the Monterey landscape. There is lots of Stevenson memorabilia here. Admission required. Closed Wed. and noon to 1pm. Hourly tours, 10am-4pm.

FISHERMAN'S WHARF

You know you're near Fisherman's Wharf when you hear the hoarse yelping of sea lions begging food from tourists. The wharf is crowded and touristy. It is lined with tourist seaside restaurants and stands selling little seafood cocktails. Some of the restaurants offer early bird specials of fresh seafood. The general atmosphere of the wharf, however, is gaudy and circus like. Sport fishing and sightseeing cruises are available from the wharf, as are whale-watching tours during the winter months. (Check with several tour companies to compare prices). A free shuttle bus to the wharf runs every 15 minutes from 9am-10pm daily, from Memorial Day to Labor Day, and on weekends only after Labor Day. All-day parking is available at the East Customs House garage for a small fee. Between the wharf and Cannery Row is a small stretch of beach and a breakwater where the more sedate sea lions bask on rocks. The adjacent strand of beach is a popular spot for snorkeling and scuba diving.

Fisherman's Wharf at Monterey

CANNERY ROW

The canneries rumble and rattle and squeak until the last fish is cleaned and cut and cooked and canned and then the whistles scream again and the dripping, smelly, tired Wops and Chinamen and Polaks, men and women, straggle out and droop their ways up the hill into the town and Cannery Row becomes itself again – quiet and magical.

John Steinbeck, *Cannery Row*

Cannery Row began at about the turn of the century with the building of one packing plant for the sardines, used as bait by salmon fishermen.

With the introduction of larger, more efficient nets and seines, and modern packing systems, new canneries opened. Cannery Row became a center for the sardine industry. Small businesses sprang up to serve fishermen and cannery workers, and cheap rooming houses opened up on the blocks behind the canneries. In the middle of all this industry, a biologist, Ed "Doc" Ricketts, opened a laboratory at the ocean's edge, where he supplied sea specimens for larger research facilities and conducted his own experiments. His approach to the study of marine life along this central coast was innovative: he identified plants, animals, invertebrates and micro-organisms according to the habitat in which they lived rather than by genus or species. He noted that several distinct habitats existed along the coastline, co-dependent on each other. Into this teeming, smelly, rough neighborhood wandered a local writer, John Steinbeck, raised just over the hills in the farm country of the Salinas Valley, who was developing a penchant for writing about the little guy, the lowlife, the down-and-outers.

What was there, really, that made this row of canneries – redolent with the smell of fish – so romantic? Perched on the edge of a beautiful natural setting, Cannery Row's poet laureate, Steinbeck, vividly captured the rhythm and atmosphere of this jumble of canneries, warehouses, whorehouses, flophouses and tiny stores.

Over 250,000 tons of sardines were hauled in each year and processed through the two dozen plants along this row. Ricketts, Steinbeck's close friend, was one of the naysayers who warned that overfishing might destroy the industry. The yearly haul did indeed shrink, and was depleted completely by 1951. Workers and fishermen left, stores closed, and Cannery Row became a corrugated ghost town. In the 1960s and 70s, a few seafood restaurants opened, and suddenly making developers and various commissions aware of the tourist potential of the area. The row of rusted canneries and rotted flophouses has become prime real estate for tourist-oriented developing, with proposals for hotels, cute stores, malls and a wax museum. The row has its patrons too, fighting to protect its historical ambience (765 Wove St., Tel. 649-6695).

Walk a block behind the strip of tourist traps to catch a taste of the old world. A few tiny clapboard and shingled houses, old flophouses and dormitories still stand. The railroad tracks are neglected and overgrown with weeds. A few of the stores on the row date back to earlier days. *Kasila's*, at 851 Cannery Row, is a funky old bar and sandwich shop. The *Old General Store* at 835 Cannery Row was once a Chinese grocery store – on which Steinbeck modeled Lee Chong's store in his book. In the back is a room of Steinbeck memorabilia. Across the street, Doc Ricketts' old laboratory has been converted into a dance club, bordered by restaurants with great views serving fresh seafood.

Opened in 1984, the **Monterey Aquarium** in the old Hovden Cannery at the end of Cannery Row, displays some of the marine life from the teeming oceanic environment in the North Bay area. 886 Cannery Row. Open daily 10am-6pm winter; 9:30am-6pm summer. Admission charge, Tel. 648-4888.

The deep reefs, the sandy sea floor, the shale reefs, the open sea and the wharf each support their own community of plants and animals. The kelp forest exhibit towers over the viewers' heads and shows how big these plants really are. During the summer, the aquarium conducts a number of half-day field trips and field courses on the marine environment and the marine biology of the Monterey Bay area.

Further east, on El Estero Dr. is the **Dennis the Menace Playground**, a collection of imaginative playground equipment for children of all ages.

Around Monterey

Due east of Monterey, at the junction of Highway 68 and U.S. 101, lies the farm country of the Salinas Valley, a world away from the smells and sights of Monterey. This area, and the town of **Salinas** itself, was immortalized in the works of John Steinbeck. The Nobel Prize-winning writer was born in Salinas in 1902 in a house that still stands at 132 Central Ave. (now a restaurant). He lived elsewhere most of his life, but he is buried here, and his modest grave can be seen at the Garden of Memories at the outskirts of town, 768

Abbott St. The **Steinbeck Festival** is held in August in Salinas. **Steinbeck House**, at 132 Central Ave., is John Steinbeck birthplace (Tel. 424-2735).

Salinas is also the place to catch the **California Rodeo** in July, kicked off by a big western dance on Saturday night. The competition draws the country's top cowboys and about 50,000 spectators. It's hot and dusty, so wear your ten gallon hat, Tel. 757-2951.

Salinas doesn't attract many tourists, and most of its inhabitants today are farmers and Mexican immigrant field workers.

South of Salinas on U.S. 101 and just east of Soledad, the spires and jagged teeth of **Pinnacles National Monument** jut out of the surrounding gentle hills. The pinnacles are the partial remains of a volcano, the other part of which lies far to the southeast. The San Andreas Fault, which runs right past this area, split up the volcanic formation, leaving these jagged shapes. The terrain offers rugged hiking trails; the sheer walls challenge rock climbers. Although there are roads that approach the monument from both east and west, they do not connect.

The Pinnacles National Monument, on the west side of the San Andreas fault, has shifted 195 miles (315 km) north over the last 23 million years or so. The volcanic remains have been polished and eroded by the elements to form sharp spires thrusting up from the surrounding rounded hills; there are caves and canyons in the area. Spring is the best time to visit the park, when the trees are green and the slopes are covered by a multi-colored carpet of wildflowers. There is one campground in the monument, at Chaparral, and one private campground outside the eastern boundary. The western Ranger Station at Chaparral and the Bear Gulch Visitor Center at the eastern entrance provide information and exhibits, as well as evening programs at both campgrounds. For information contact Park Headquarters, Pinnacles National Monument, Paicines, 95043, Tel. 389-4485.

Located in the Salinas Valley just west of Soledad, the **Paraiso Hot Springs** bubble up with healing mineral waters. It is about an hour's drive from Monterey. The setting is tranquil and strict rules help sustain the area's natural state. There are outdoor and indoor pools in which to relax, as well as a library, recreation room, and free cookies and coffee. Take the U.S. 101 to Soledad, then follow the Arroyo Seco Road west to Paraiso Springs Road, all the way to the springs. There are hook ups for trailers, and simple accommodation, Tel. 408-678-2882.

Just north of Monterey on Highway 1 is Castroville, a small farmtown at the mouth of the Salinas Valley which is renowned only for its claim as the artichoke capital of the world and home of the annual Artichoke Festival in September. At the end of the main street of town is the **Giant Artichoke** housing a gift shop and restaurant. The speciality is french-fried artichoke. Incidentally, in the campaign to promote artichokes in 1947, an aspiring young actress named Marilyn Monroe was crowned the first California Artichoke Queen.

If you are driving, stop at the fresh fruit and vegetable stalls on the road-side. The abundance of excellent products at low prices will serve you for the rest of the trip.

To the north of Castroville, on Route 1, is the tiny fishing village of **Moss Landing**. It's just opposite the gigantic power station. Cross the bridge that spans the tiny estuary to enter the town itself. This is a real fishing village. Near the fishing boats is a row of small dilapidated bait shops, garages and bars. Here the fishermen haul in catches of salmon, albacore and other fish, without catering to tourists.

SANTA CRUZ

Santa Cruz is situated at the northern end of Monterey Bay, where ocean, forested mountains and fields combine to create absolutely gorgeous scenery. The sandy beaches are sheltered by the northern promontory, and the water is fairly warm with comparatively gentle surf. The northern promontory also protects Santa Cruz from the fog that envelopes most of the central coast.

Like many Californian coastal towns, Santa Cruz began as a Spanish mission which developed because of the abundance of local resources: lumber, fishing and agriculture. Today it is still a commercial center for farmers, flower growers and the region's many wineries. By the turn of the century, resort hotels had opened along the beach, and with the completion of a narrow gauge railroad link with Los Gatos, Santa Cruz became a full-fledged vacation town, which it has remained.

Perhaps because of the influence of the highly innovative University of California at Santa Cruz (UCSC), and because of its semi-isolated location, Santa Cruz is a trendy rural center with artisans living in the hills, a vibrant cultural life, a strong environmental protection movement and a variety of cults thrive.

In contrast, the beach, boardwalk and old ornate amusement park are crowded with cruisers – from punks to gays and staid, well-dressed couples sharing a sentimental cotton-candy cone.

HOW TO GET THERE

From the San Francisco Bay area, the Route 17 freeway crosses over the Santa Cruz mountains from suburban Santa Clara Valley. On a busy weekend, the traffic can crawl along, bumper to bumper. Route 9 is even slower, winding through deeply shaded redwood canopies and small towns that seem a thousand miles away from any urban area. Highway 1, the Pacific Coast Highway, extends from the spreading suburbs to a peaceful coastline of state parks, beaches and small towns. From Monterey in the south, Highway 1 is alternately freeway and small road. Even if traveling along the faster U.S. 101, you must cut over Highway 1 from either Marina or Gilroy.

Although it is possible to travel by local transit systems to Santa Cruz, this is very time consuming. *Greyhound* is much faster, serving both Santa Cruz and Watsonville. Santa Cruz's public bus system is efficient and extensive, reaching all corners of this relatively spread out county. The transit terminal, off the Pacific Garden Mall at Walnut and Pacific, clearly displays schedules, as well as art from local schools. There are two other transit centers at Capitola and Watsonville. A rider's guide, called *Headways*, details the system's routes and schedules. From Memorial Day to Labor Day, a summer shuttle runs every 15-20 minutes, connecting the **County Government Center**, the metropolitan center and the wharf area, Tel. 425-8600.

Santa Cruz has been a paradise for both recreational and racing cyclists for many years, and it hosts many races. Extensive cycling lanes on roads and separate bike paths

Santa Cruz – the beach

criss-cross the city leading into the rural hills and flatlands. The Bike-centennial Pacific Coastal Route from Oregon to Baja runs through Santa Cruz. The **Santa Cruz Cycling Club** offers weekly rides that visitors can join, Tel. 423-0829. The club also distributes an excellent map of local routes, available in cycling shops. Another map of local cycling routes is supplied by the **Santa Cruz Transportation Commission**, 701 Ocean St., Santa Cruz, 95060, Tel. 454-2340.

ACCOMMODATION

Bed & Breakfast Inns abound in Santa Cruz County. Some are in old Victorian buildings a few blocks from the boardwalk, others are in country farmhouses. Here are a few of them:

Babbling Brook Inn: 1025 Laurel St., Tel. 427-2437 or 800-866-1131.

Darling House: 314 West Cliff Dr., Tel. 458-1958.

Inn Laguna Creek: 2727 Smith Grade, Tel. 425-0692.

Some other hotels and motels:

The Tyrolean Inn: 9600 Highway 9, Ben Lomond 95005, Tel. 336-5188. A little bit of the Austrian Alps in the midst of redwood country. Cozy cabins and friendly atmosphere. Accessible by bus from downtown Santa Cruz. $43-$56.

La Plaza Motel: 505 Riverside Ave., Tel. 426-2899. Across the street from tennis courts. $32-$120.

Dream Inn: 175 West Cliff Dr., Tel. 426-4330, Res. 800-662-3838 (CA), 800-421-6662 (US., Can.). Heated pool, spa, sauna, restaurant, lounge. $100-$205.

Youth Hostels

Hostelling International Santa Cruz AYH-Hostel: 511 Broadway St., Tel. 423-8304. AYH or IYHF Membership required. Open between 7-9am and 5-10pm. Closed during the day. Kitchen facilities and lockers available.

Camping

Camping options are plentiful, and since there are many state parks in the immediate Santa Cruz area, it is generally possible to find camping spots even on crowded weekends. Camping facilities range from trailer lots to primitive and isolated sites for hikers and cyclists. It is best to make reservations. For information call the State Parks Dept. Tel. 426-0505.

Some stunning camping areas for vehicles and hikers can be found in Big Basin State Park, Tel. 338-6132 or 800-444-7275.

For Tent Cabin Reservations call 800-874-8368.

FOOD

El Palomar: In the old *Paloma Inn*, 1336 Pacific Garden Mall, Tel. 425-7575. Unusual, delicious Mexican food, from Michoacan in the south. Reasonable prices, but you might get a stiff neck gazing at the beautifully decorated high ceiling. Live music on Friday and Saturday nights.

Georgiana's Café: 1522 Pacific Ave., Tel. 427-9900. Located in a bookshop. Apart from books, it offers soups, salads, sandwiches, pastries, espresso and granita.

Beach Street Café: 399 Beach St., Tel. 426-7621. Breakfast and lunch, affordable prices.

Pon's Chinese Food: 1002 Soquel Ave., Tel. 429-8209. Cantonese and Szechwan cuisine. Clean and friendly environment at reasonable prices.

Anna Maria's Italian Restaurant: 55-C Municipal Wharf, Tel. 458-9534. At the top of Santa Cruz Wharf (use stairs or elevator). Full unobstructed view of the Bay. Seafood, chicken, steak and handmade pasta.

Zoccoli's Delicatessen: 1534 Pacific Ave., Tel. 423-1711. When you have tired of sprouts on crackers, taste the lasagna lunch special here.

IMPORTANT PHONE NUMBERS

Area Code: Tel. 408.
Emergency: Tel. 911.
Santa Cruz County Conference and Visitors Council: 701 Front St., Tel. 425-1234.
Public Transit Information: Tel. 425-8600, or Tel. 688-8600.
Greyhound Peerless Stages: Tel. 423-1800 or Tel. 722-4457.
Green Tortoise: Tel. 462-6437.
Amtrak: Tel. 800-872-7245.
Santa Cruz Airporter: Tel. 423-1214 or 800-497-4997. To San Jose Airport and San Francisco Airport.
California State Parks Dept.: Tel. 426-0505.

What to See

Information on the Santa Cruz area can be found at the local Convention and Visitors Center and the Chamber of Commerce. The local free weekly paper, *Good Times*, has full listings of Santa Cruz's night life, which includes a dozen or so local bars and clubs showcase music, influenced by the music scene in nearby San Francisco. The university is the venue for exhibits, films, concerts, lectures and drama. For cultural events at the university call: **UCSC – Performing Arts Com-**

plex, Tel. 459-ARTS (calendar information) or 459-2159 (tickets).

The flower-lined **Pacific Garden Mall's** relaxing small-town atmosphere is distinctly Santa Cruzian with aspiring singers crooning stoned-out versions of Dylan songs and a store sponsored by Greenpeace, the activist environmental protection group. It seems that here too, as in all of California, the smart, expensive yuppified shops have been taking over the quaint stores in the past few years. Much of the old western architecture has been preserved. The shops are unusual, the restaurants varied and surprisingly reasonable, the book stores eclectic, and the cafes hip and intellectual. The mall's stores have a special atmosphere. They extend along the side streets to Front St. Both Pacific and Front extend beyond the commercial section to the beach area.

The **Octagon**, set in a beautiful old building, is a small historical museum featuring local exhibits, 118 Cooper 11am-4pm, Tues.-Sun., Tel. 425-7278. The **Art Museum of Santa Cruz County** presents

nationally circulated exhibits, 705 Front St., 11am-4pm Tues.-Sun.; 11am-8pm on Thursday. Admission charge except on Sunday, Tel. 429-1964.

The Mystery Spot, 1953 Branciforte Dr., offers half-hour guided tours through mysterious phenomenon of nature. Balls roll uphill, visitors lean at precarious angles and laws of gravity seem to be reversed. Open daily 9:30am-5pm, Tel. 423-8897 or 426-1282.

The Santa Cruz **Boardwalk**, built in 1907, is the last of the elegant old amusement parks extant on the West Coast. 400 Beach St. Admission free. Individual rides charged, with various ticket plans available. Open daily from Memorial Day to Labor Day, and weekends the remainder of the year, Tel. 423-5590.

Shooting galleries, organ music, teenage boys trying to win kewpie dolls for their girls – all the grand old amusement park scenes are here. The people parading along the boardwalk range from the sedate to the ultra-hip, while the architecture and props belong to another era. The oldest ride is the **1911 carousel**, with a pipe organ and seventy hand-carved horses, some of which are more valuable today than live ones. The **Giant Dipper roller coaster** is wild, rated as one of the world's top ten. Yet even at an old time amusement park time marches on, and the vintage arcade games are being elbowed out by Pac-Man and Dragon-Slayer. The **Coconut Grove Ballroom**, built in 1907, hosted most of the major big bands during the 1940's swing era, and still showcases that same sound in regular concerts today.

Time for a break

Beachfront Santa Cruz throbs with action. Across from the Boardwalk are cheap beach joints with big gaudy signs that you would expect to find at Coney Island. Young kids zoom up and down in revved up "wheels". It is only appropriate that this is the spot for an annual vintage 1950s and 60s car contest, when gleaming '56 Chevys roll out. The **Clam Chowder Cook-off and Festival** in February draws thousands of contestants and even more volunteer tasters, but it is hard to imagine anything surpassing the **Brussel Sprouts Festival**, held every October. The festivals are held at the beach area.

Commercial fishermen operate out of the adjacent **municipal wharf**, where there are a number of small restaurants, bait shops and small bars. It is usually possible to see sea lions, happily frolicking on the lower scaffolding of the wharf. Open daily, 5am-2am, Tel. 429-3628.

It's a nice bike ride and an exhilarating walk to **Lighthouse Point** from the wharf area. Seals and surfers hang out here. The **Santa Cruz Surf Museum**, which recently opened in the lighthouse, depicts Santa Cruz as a long-time surfing center, and surfing as a consuming passion. Open daily. Hours vary. Admission free, Tel. 429-3429 or 462-0331.

Take West Cliff drive to the abutment of land that marks the end of Monterey Bay until you reach the **Natural Bridges State Park**. Here the surf has pounded holes through the jutting walls of cliff. Located just west of the park, on Delaware St., is the **Long Marine Laboratory**, maintained by UCSC. Open Tues.-Sun. 1-4pm, Tel. 459-4308 or

459-2883. East of the Boardwalk across the San Lorenzo River is the **Santa Cruz City Museum**. Just look for the stone whale. Located at 1305 E. Cliff Dr., 10am-5pm Tues.-Fri., 1pm-4pm Sat.-Sun., Tel. 429-3773. Inside, the displays focus on local tidepools, mammals, geological history and Indian culture.

Hills covered in redwoods slope gently down to the ocean at the beautiful campus of **UCSC**, which is unique in the UC system and considered one of the most innovative schools in the country. It is really a cluster of interdependent small colleges. Each college is a small, self-contained, architecturally distinct community. Each has its own classrooms, resident halls, library, etc.; the colleges are inter-connected through courses and extramural activities. The emphasis here is on the writing of theses, not on getting good grades on exams grades. The visitors center in Kresge Hall provides information and guided tours, Tel. 459-0111.

Along the coast and in the valleys to the east, apples, figs, corn, berries and other seasonal fruits and vegetables are grown; this is also a wine region. A visit to one of the farms gives one an opportunity to observe the countryside and a chance to purchase fresh produce, sometimes at bargain prices, as well as a chance to meet the locals. Many farms encourage and welcome visitors, but it is best to call ahead. A self-guided tour map is available, with a detailed listing of local farms, ranches and produce. The Chamber of Commerce and Convention and Visitor Bureau distribute these maps. Also available is a list of regional wineries dotting the countryside.

Within the coast, the hills and the canyons around Santa Cruz are many state parks. **Henry Cowell Redwoods State Park**, along Route 9, is a short ride north of Santa Cruz, and includes 4,000 acres of magnificent redwood forest. There are 15 miles (24 km) of hiking and riding trails, as well as camping facilities. The popular trail looping through Redwood Grove begins and ends at an exhibit shelter. The largest part of the park is accessible only by foot or on horseback. **Fall Creek State Park**, a part of Henry Cowell State Park, is strictly a hikers' park, with no roads. It is heavily forested, with deep canyons. Campfire programs and guided hikes are conducted in the summer. Park headquarters can be contacted at Tel. 335-4598.

Adjacent to the Henry Cowell State Park is **Roaring Camp and Big Trees**, where old-fashioned steam-powered trains chug along a winding narrow gauge rail line. This is a faithful recreation of the lines that carried giant redwood logs from forest to sawmill. Every Memorial Day weekend there is a three-day re-enactment of the Civil War period, including battles staged with infantry, cavalry and artillery battle tactics. Take Route 9 to Felton, turn southeast on to Graham Hill Rd., and continue half a mile. Admission fee. Open daily in summer, and weekends and holidays year round. Trains start in summer at 11am or noon, on a varying schedule, Tel. 335-4484 or 335-4400. The covered wooden bridge in Felton is not the awesome sight lauded by the local brochures, but it is a quaint photo spot.

Further to the north is the 16,000 acre **Big Basin State Park**, an immense primeval redwood forest preserve on the ocean-facing slopes of the Santa Cruz Mountains. There are 60 miles (95 km) of trail in this park. From the park headquarters, just opposite the campground, is the popular Skyline-to-Sea trail. A short trail (20-25 minutes walk) is the Redwood route next to parking lot at the entrance to the reserve. This will lead the visitor to interesting trees, such as the "Chimney Tree" with a hollow

trunk through which you can see the sky. There is also "Mother of the Forest" which, though it is the tallest in the forest (329ft/112m) is less impressive than "Father of the Forest", a wonderful example of the dimensions which these trees can reach. This is a much visited park, but since most visitors come for a picnic or short stroll through the most accessible redwood groves, it is easy to find uncrowded trails and quiet solitude in shaded canyons or beside misty waterfalls. Guided hikes and evening campfire programs are held from mid-June to Labor Day. Pick up a trail map at the Visitor Center. The park has four major camp-grounds and backcountry camping is allowed. Permits are required. To reach Big Basin, drive north on Route 9 to Boulder Creek and turn north-west on Route 236 to the park, Tel. 338-6132 or 800-444-7275. Admission charge.

SAN FRANCISCO

San Francisco is perhaps best typified by its annual September "City Fair", where apple pie contests have been replaced by contests for the best quiche; Quilting bees have been replaced by garbage can painting; and bronco-riding and cattle-punching has given way to stunts on skateboards and small bicycles to breakdance rhythms. In addition to the usual burgers and fries, you'll find chow mein and egg roll, sushi, enchiladas, felafel, curry, souvlaki, piroshkis, Thai broiled fish, Salvadoran rice, Ethiopian injira, and New York kosher pastrami-on-rye with a pickle on the side. At the entrance to the fair, municipal and civic organizations hand out flyers urging support for various projects, from recycling bottles and newspapers to supporting mobile libraries for the elderly – all this with a heavy sprinkling of the spiritual.

San Francisco, with a population of 750,000, has the richness, diversity and the crowded neighborhoods of a major urban center, without the hectic pressure of a big city. The glass and concrete financial district, with its crowds in dark business suits, could be Wall Street, yet the neighborhoods of small houses and fenced-in yards just a bus ride away might be found in any small town. The streets and alleys of Chinatown toward the east end of the city are packed with crowds, noise and delicious smells; but at the nearby tree-covered western slopes of the city, soothed by the rhythm of surf and foghorn, you would hardly believe there's a city behind you at all.

San Francisco is a city that conjures up many different images: It is the bastion of old-world, cosmopolitan urbanity, its ethnic fabric rich with diversity; it is the epitome of wealthy, cultured, self-absorbed hedonism, a place where the leisure-loving, the young and the upwardly mobile make money and spend it on expensive toys; homosexuality is open and almost fashionable; and there are enough self-liberating, consciousness-raising, spiritually awakened groups, cults and movements to warrant their own yellow pages. Experimental art and theater proliferate; new ideas spring from the cultural soil and every second clerk or waitress claims to be an artist, writer or musician.

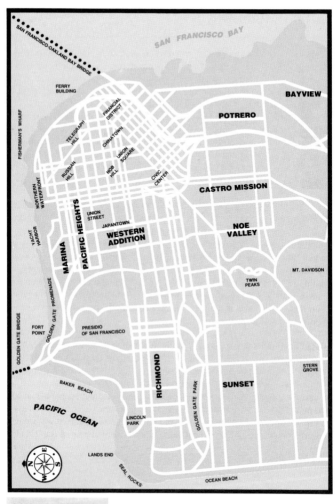

SAN FRANCISCO

There is, obviously, a more serious side to the city as well. San Francisco is a rapidly changing city. It was at one time the farthest point west one could go. Now it seems as if the Far East has been extended to the California shore. The strong ties between San Francisco and the Far East come from several sources. Chinese and other Asian groups have median incomes exceeding those of Whites. They are hard-working, persistent and family-oriented. A higher percentage of their children attend college, often in the most technical fields and advanced sciences. Chinatown and the surrounding area, one of the most densely populated areas in the country, has been bursting its seams for quite a while now and has spilled over not only into the neighboring Italian neighborhood, but also into suburban neighborhoods far away.

San Francisco, located on the tip of a peninsula which separates San Francisco Bay from the Pacific Ocean

The decrepit Tenderloin area has suddenly had an influx of Cambodians and Indonesians, as well as a steady influx of immigrants from Asian countries in political turmoil – Laos, Vietnam, Cambodia, Thailand and especially the Philippines. Moreover, trade with Asia has soared. Cities in the Pacific are growing rapidly. With one exception, the eight largest banks in the world are from the Pacific nations, and Pacific investors are buying up San Francisco property.

Added to this ethnic mélange is the influx of immigrants from unstable Latin American countries – El Salvador, Nicaragua and Peru – and from Mexico, many of whom are not legally registered.

A casual survey of Latino neighborhoods reveals a great surge in numbers and nationalities. The Latinos have not been integrated into American society as rapidly as the Asians, but they bring with them rich cultures and often a powerful sense of political radicalism. The traditional profile of San Francisco as a city of career-conscious single yuppies, prosperous gay entrepreneurs, Victorian houses and bohemian poets is partial at best. The city is in the process of change, from its foundations upwards.

The term "Pacific Rim" is vogue in California, and has become as common as the concepts "Third World", "Middle East" or "Old World". It hints at a new global orientation, towards the coasts lining the huge expanse of the Pacific. San Francisco, in the city's finest tradition, is on the cutting edge of change.

San Francisco of today is a city for the traveler, food-lover, walker, music-lover: eat in a burnished, padded grillroom, or survive on burritos; have the valet park your car or get around by bus, subway and cable car; hear the biggest names in classical or rock music, or rub shoulders with a struggling artist in a doorway on a windy night.

Orientation

San Francisco is located at the tip of a peninsula extending north from the

San Mateo hills. The peninsula separates the San Francisco Bay from the Pacific Ocean. The bay's narrow, and only, entrance from the Pacific was ignored for over two hundred years after the first explorations of the coast.

Across this narrow strait to the north lies the peninsula of Marin. To the east, across the bay, lie Oakland and Berkeley and a series of suburban communities.

The first European settlement, built by the Spanish in 1776, included a presidio at the western tip of the peninsula, and a mission. The settlement that grew up around these two points remained small for years. At the time of the discovery of gold, the settlement had only several hundred inhabitants, and was of secondary importance to Monterey and other towns.

The sparks of the gold rush ignited an explosion of growth. The port developed at the northeast bend of the peninsula. Early photographs show a veritable forest of masts. The city expanded in a ragged progression of tents, shacks and muddy streets up the hills. From the very beginning, San Francisco was an ethnic patchwork. Gold-hungry immigrants streamed in from all over the world. Europeans, Americans, Mexicans, Central Americans and Chinese were thrown together into the maelstrom that was young San Francisco.

The core of old San Francisco was in the hilly northeast corner, from whence the city fanned out. The original area included the wharves of the Embarcadero, the Barbary Coast (whose dance halls and brothels were eventually replaced by the towers of the Financial District), Union Square vicinity, Chinatown, North Beach and Fisherman's Wharf.

Telegraph Hill, between the Embarcadero and North Beach, eventually became a neighborhood for Italian workers and fishermen, and is easily recognized today by Coit Tower at its peak. West of downtown rise Nob Hill and Russian Hill. On Nob Hill the industrial and financial overlords of the rapidly growing city built their mansions.

From the Embarcadero, the main thoroughfare, Market Street, slants to the southwest. The area south of Market St., SOMA, was, until recently, a

San Francisco – between the hills and San Francisco Bay

rundown collection of warehouses and lots, but artists, dance clubs and trendy restaurants are now moving in. Further along the axis of Market St. is the expansive layout of public buildings around the Civic Center. Neither of the neighborhoods bordering the Civic Center – the Tenderloin area to the northeast, and the Western Addition to the west – is especially attractive or safe. A small Japantown clings to the northern edge of the Western Addition. Further along Market St., and just to its south, is the predominantly Mexican and Latino Mission District. Market street leads up to the gay Castro St. neighborhood, and to Twin Peaks Park.

Twin Peaks and the adjacent Mt. Davidson, the highest point in the city at some 1,000 ft. (340m), provide breathtaking panoramas of the entire city spreading below in every direction. From here it is easy to see how the southern reaches of the city blend into the suburbs of Daly City (reputedly the inspiration for Malvina Reynolds' famous song about suburbia, *Little Boxes*).

West of the restaurants and malls of Fisherman's Wharf, along the city's northern shore, rises the promontory of Fort Mason, which houses the National Park Service and a youth hostel. The old red-brick military buildings on the docks have been converted into studios, museums and workspace for various grassroots organizations. Beyond Fort Mason lies the Marina, used for pleasure crafts. To the south of the Marina rises Pacific Heights, a pretty neighborhood of old houses squeezed side by side. On the way up is Union Street lined with refurbished Victorian buildings and renown for its singles scene.

Further west lies the residential Richmond neighborhood, with its excellent restaurants along Clement St. To the south stretches the green belt of Golden Gate Park, with Haight-Ashbury at its eastern end and the ocean at the west. Public beaches stretch in both directions from here. To the north they rise into high and rugged bluffs fringed by forest and hiking trails. Situated on Fort Point is part of a large army base, the Presidio. Most of the shoreline includes a recreational strip. At the northernmost point, above Fort Point, the Golden Gate Bridge stretches north toward Marin. Grass and walking paths follow the rocky shore east back to the Marina.

San Francisco's famous fogs obscure the Golden Gate Bridge and block the sun from the western neighborhoods, while the sun still shines on the inland districts buffered by the hills. Sometimes the fog rolls over the whole city, bringing with it dampness and chill. Mark Twain said that the coldest winter he ever experienced was a summer in San Francisco. A heavy sweater might be necessary, even in summer. The weather can change sharply, not only from neighborhood to neighborhood, but within the day. Summer temperatures are generally moderate and comfortable. Cold days of damp fog or heavy rain may be interspersed with warm clear days.

The variety of tightly-packed neighborhoods, each with its own center and identity, makes exploring this city a joy. The most popular sites are concentrated in the old hilly northeastern section of the city. These neighborhoods can easily be explored on foot.

The public transportation grid is comprehensive, but you must take the time to figure it out. You can easily get from one place to another and tour each individual area on foot; this can be a lot more convenient than touring with a car.

How to Get There

By air: San Francisco International Airport (SFO), serves airlines from around the world, without the chaos of a major airport. It is located 14 miles (22 km) south of the city on a small peninsula stretching into the bay.

The various airlines are divided between the three terminals – North, Central and South. The upper tier of the terminals is for departures, the lower for arrivals. Street traffic moves smoothly at the arrival level; Airport Information will handle all enquiries about transportation, hotels, etc.

San Francisco's individuality is obvious even at the airport: For travelers with time to kill the airport's art museum and guided tour of the airport are attractive alternatives to reading a cheap novel.

The airport is easily and quickly reached by car via the Freeway 101. During rush hours, the highway may be congested in the city itself, but traffic generally flows fairly fast outside the city. Barring a major traffic jam, it takes about half an hour to reach the airport from the city center.

Public and private transportation from the airport to downtown San Francisco is relatively convenient and inexpensive. If you require public transportation, make sure to specify when seeking information (otherwise you may only get information about private *Airporter* buses). *San Mateo County Transit (SamTrans*, Tel. 800-660-4287) buses make the trip between downtown and SFO about every half hour, from early morning to about 1:30am. These buses arrive downtown at the Transbay terminal a few blocks south of Market. From there, local public transportation can be gotten right at the terminal entrance. The terminal is not in the best of neighborhoods, nor are there many facilities for the tourist in the immediate vicinity, something you should consider if arriving at a late hour.

To get to the east bay area – Oakland, Berkeley – the ride downtown is unnecessary. Take the *SamTrans* bus that goes to the Daly City terminal of the *Bay Area Rapid Transit (BART)* system, where the sleek futuristic train will whoosh you under the city and bay.

The *Airporter* bus service runs a shuttle from the airport to the terminals, including to its downtown terminal in Union Square. Buses run every 20 minutes, from 5am-midnight, Tel. 495-8404.

Smaller shuttle and van services go from door to door for a few extra dollars. Direct private transportation can also be obtained for outlying destinations, such as Napa. Inquire at the airport for both services. Representatives of the major car rental firms are located in the terminals.

Major airports in Oakland and San Jose also provide full flight schedules for major national and regional carriers. The airport at Oakland has been extended and renovated, and now services many San Francisco-bound travelers. The *BART* train, which stops regularly at the airport, offers the best connection between the airport and the center of San Francisco.

San Francisco International Airport (SFO) Information: Tel. 761-0800.

By land: *Greyhound* serves San Francisco; its terminal is open 24 hours, but is located on the south side of Market St. – the wrong side if it happens to be late at night.

Behind the Transbay terminal is *Green Tortoise*, Tel. 821-0803 or 956-7500, the bunk-bedded bus line that offers somewhat adventurous and unconventional trips to destinations around the state and country. There are frequent and cheap trips to Los Angeles, up the coast, to Yosemite, or across the country.

By train: *Amtrak* stops (or starts) in Oakland. A free shuttle bus connects the *Amtrak* station and the Transbay Terminal in San Francisco. The shuttle trip takes about half an hour.

By car: The fastest way to get from Los Angeles to San Francisco by car is to take the I-5 along the western edge of the San Joaquin Valley, and then to go west along I-580 to the bay area. U.S. 101 is not as spectacular as the Pacific Coast Highway or as fast as I-5, but it's more interesting than the valley route. The coastal route along Highway 1 through Big Sur is a breathtaking drive. From the Monterey and Santa Cruz areas, several routes approach the bay area. U.S. 101 swings east into the Santa Clara Valley, enters San Jose, and approaches the east bay. Highway 1 becomes a freeway south of Santa Cruz, and connects with Highway 17, which crosses over the Santa Cruz mountains to the network of freeways running on both sides the bay. Highway 1 continues up the coast as a small road, passing state beaches, gentle hills and several small towns before reaching the lower edges of suburbia. Another alternative route runs on Route 9 from Santa Cruz, and passes under a canopy of towering redwoods.

From the north, whether driving along Highway 1 or U.S. 101, the two roads merge and U.S. 101 takes over as the highway crosses the Golden Gate Bridge. From Sacramento, Tahoe, Reno and the east, the transcontinental I-80 leads directly to the Oakland Bay Bridge.

Local Transportation

In 1873, the cable car was invented in San Francisco, to replace horse-drawn carriages for which the city's steep hills were too taxing. In 1912, first publicly owned municipal transportation system in the country was launched by San Francisco, and it is no wonder that San Francisco has a superb public transportation system today, both within the city limits and connecting its satellite communities. There is such an array of overlapping and inter-connecting systems – cable cars and trolleys, buses and municipal subway, *BART, AC Transit, Sam-Trans, CalTrain* and *Golden Gate Transit*, plus shuttles between the various systems – that it can be baffling to a visitor. A variety of tickets, designed to save money for the regular traveler and encourage the use of public transportation, is available.

MUNI, the principal municipal transportation system, has several components: trolley cars, cable cars, buses and the metro (subway) system. Trolleys are the cars attached to overhead wires (that spark occasionally), and cable cars are the squat, multi-colored open cars that run up and down the hills near the city center. The fare is the same for all systems except the cable cars, which cost considerably more. Free transfers are good in any direction for 90 minutes. Exact change is required. A $35 *MUNI* Fast Pass allows unlimited travel for one calendar month on *MUNI*

(including the cable cars) and *BART* (*Bay Area Rapid Transit* – see below), within the city limits. They are available at *MUNI* ticket outlets, and if you are planning an extended stay in the city they are well worth considering. In addition, an all-day pass, good for the entire *MUNI* system, is available at automatic ticket machines located along the cable car lines.

The **cable cars** themselves are not motorized: a big motor at the cable car station pulls a steel cable, guided by an intricate network of pulleys, through a trench beneath the tracks. The cable is held and released by a grip on the car that works like a pair of pliers. The brakes are mechanical. This system was widely used in San Francisco (as well as in other cities), until it was supplanted by the trolley on all but the steepest routes. After the 1906 earthquake, the trolley replaced the cable cars on most routes. The cable car system, over-hauled in 1984, is an official National Historic Landmark.

The cable cars operate along three routes today. The *Powell-Hyde* line begins at Powell and Market streets and ends at Victorian Park near the Maritime Museum and Aquatic Park. The *Powell-Mason* line also begins at Powell and Market but terminates at Bay Street, just three blocks from Fisherman's Wharf. The *California Street* line runs from the foot of Market Street to Van Ness Avenue. Cable car riders should, if possible, purchase tickets before boarding from the self-service ticket machines at all terminals and major stops. There is usually a lengthy line waiting to board the cable-cars, and you must expect to wait as long as an hour during the summer season. The station with the shortest line is the one on Van Ness Ave.

The cable car – one of San Francisco's trade-marks

Hop off any Powell St. line, at Washington and Mason, for a visit to the **Cable Car Museum**, the humming center of the cable car operation. Open 10am-6pm daily. Admission free. Tel. 474-1887. The building was restored on the original foundation in 1984 and presents a wide display of historical exhibits and memorabilia on the cable car, including the original prototype car. A 16-minute film is shown continuously.

The five-line **metro** train system, operating both above and below ground, is the newest addition to the *MUNI* system. Downtown, between the Embarcadero and the Civic Center, it follows the *BART* route. It then branches off to the west and southwest, reaching Castro St., the Twin Peaks area, and the San Francisco Zoo near the beach. Another line heads for the beach, just south of Golden Gate Park. It operates from 5am-12:30am weekdays.

BART is the sleek futuristic system that shoots from Daly City in the south, through downtown, and beneath the floor of the bay to Oakland, Berkeley and other East Bay cities and suburbs. The tube under the Bay, over three-and-a-half miles (5.5 km) long, is one of the longest underwater crossings in the world.

Within the San Francisco area (from Balboa Park to the Embarcadero stations) a *MUNI* pass is also valid for *BART*. Take time to study the charts and the system before using it. Everything, from the ticket purchase to entry through the gate, is automatic. There are various longer-term, regular-use tickets available as well as arrangements between companies on ticket use. Should the automatic ticket system baffle you, there is an attendant at every station. If you walk out from a *BART* station into San Francisco, a two-part transfer at the station will allow you to ride on *MUNI* (not the cable car) to your destination and back to the *BART* station. One can also take a bicycle aboard *BART* lines. If traveling through a pneumatic tube all day thrills you, you can buy the *BART* excursion ticket which allows you to tour all the *BART* stations for up to three hours. The catch is that you can only exit from the station you entered; exiting anywhere else will nullify the excursion ticket.

The *Transbay Transit Terminal*, at 1st and Mission, is the San Francisco center for three bay area bus lines. *AC Transit* (Tel. 800-559-INFO) operates between San Francisco and the East Bay, and among the East Bay communities themselves. The terminal also houses *SamTrans* (Tel. 800-660-4287), connecting to the airport and to peninsula cities as far south as Palo Alto.

Golden Gate Transit (Tel. 332-6600), connects Marin County to the city via the Golden Gate Bridge, as well as serving the cities within Marin County. The connections within Marin can sometimes be sporadic, but bus no. 76 can bring you from downtown San Francisco right to the wild edge of the Pacific in the Marin Headlands Reserve.

CalTrain (Tel. 800-660-4287), with a terminal at 4th St. and Townsend, operates commuter trains between San Francisco and San Jose, and links with the *Santa Clara County Transit System*. Weekday shuttle buses run between the terminal and the Financial District at the peak commuting hours. Also located here is the San Francisco station for *Amtrak*, with shuttle buses stopping along 4th St. for connections with *Amtrak* trains at the Oakland train station.

Accommodation

As might be expected, San Francisco offers a wide range of accommodation, something to suit the taste, needs and budget of almost any traveler.

The classic old San Francisco hotels include the *St. Francis*, the *Sir Francis Drake*, the *Fairmont* and the *Mark Hopkins*. All these are in the area of Powell St. or the adjacent Nob Hill. Some afford fantastic views, as well as tasteful luxury. They are, as one might guess, quite expensive.

Other, newer luxury hotels have sprouted in the central areas of the city. There is the *Hyatt*, at the Embarcadero, and several others in the area of Fisherman's Wharf.

On Geary St., near the Marina neighborhood, you'll find more standard motels at various prices. At the lower end of the spectrum, there is a concentration of cheap, but still decent and safe hotels and hostels in the Tenderloin area and the area south of Mission St. The neighborhood may be questionable at a late hour, but the facilities themselves are generally secure. The best bet, in this price range, is one of the youth hostels in and around the city.

In recent years, the number of Bed & Breakfast Inns in the city has increased. Some of these are located in beautifully restored Victorian buildings.

For information, referrals, and brochures on local B&Bs, contact the Association of Bed & Breakfast Innkeepers of San Francisco, Tel. 921-7150.

LUXURY HOTELS ($140 AND UP)

Each of these is opulent in its own way. The service is superb and the rooms are distinctive, often individually designed. Most have a turn-of-the-century atmosphere.

The Fairmont: 950 Mason St., Tel. 772-5212, Res. Tel. 800-344-3550 (U.S.), 800-527-4727 (Can.). Spa, restaurant, lounge.

Four Seasons Clift: 495 Geary St., Downtown, Tel. 775-4700, or Tel. 800-332-3442. Perhaps the best hotel in town. Great location, spacious rooms and excellent service, making it one of the most desirable hotels in the whole of California.

Mark Hopkins Inter-Continental: 1 Nob Hill, Tel. 392-3434, or Tel. 800-327-0200.

Sir Francis Drake Hotel: 450 Powell St., Tel. 392-7755, Res. Tel. 800-227-5480. Spa, restaurant, lounge.

Hyatt Regency: 5 Embarcadero Center, Tel. 788-1234, Res. 800-233-1234. Different from the traditional hotels, this modern luxury hotel has a lobby like an immense greenhouse and a famous revolving bar high above the streets.

Sherman House: 2160 Green St., Pacific Heights, north of Union Square, Tel. 563-3600, Res. 800-424-5777. Only 15 rooms in this first-rate hotel. Advisable to reserve rooms well in advance. European style decor and service create an old-world atmosphere not easily forgotten.

**MODERATE HOTELS
($100-$140 PER NIGHT)**
Cartwright Hotel: 524 Sutter St., Tel. 421-2865, or Tel. 800-227-3844. Cozy and central, with individually designed rooms.

Hotel Beresford: 635 Sutter St., near Mason: Tel. 673-9900, Res. Tel. 800-533-6533. A very warm, friendly Victorian-style hotel, with gaslight lamps. Attached is the *White Horse Tavern*, a replica of the 18th-century original pub in Edinburgh.

Lombard Hotel: 1015 Geary St., Tel. 673 5232, or Tel. 800-227-3608. Pleasant hotel with different rooms in terms of quality and price. Better ask to see room before checking in. Close to many tourist centers.

**INEXPENSIVE HOTELS
(LESS THAN $100 PER NIGHT)**
Adelaide Inn: 5 Adelaide Place.,

Tel. 441-2261. Clean, no private baths. Small, *pension*-like establishment, with kitchenette for guests. Continental breakfast.

The Red Victorian Bed and Breakfast Inn: 1665 Haight St. Tel. 864-1978. In the heart of the Haight right next to the funky movie house of the same name. If there was ever such a thing as a hip B&B, this is it. Beautiful Victorian decor, individually decorated rooms. A little expensive, but definitely unique.

Allison Hotel: 417 Stockton St., Tel. 986-8737, Res. 800-628-6456.

Beresford Hotel: 635 Sutter St., Tel. 673-9900, Res. 800-533-6533.

Commodore Hotel: 825 Sutter St., Tel. 923-6800, Res. 800-338-6848.

Fitzgerald Hotel: 620 Post St., Tel. 775-8100, Res. 800-33-HOTEL.

Hotel Verona: 317 Leavenworth St., Tel. 771-4242, Res. 800-422-3646.

Powell Hotel and Powell West Hotel: 28 Cyril Magrin St./111 Mason St., Tel. 398-3200, Res. 800-652-3399 (CA), 800-368-0700 (U.S., Can).

Star Motel: 1727 Lombard St., Tel. 346-8250, Res. 800-835-8143.

YOUTH HOSTELS
There are five youth hostels in the Bay area which are located right on the bay or the ocean:

San Francisco International Hostel: Building 240, Fort Mason, Tel. 771-7277. Located in a Civil-War era building, with easy bus or walking access to all major areas of the city. Recommended.

Golden Gate Hostel: Building 941, Fort Barry, Sausalito, Tel. 331-2777. The building is a historical landmark, set within miles of hiking trails in the gorgeous Marin Headlands, accessible to hills, lagoons, beaches and Muir Redwoods, as well as to Sausalito itself.

Point Reyes Hostel: Point Reyes Station, Tel. 663-8811. An old ranch house, situated near the quiet beaches, estuaries and sand dunes of beautiful Point Reyes National Seashore. Reservations are recommended, especially on weekends.

Montara Lighthouse Hostel: 16th., Cabrillo Highway 1, Montara, Tel. 728-7177. Set in the old light station itself, 25 miles (40 km) south of San Francisco, near trails, boating facilities and tide pools of the marine reserve.

Pigeon Point Lighthouse Hostel: Pigeon Pt. Rd., Highway 1, Pescadero, Tel. 879-0633. 50 miles (80 km) south of San Francisco, in a series of old Coast Guard bungalows, near tidepools, trails and redwoods.

All these hostels are easily accessible by public bus, *BART* or commuter train. Call the hostel itself for exact transportation.

Food

Just walking through a crowded San Francisco street will whet your appetite. Everywhere you turn there are restaurants, with a variety to suit any taste and budget.

The classic old San Francisco restaurants combine sparse decor with food cooked on an open grill. Fresh fish grilled on intensely hot mesquite charcoal is a local favorite. There is no so-called "local cuisine", because there is so much of every kind of cooking throughout the city.

Chinese restaurants offer an informal lunch-counter atmosphere, a nice alternative to greasy diners. The plethora of Chinese restaurants has been supplemented in recent years by other Asian restaurants: Cambodian, Laotian, Thai, Filipino and, of course, Japanese. One need only sample a few of the Asian ethnic restaurants in San Francisco to realize that each cuisine is distinctive. Similarly, Latin American restaurants have been springing up, exposing the city to foods from El Salvador, Nicaragua and Peru. There are also the French, Russian, Persian, Basque and Greek restaurants.

Not surprisingly, San Francisco has been in the forefront of developing gourmet vegetarian restaurants featuring vegetables you've probably never heard of.

Diners and fast-food stands can also be found here, as can lots of great ice cream stands – although in San Francisco you don't eat ordinary ice cream; head for North Beach for the famous Italian gelato. Some restaurants are described below grouped according to district.

FINANCIAL DISTRICT/DOWNTOWN

The downtown and Montgomery St. environs have no shortage of old, brass-polished San Francisco bars and restaurants. Some of the best seafood, especially grilled fish.

Tadich Grill: 240 California, in the

Financial District, Tel. 391-1849. The lines can be long with people waiting for the superb seafood.

Jack's Restaurant: 615 Sacramento St. The bare, simple surroundings belie the quality that have made this a San Francisco by-word. Moderate prices.

Scott's Seafood: 3 Embarcadero. Tel. 981-0622. A branch of the original on Lombard St., serving the same menu of seafood that is reputedly among the best in the city. Moderate prices.

Sam's Grill: 374 Bush St., Tel. 421-0594. Another classic standby, with curtained booths for a special rendezvous. Delicious grilled fish and sourdough bread. Reasonably priced.

John's Grill, 63 Ellis St., Tel. 986-0069. Moderate prices.

CHINATOWN

Empress of China: 838 Grant Ave., Sixth Floor, Tel. 434-1345. Chinese cuisine amidst Oriental splendor matched by great views. Lunch until 11pm. Moderate prices.

Golden Dragon Restaurant: 816 Washington St., Tel. 398-3920. Chefs from Hong Kong prepare Cantonese food in the heart of Chinatown. Breakfast, lunch and dinner daily 8am-midnight. Inexpensive.

Hang Ah Tea Room: 1 Hang Ah St. off Sacramento St. near Stockton, Tel. 982-5686. This small café near the Chinese Playground serves authentic Chinese dim sum and dinners. Daily 10am-9pm. Inexpensive.

Lotus Blossom Restaurant and Gold Coin Lounge: 750 Kearny St., Tel. 433-6600. This Financial District-Chinatown crossroads offers dancing and entertainment Thursday-Sunday. Buffet breakfast daily, lunch Monday-Friday, dinner nightly until 10pm, Sunday brunch noon-2pm. Moderate prices.

Oriental Pearl Restaurant: 760-778 Clay St., Tel. 433-1817. Contemporary Chinese cuisine in an elegant setting. Lunch and dinner Monday-Friday 11am-9:30pm, Saturday-Sunday 10am-9:30pm. Inexpensive.

Royal Jade Seafood Cuisine: 675 Jackson St., Tel. 392-2929. Dim

sum and seafood dinners. Friendly service. Breakfast, lunch and dinner daily 9am-10pm. Moderate prices.

NORTH BEACH

Eating out and hanging out in North Beach is a local sport which is extremely easy and inviting to take up. Many restaurants run lunch specials, which often consist of a heavy meat-and-pasta meal.

The Basque Hotel and Restaurant: 15 Romolo Place, Tel. 788-9404. Family Style, French Basque restaurant. Dinner Tuesday-Sunday 5-10pm. Inexpensive.

Gold Mountain Restaurant: 644 Broadway, Tel. 296-7733. Chinese Cuisine in a cosmopolitan atmosphere. Breakfast, lunch and dinner daily 8am-9:30pm. Inexpensive.

Anthony's: 1701 Powell St., Tel. 391-4488. Italian Cuisine. Wood-fired prime steaks and pasta are specialties. Dinner nightly 5-11pm. Inexpensive.

Maykadeh Persian Cuisine: 470 Green St, Tel. 362-8286. The Persian haute cuisine served here is exotic to the American palate. Even the Middle Eastern Basmati rice stands out. The *ghorme sabzee*, roughly translated as braised and spiced lamb, is worth trying. Then again, just about everything is. Portions are large. Lunch Monday-Friday 11:30am-2:30pm; dinner Monday-Thursday 5-10pm, until 11pm Friday; lunch and dinner Saturday noon-11pm; Sunday noon-10:30pm. Moderate prices.

Capp's Corner: 1600 Powell St., Tel. 989-2589. Powell and Green. A small and very well-known North Beach joint, with celebrity pics all over the walls, and the large Italian lunch specials scribbled daily on the board. Lunch Monday-Friday 11:30am-2:30pm; dinner Monday-Friday 4:30-10:30pm; open Saturday-Sunday 4-11pm. Inexpensive.

Basta Pasta: 1268 Grant Ave., Tel. 434-2248. Fresh pasta, home cured prosciutto and pizza baked in a wood-burning oven make this a favorite spot, especially for late-night dining. Lunch and dinner daily 11:45-1:45am. Inexpensive.

Buca Giovanni: 800 Greenwich St., Tel. 776-7766. The underground dining room with cave effects sets the stage for an elegant Tuscan-style dining experience. Dinner Monday-Saturday 5:30-10:30pm. Moderate prices.

THE MISSION DISTRICT

Jack in the Box: Fourth and Mission Sts., Tel. 543-3081. This fast-food restaurant features teriyaki bowls, chicken caesar sandwich, grilled sourdough burger, chicken fajita pita and salads as well as hamburgers and tacos. Daily 6am-midnight. Inexpensive.

El Oso Restaurant: 1153 Valencia St., Tel. 550-0601. Spanish cuisine. Menu items include tapas and paella at a restaurant enlivened with eccentric decor and live piano music. Lunch Monday-Friday 11:30am-3pm; dinner daily 6-11pm. Inexpensive.

CIVIC CENTER

Hayes Street Grill: 320 Hayes. Tel. 863-5545. The grilled fish and sourdough bread have made this place a big hit. Lunch Monday-Friday 11:30am-2pm; dinner Monday-Thursday 5-9:30pm; Friday

5-10:30pm; Saturday 6-10:30pm; Sunday 5-8:30pm. Moderate prices.

Ananda Fuara: 1298 Market St., Tel. 621-1994. International vegetarian dishes in a tranquil atmosphere. Monday-Saturday 7am-7pm, until 3pm Wednesday, closed Sunday. Inexpensive.

Spuntino: 524 Van Ness Ave., Tel. 861-7772. Italian "quick bites" spark the taste buds of inveterate nibblers: *insalate*, *pizette*, *pasta*, *panini*, pastries, espresso and *gelato*. Monday 7am-10pm; Tuesday-Thursday 7am-11pm; Friday 7am-midnight; Saturday 10am-midnight; Sunday 10am-9pm. Inexpensive.

SOUTH OF MARKET
Eddie Rickenbacker's: 133 Second St., Tel. 543-3498. Down-to-earth American cuisine. Open daily for lunch 11am-3pm; dinner 5-9pm; open until 10pm Friday. Moderate prices.

Annie's and Annie's Billiards: 20 Annie St., Tel. 777-1102. Tucked in a quaint alley just off Market Street, two blocks north of Moscone center, Annie's offers continental cuisine complemented by soft piano music. Lunch Monday-Friday 11am-3pm. Bar and billiards open all evening. Inexpensive.

UNION STREET
Perry's: 1944 Union St. Tel. 922-9022. A popular and busy place. The grilled food is excellent. Open daily 9am-2am.

Luisa's: 1851 Union St. at Octavia, Tel. 563-4043. Romantic candlelight atmosphere and European-style service. Dinner served nightly 5-11pm. Moderate prices.

L'entrecote de Paris: 2032 Union St., Tel. 931-5006. The fashion-conscious gravitate to this bistro known for its house specialty – Entrecote with Sauce Café de Paris. Serves French seafood and other French specialties. Lunch and dinner Monday-Thursday 11:30am-11pm; open until midnight Friday-Saturday, until 10pm Sunday. Moderate prices.

Sushi Chardonnay: 1785 Union St., Tel. 346-5070. All-you-can-eat dinner buffet, serving Japanese foods. Lunch Monday-Friday 11:30am-2pm; dinner Monday-Thursday 5:30-10:30pm; Friday-Saturday 5:30-11pm; Sunday 5-10pm. Moderate prices.

CLEMENT STREET
Just a stroll down this aisle of restaurants, cafés, diners and pubs will make you hungry even if you have just eaten a prime steak and eggs.

Alain Rondelli: 126 Clement St., Tel. 387-0408. French contemporary foods in a warm and elegant atmosphere. Dinner Tuesday-Sunday 5:30-10pm. Moderate prices.

JAPANTOWN
Isobune: 1737 Ost St., Japan Center, Tel. 563-1030. A sushi restaurant, in which platters of sushi come around by boat on a small stream. Besides the novelty, the morsels are so delicious you'll be tempted to reach for more and more (the bill is calculated by the number of plates).

Mifune: 1737 Post St., Tel. 922-0337. Delicious and reasonably priced Japanese noodles.

HAIGHT-ASHBURY

Ben and Jerry's Ice Cream and Frozen Yogurt: 1480 Haight St., Tel. 249-4685. Ice cream and frozen yogurt, espresso, cappuccino and ice cream cakes. Sunday-Thursday 11am-11pm; Weekends until midnight.

FISHERMAN'S WHARF

Fridays: 685 Beach St., Tel. 775-8443. Contemporary American Cuisine – steak, ribs, burgers, seafood, sandwiches, salads and pastas. Lunch and dinner daily 11:30am-midnight. Moderate prices.

Yet Wah restaurant: Pier 39, Tel. 434-4430. Serving food from all over China, including live crab, lobster and fresh fish from a tank. Lunch and dinner served daily, 11am-10pm. Inexpensive.

EMBARCADERO

Gaylord (India) Restaurant: 1 Embarcadero, Tel. 397-7775. Authentic Indian cuisine in an elegant setting with panoramic views of the bay and the Marin Headlands. Lunch daily 11:45am-2pm, dinner daily 5-11pm. Moderate prices.

Il Fornaio Cucina Italiana: 1265 Battery St., Tel. 986-0100. Italian Cuisine. Tuscan scenes adorn the walls. Breakfast Monday-Friday 7-10:30am, brunch Saturday-Sunday 8am-1pm. Lunch and dinner Monday-Thursday 11:30am-11pm; Friday and Saturday until midnight; Sunday 1-11pm. Moderate prices.

Clubs

The music scene in San Francisco changes constantly. There is a wide variety of styles and music from S.F.'s traditional jazz to the latest fad. The listings here are, of course, only partial. Check the local newspapers and entertainment weeklies.

Big Heart City: 836 Mission St. Tel. 777-0666. An upscale Victorian atmosphere combined with the latest entertainment technology keeps crowds coming back at this

multimedia nightclub, espresso café and Thai restaurant. Live music, a computer interactive video lounge and dancing. 7am-2am daily.

Club Interlude: Holiday Inn Golden Gateway, 1500 Van Ness Ave. at California, Tel. 441-4000. Contemporary music in a distinctive atmosphere. Cocktails daily 11am-2am; lunch served daily 11am-2am; special "Pizza Hut" snack menu daily 2-10:30pm.

Club 181: 181 Eddy St. (Downtown) Tel. 673-8181. A fashionable supper, bar and billiards club attracting a diverse crowd, Club 181 serves candelabra-lit, new American cuisine. A mellow jazz band performs until 10pm, when the music picks up with a featured band, D.J. and dancing. Wednesday-Sunday 7pm-2am; Friday until 3am.

Johnny Love's: 1500 Broadway at Polk, Tel. 931-8021. Fast becoming one of San Francisco's hottest night spots, Johnny Love's jumps with live music and dancing nightly. Johnny "Love" Methany himself is on hand to set just the right mood. Supper club atmosphere complemented by live jazz and American bistro-style menu that changes weekly. Bar open daily 5pm-2am, dinner nightly 6-10pm.

Rock & Bowl: 1855 Haight St., Tel. 826-BOWL. Bowl and boogie at this combination nightclub/bowling alley. A 9-foot by 12-foot screen in the middle of the alley coupled with 25-inch screens over each lane play rock videos enhanced by a high-quality sound system. Bowl the night away or party around pool tables. Thursday 9pm-12:30am; Friday 10pm-2am; Saturday 9pm-2am.

Important Phone Numbers

Area Code: 415.
Visitor Information Center:
At Powell and Market, below street level, near the entry to the *BART* station. Hallidie Plaza, P.O. Box 429097, San Francisco, 94142-9097, Tel. 391-2000.
San Francisco International Airport (SFO) information: Tel. 761-0800.
Greyhound: Transbay Terminal, 425 Mission St. at First St., Tel. 800-231-2222.
Green Tortoise: Tel. 821-0803, 956-7500 or 800-TORTOISE.
Amtrak: Ferry Building, Suite 130, foot of Market St., Tel. 800-872-7245.
San Francisco Municipal Railway (MUNI): Tel. 673-MUNI. Info from 9am-5pm.
AC Transit: Tel. 800-559-INFO. Buses to and within east bay area.
SamTrans: Tel. 800-660-4287. To San Mateo County, and south along the peninsula.
Golden Gate Transit: Tel. 332-6600. Buses to and within Marin County.
CalTrain: Tel. 800-660-4287. Regional trains.
Bay Area Rapid Transit (BART): Tel. 788-BART.
Traveler's Aid Society: Tel. 255-2252.
Events: Tel. 391-2001 (for a recorded message listing daily events and activities).
Ambulance: Tel. 931-3900.
Road Conditions: Tel. 557-3755.
Senior Citizens' Information: Tel. 626-1033.
National Park Service: Fort Mason, Tel. 556-0560. General information, and specific information on places within the Golden Gate National Recreation Area.

Getting to Know the City

The abundance of attractions available to the tourist is likely to be confusing at first, since this beautiful city is packed with wonderful things that should not be missed. To help overwhelmed visitors, the city of San Francisco initiated, in 1938, an all-encompassing route that includes most of its treasures. This route, more commonly known as the 49-mile drive, takes approximately half a day to complete, and is clearly sign-posted throughout town in blue and white signs carrying the emblem of a sea-gull. The route includes Chinatown, Telegraph Hill, Golden Gate Park, the Civic Center and more. It may be undertaken in your own car or with one of the tourist companies, such as *Gray Line*, that runs the four-hour tour (known as Tour 1) several times a day (Tel. 558-9400 or 800-826-0202).

THE FINANCIAL DISTRICT

The theme of this area is, predictably, money. See how it is made, where it goes and how it is spent.

The **Museum of Money of the American West**, in the Bank of California, 400 California St., Tel. 765-0400 will give you an idea of the fever that the discovery of gold in California really caused. Continue your tour at the **Old Mint Museum** for still more dreams of gold. 5th and Mission. Open Mon.-Fri.10am-4pm. Admission free. Tel. 744-6830.

The **Wells Fargo History Room** at the Wells Fargo Bank, 420 Montgomery St., Tel. 396-2619, gives a history of the bank. An interesting stop. Open during banks working hours. Admission free.

Enter the old **Monadnock Building**, at Third St. and Market to glimpse the new wall and ceiling murals that look as if they might have come from a Renaissance Piazza.

The tall sleek **Transamerican Pyramid** at Montgomery between Clay and Washington stands out among the other towers and has become a San Francisco landmark. This is the tallest building in town at 853ft. (290m). There is a good viewing area on the 27th floor.

Transamerica – the tallest building in San Francisco

which is open to the public Mon.-Fri. 9am-4pm. Next to the pyramid is Redwood Park, a small peaceful haven of green, where lunch-time concerts are performed throughout the summer. On the eastern edge of the Financial District, the Embarcadero has been renovated (but the ugly freeway cuts off the entire view of the east bay). At the foot of Sacramento street stands the three-level **Embarcadero Center**, Tel. 772-0585. Attached to this complex of expensive stores is the *Hyatt Regency*, which has a high, translucent atrium and a famous revolving bar, the *Equinox Lounge*, at the top where you can nurse your drink for the 45-minute spin. Jacket and tie necessary. The interior of this hotel is very impressive and turns the place into a popular attraction even for those who cannot afford its prices.

Also at the Embarcadero Center, the **Levi Strauss History Room** relates how an immigrant tailor and his company transformed workpants into international fashion. Mon.-Fri. 10am-4pm. Admission free.

DOWNTOWN

Downtown and the Financial District can be spoken of separately or together. Market St. is their common southern boundary. The plaza where **Powell and Mason** meet **Market**, coming in from the seedy Tenderloin district to the west, is a small downtown hub of sorts. This is where the Powell

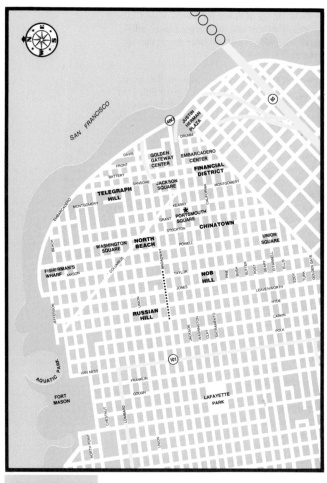

**DOWNTOWN
SAN FRANCISCO**

St. cable car turntable, heading to Ghiradelli Square, is situated. During the summer there is always a line of tourists waiting for the cable car.

Downstairs, to the side of the plaza is the city's main Visitor Center. The *BART* and *MUNI* metro station here can supply information on all the municipal systems – rail, trolley, bus, and cable.

A few blocks up Powell street is **Union Square**, a popular spot with office workers and street performers during weekday lunch hours. The street's flower stalls on the street corners do a brisk business with the executives. Around Union Square are the big department stores, *Macy's* and

Magnin's. On the east end of Union Square is a *Bass* ticket office and booking service selling tickets for a wide variety of theater events throughout the city.

On the west side of Powell St., opposite the square, is the dignified, *St. Francis Hotel*. Up the hill, west of Union Square is the wealthy neighborhood of **Nob Hill**, known locally as Snob Hill. In addition to the *St. Francis*, there are other classic, established and opulent San Francisco hotels on Powell St. and on the slopes of Nob Hill. These include the *Fairmont Hotel*, 950 Mason, the *Sir Francis Drake*, Sutter and Powell and the *Mark Hopkins*, California and Mason. All these hotels have elegant bars, cocktail lounges, or restaurants on their higher floors, offering fine views of the city.

The **Tenderloin** district, just west of the downtown area around Powell and Market, is a decrepit area of drunks, pushers, addicts, peep shows, porno movies, depressing residential hotels and boarded-up shops. Yet something new is stirring here, with immigrants from Vietnam and Cambodia moving in. A number of very good, reasonably priced restaurants have sprung up. As threatening as it may appear, it is (relatively) safe to walk around during the day. If you feel a bit adventurous about discovering interesting eateries, this is the place to go.

CHINATOWN

The old Chinatown, squeezed in roughly between Powell and Kearny, Bush and Broadway, is crammed with crowds, shops, colorful Chinese signs, and the delectable smells of Chinese food. Two cable car lines skirt Chinatown. Two blocks up the hill to the west run the two Powell St. lines. The California St. line, running between the Embarcadero and Van Ness, crosses Grant St. just where it turns into the crowded, brightly-lit and touristy main boulevard of Chinatown. Grant, lined with innumerable shops, runs north into Broadway and the Italian section of North Beach. This stretch and the surrounding streets are easily walkable. On Stockton, a block up from Grant, and on some of the

Celebrating the Chinese New Year in Chinatown

A taste of China on Grant Street

sidestreets, the signs and restaurant menus may be only in Chinese. The main activity in Chinatown is simply to stroll around, browse in the Chinese spice shops, examine all the strange little gadgets and trinkets being sold, stare at the meats hanging in the butcher shop windows, photograph the old men playing various games in Portsmouth Square, watch the rush of people, and breathe in the enticing aromas which beckon you from one restaurant to the next.

It is amazing how many good restaurants there are along the Chinatown streets. Each seems to have its own clientele, and many have newspaper clippings taped to the window proclaiming that particular place as positively the best Chinese restaurant in the city. Avoid the ones with gaudy, contrived settings and a primarily tourist clientele. You may make some fine discoveries of your own if you seek out that special hole-in-the-wall with bare walls, chipped linoleum tables, Chinese menus and Chinese customers.

The number of specific sites to see in Chinatown is limited. There is the large, ornate Chinese gate at Grant and Bush, which was given to the city as a gift from the Rep. of China in 1969. In addition to serving as a community center, the **Chinese Culture Center** houses a museum for the appreciation of Chinese arts and culture, with regularly changing exhibits. Located at 750 Kearny St., 3rd floor of *Holiday Inn*. Open Tues.-Sat. 10am-4pm. Admission free. Tel. 986-1822.

The museum of the **Chinese Historical Society of America** is concerned mainly with the role of the Chinese in the California Gold Rush, and the subsequent rapid development of the West Coast. Located at 650 Commercial St. Open Tues.-Sat. noon-4pm. Donation requested. Tel. 391-1188.

You can also visit a Chinese shrine, such as the **Tien Hou** Temple, 125 Waverly Place, which is one of the first Chinese buildings in the city; or visit the less interesting **Jeng Sen** Temple at 146 Waverly Place or **Norras** at 109 Waverly Place.

NORTH BEACH

North Beach abuts Chinatown at Broadway, and extends north along Columbus Ave. toward Fisherman's Wharf, and east up the steep slope of Telegraph Hill. An old Italian neighborhood, lined with small delis, bakeries, restaurants and cafés, it became a magnet for the emerging "Beat" movement in the early 50s.

"I saw the best minds of my generation destroyed by madness, starving hysterical naked..." – with that line from the poem *Howl*, delivered in a semi-chant in a small North Beach forum, Allen Ginsberg helped bring to the public's attention the new Beat poetry and literature that had been developing in San Francisco during the post-war years. Ginsberg and Jack Kerouac, Lawrence Ferlinghetti and others in the forefront of the movement headed to San Francisco because of the freer atmosphere, and congregated in North Beach because of the cheap rents and the village-like surroundings.

Ferlinghetti's *City Lights Bookstore* at Columbus and Broadway showcased the works of the Beat poets even when they were banned, and became a focal point for a new era of artistic, intellectual and social rebels.

In the clubs on **Broadway**, post-war free-form jazz bloomed, and comedians such as Lenny Bruce and Mort Sahl honed a comedy edged with piercing political and social criticism. A few years later, the clubs featured the folk and protest music which emerged as a powerful influence in the early 60s.

A street in Chinatown

As the glitter of these clubs began to fade, the old clubs became strip joints and new ones opened. Their flashing signs lined the street and dazzled the eyes. Glib "barkers" at the entrances lured in tourists with "free peeks". The big signs were eventually turned off, left hanging above boarded-up doors. Only the strip joints remain. The girls themselves often try to lure in patrons.

Broadway deteriorated, becoming the center of San Francisco's sleazy side, bastion of punk music, the cruising hangout for kids from the suburbs hunting down a little big-city action. There was a rise in crime, and although it is safe to walk the brightly lit street, it is not recommended to veer into one of the small side-streets at a late hour. Grassroots groups and city planners are considering the problem of the Broadway strip, and may try to transform it into a district of small theaters.

Concurrently, there is a marked increase in the numbers of Chinese signs which have crossed over Broadway. Many of the old, reliable, family-owned Italian stores have closed. On the sidestreet cafés, people park themselves at tables with notebooks and sketchpads. A few survivors from the old days hang out at *Vesuvio's*, near *City Lights*. *City Lights* itself is still open; its basement provides a peaceful respite from Broadway's bright rush. On Columbus, just north of Broadway, there are clusters of cafés and restaurants from which one can watch the passing parade: old Chinese, young punks, open-eyed tourists and hip young professionals.

Washington Square, near Columbus, is a nice place to enjoy a bit of greenery. All sorts of characters float by here. It is the perfect place for a picnic, with several good delis and bakeries bordering it. The slope of **Telegraph Hill** begins to the east of Washington Square. It is a steep walk, through some beautiful staired streets that are quiet even though they are right in the heart of the city. Bus 39 reaches the famous **Coit Tower** at the top of Telegraph (Tel. 362-0808).

The tower was erected in 1933 during the Depression by famous philanthropist Lillie Coit. Admission required for the climb or elevator ride to the top. Open daily 10am-7pm. The view from the base, a smidgeon lower, is just as spectacular and is free. The murals in the circular hall surrounding the lobby are impressive. They are wonderful examples of the populist frescoes which

Downtown and the bay, from Telegraph Hill

emerged from the school of modern industrial realism in American art. At the time they caused such a stir because of their clear political implications, about the role and destiny of workers that they had to be modified a bit.

For a visual feast continue down the east side of the hill, towards **Filbert Street**. Along with a few old wooden houses, pre-dating the 1906 earthquake, a pocket-sized paradise clings to the slope. The lovely overflowing garden was the creation of Grace Marchant who moved here in 1949 at the age of 63. She began by hauling away the bedsprings, tires and other garbage. By the time of her death at the age of 96, Marchant had transformed the neglected hillside into a lush, wild corner that attracted birds, wildlife and people.

Lombard Street

Bus 39 runs between Coit Tower and Fisherman's Wharf. A popular route for a day's excursion could include the cable car ride up Powell St. to Ghiradelli Square, a stroll along the docks and colorful tourist traps of the wharf area, the bus 39 ride to Coit Tower, a ride or walk back to Washington Square and North Beach, continuing by foot across Broadway into Chinatown, and a walk, bus or cable car (Powell is two steep blocks west of Chinatown) back downtown or wherever you need to go. This route invites detours and diversions. One popular place that every tourist must experience once is "the crookedest street in the world", **Lombard Street** (between Hyde and Leavenworth, in the northwest corner of North Beach).

FISHERMAN'S WHARF

Fisherman's Wharf is an overpriced tourist trap, but it is worth a visit, simply to see the colorful crowds against the bay shining in the sun. The view from the bay-side tables at old established seafood restaurants such as *Castagnola's* and *Alioto's* is beautiful, but the food is over-priced here, as it is at the sidewalk crab stands. There are several shopping complexes, housed in gutted old brick warehouses. At **Ghiradelli Square** (named after the chocolate manufacturer) the shops are arranged around an open square, with lavish and expensive restaurants. It is worth indulging in Ghiradelli chocolate, despite the high prices and long lines (Tel. 775-5500).

The marina at Fisherman's Wharf

At the foot of Polk St., just beyond Ghiradelli Square, is the **National Maritime Museum**, part of the small **Aquatic Park** near Fisherman's Wharf. Open daily 10am-5pm. Tours daily, Admission charge, Tel. 929-0202. The museum houses a wide range of sailing ship models, old photographs and artifacts. The photographs illustrate the phenomenal growth of the San Francisco port from a collection of tents to a sprawling city. Connected to the museum are several historic sailing ships berthed at nearby **Hyde Street Pier**. They include an old car ferry, steam schooner, tugboat and the *Balclutha*, a Cape Horn sailing ship. Hyde Street Pier has convenient hours – 9:30am-5pm (winter), 10am-6pm (summer) – and offers guided tours, self-guided tours, films and demonstrations. Beyond them, along the Embarcadero and the ferry to Alcatraz is another historic ship: The *Pampanito* at Pier 45, a World War II submarine. Admission charge, Tel. 929-0202.

On Hyde St. just opposite the cable car landing is another venerable institution, the *Buena Vista*, claiming to be the place where Irish coffee was first served. It's still good after all these years, and this is one of the few wharfside spots patronized by indigenous San Franciscans.

At the **Cannery**, Tel. 771-3112, east of Ghiradelli, the shops are a shade lower in price but just as touristy. Amid the boutiques and cute card stores are art galleries with some high-quality art. Further along Jefferson, are the Wax Museum, Ripley's Believe It Or Not and other similar touristy establishments.

Fisherman's Wharf itself operates as a real wharf with real fishermen; about five in the morning they unload their haul, with the seagulls hovering above. Chartered boats and cruises can be arranged for on the wharf.

The wharf area attracts a wide variety of street performers. Some move up to places with roofs, while others fade into the sunset. Well-known attractions include the jukebox man, who will pop out of his little box on the insertion of a coin and play a tune on his trumpet and the fellow in the Captain Kidd get-up with the parrot on his shoulder who wants money just for being photographed (even though the bird does all the work).

The **Anchorage** is yet another mall, 2800 Leavenworth St., Tel. 775-6000. **Pier 39** is newer, extending out over the water, at Beach St. and Embarcadero, Level 3, Stairway 2, Tel. 981-PIER. *Only in San Francisco*, at the entrance of the pier, offers free information and maps, but on little else other than the pier itself. One worthwhile spot here is the old *Eagle Cafe*, which was moved from the Embarcadero and was one of the old fishermen's and longshoremen's cafés during the port's heyday.

Near **Pier 41**, just west of Pier 39, is the docking point for the *Red & White Fleet*, which operates ferries to Alcatraz, Angel Island, Sausalito, and Tiburon. Eat at one of several restaurants in Tiburon and save a few dollars on the ferry ticket. *Red & White* also supplies free maps, Tel. 546-2700 or 800-229-2784 (CA), 800-229-2874 (U.S.) Sausalito and Larkspun can be reached by *Golden Gate Ferries*, leaving from the terminal at the edge of Market St., Tel. 332-6600.

The *Blue and Gold Fleet* runs loop tours between the Golden Gate and East Bay bridges. One-and-a-half-hour tours from Pier 39, near Fisherman's Wharf, Tel. 546-2896.

In the middle of the entrance of San Francisco Bay, with an enticing view of the sunset beyond the bridge, the silvery towers of the city and the green mountains to the north, sits **Alcatraz**, "the rock". Alcatraz, an a-typical national park, is worth a visit; a complete visit lasts about two hours. Wear good walking shoes and bring some warm clothes even in summer. Boats leave every 45 minutes from Pier 41 at Fisherman's Wharf, from 9:30am to 2:45pm Mon.-Fri. and with greater frequency on weekends and holidays. Advance purchase of tickets is recommended in the summer. For more information, contact *Red and White Fleet*; Tel. 546-2896.

A tour of Alcatraz makes it easier to understand how, surrounded by tantalizing beauty, hardened criminals in this former maximum security federal prison must have reached the depths of hopelessness. On Alcatraz, rehabilitation was an unknown word. Guards were everywhere, discipline harsh, the routine rigid, endless and boring. America's most notorious gangsters – Al Capone, Machine-gun Kelly and Doc Barker – were incarcerated here. It is hard not to admire the desperate determination of the 39 men who tried to escape across the expanse of freezing cold water with its strong currents. Ten died and most were recaptured; five were never found.

The famous prison of Alcatraz,

Six years after it was abandoned as a prison, Alcatraz was seized by 85 Indians who declared it

an Indian cultural center; their "occupation" of "the rock" lasted one-and-a-half years.

FORT MASON

Situated on the promontory between San Francisco's Marina and Fisherman's Wharf, Fort Mason has two main functions. The upper part houses the headquarters of the National Park Service, which is the central information source for all the scattered portions of the Golden Gate National Recreation Area in San Francisco and Marin County. An AYH youth hostel is also located here.

The lower part of Fort Mason, among the old docks and brick military buildings, serves as a "regional cultural center". In more concrete terms, it is a collection of innovative, political, social, cultural and counter-cultural grassroots organizations. It is a fairground, classroom, dance studio and performance center. It is home to Mexican Museum, Greenpeace, Friends of the River, and the Young Performers Theater among others. There are many offbeat, unusual exhibits, activities and tours that give the tourist an opportunity to see beneath the city's touristy veneer.

Do not miss out on a visit to the S.S. *Jeremiah O'Brian*, last of the World War II Liberty Ships, a national monument that still sails. Pier 3 East. Laguna St. and Marina Blvd. Open daily 9am-3pm Mon.-Fri.; 9am-4pm Sat.-Sun. Admission charge. Tel. 441-3101.

The famous *Tassajara Bakery* (Tel. 822-5770), run by the San Francisco Zen Center is worth visiting just for its graceful decor. For information about Fort Mason events, call Tel. 441-5706.

EXPLORATORIUM

The Exploratorium, located in San Francisco's Palace of Fine Arts opposite the Marina, is a unique institution for the teaching of science.

The dome of the grandiose Palace of Fine Arts is

easily visible. 3601 Lyon St. Winter, opening hours are Tues.-Sun. 10am-5pm, Wed. 10am-9pm; open daily in summer, 10am-6pm, Wed. 10am-9pm. Admission charge, Tel. 561-0360.

This scientific funhouse grew out of the experience, philosophy, values and never-ending initiative of an amazing man, the eminent scientist Frank Oppenheimer, brother of J. Robert Oppenheimer, the "father of the atom bomb". Before and during World War II, Oppenheimer, like his brother, was deeply immersed in the development of atomic energy. He was involved in the early atomic tests and the application of nuclear energy toward aircraft propulsion and land research on cosmic rays. Then, like his celebrated brother, and many others, he suffered from harassment by the House of Un-American Activities Committee during the McCarthy purges of the 1950s. Suddenly finding himself an outcast, he took up cattle ranching in a small Colorado town. He remained even in this enterprise the creative experimenter who made his own tools, searching for innovative solutions.

Oppenheimer began teaching science at the local high school and urged his students to explore the wonders and reality of the scientific and natural worlds with their own hands, through direct experience and experimentation, whether it meant designing their own lab experiments or examining car parts in the local dump. Students from the obscure Colorado town began garnering state and national science prizes.

The Palace of Fine Arts, which houses the Exploratorium

Oppenheimer eventually returned to the world of academia. He also studied science museums in Europe, and in 1968 opened the Exploratorium, which, in his words, is not really a museum, but rather "the woods of natural phenomena through which to wander".

The one-time scientific pariah and his staff created a "woods" of 450 exhibits, centered around the myriad phenomena available to the human senses. Artists are much involved in planning exhibits. A harp sings in the wind. Sunbeams shoot through prisms and mirrors to create a mural. The wave organ, jutting over the water at the Marina itself, creates music from the motion of the waves.

The workshop, where the exhibits are created, is out in the open and is treated as one of the exhibits. In this enclave of educational chaos, there are no guards, no rules, and no restrictions.

CIVIC CENTER

The **Civic Center** is located on the western edge of the decrepit Tenderloin district. In one of those classic ironies of municipal layout, the center's beautiful, expansive plaza is a favorite hangout for vagrants. The plaza is also the site for large public arts exhibits. Extending for five blocks, west from McAllister and Market to Franklin, the Civic Center network includes the UN Plaza, Public Library, City Hall, Civic Auditorium, Opera House and various administrative buildings.

The **City Hall** has a dome higher than the Capitol Building in Washington, and a long pool reflecting the lights at night. Contrasted to this, the glass and white concrete **Davies Symphony Hall** (Tel. 431-5400) is very modern in design. This hall is part of the **San Francisco War Memorial** and **Performing Arts Center**, which is home to the San Francisco Ballet, Symphony and Opera as well as Herbst Theater. Open Mon.-Fri. 8am-5pm. Call for schedule; Tel. 621-6600.

The **Veteran's Building**, adjacent to the Opera House on Van Ness, houses the **Herbst Theatre**, which was the site of the signing of the United Nations Charter in 1945 and now houses large murals from the 1915 Panama-Pacific Exposition. It used to house the San Francisco Museum of Modern Art, before it moved to its new residence in SOMA. The nearby area of Hayes St., behind Davies Hall, has cafés, restaurants and some interesting galleries and bookstores.

SOMA

Formerly an area of run-down apartments, flophouses, greasy chili joints, parking lots, warehouses and factories. South-of-Market

(SOMA for short) has been going through a renaissance of sorts. In the last few years, artists have taken over some of the warehouses, and punk and rock clubs, as well as trendy restaurants and new theaters have been opened.

At 151 3rd St., stands the spectacular new building housing the San Francisco Museum of Modern Art, previously located in the Civic Center. The 225,000 sq. ft. building is crowned by a circular skylight marked by bands of contrasting black and white stone and topped with a radial pattern of the same stone. This is the West Coast's most comprehensive collection of 20th century art, including the latest developments in contemporary art. Open Tues.-Sun. 11am-6pm; Thurs. until 9pm. Admission charge; first Tues. of each month free; Thurs. 5-9pm half-price. Tel. 357-4000.

A strange and interesting museum, typical of the area's spirit, is the **Tattoo Art Museum** at 30 7th St. This museum is the private collection of the owner of the tattoo studio situated in the same building. For an adequate price, he will happily tattoo an indelible souvenir of the city on you (Tel. 864-9798).

JAPANTOWN

Japantown, also known as Nihonmachi, is a new center and not very big. The Japanese population of San Francisco is about 15,000. Japantown is located on the edge of the Western Addition, a neighborhood of low-income housing units.

Japantown basically consists of a five-acre complex of modern shops and restaurants, centered around the **Peace Plaza**. The adjoining **Buchanan Street Mall**, between Post and Sutter is a small walking area lined with cherry trees. Beyond this, there is a sprinkling of Japanese restaurants and shops on the surrounding streets.

In the center of Peace Plaza is the five-tiered **Peace Pagoda**, donated by the children of Japan in memory of the victims of the atomic bombings of Hiroshima and Nagasaki.

Japantown loyalists claim that the *sushi* rage on the Pacific coast started right here; Little Tokyo in Los Angeles makes the same claim. In any case, there are numerous sushi bars, some very well-reputed, as well as several places specializing in Japanese noodles.

If you want to extend your knowledge of Japanese culture, Japantown is the place to search for books. The bookstore here carries an enormous variety of books (both in English and Japanese) on every aspect of Japanese history and culture. On the bottom floor of the shopping complex, at the east end of Peach Plaza, there is a display of amazing wooden sculptures. They are so finely and realistically detailed that the huge sea serpents seem about to breathe fire.

Japantown, normally quiet and sedate, explodes with life during its several annual festivals. **The Cherry Blossom Festival**, held during two consecutive weekends towards the end of April, is an extravaganza. Some shows and exhibits charge admission, while many others are free. Thousands of people of all racial and ethnic groups gather for the parades, the performances, the incessant *taiko* drumming and the endless rain of cherry blossoms, a symbol of transient beauty in Japan. In August, the **summer festival** is held and shortly after that is the **Nihonmachi Street Fair**.

UNION STREET

Cow Hollow, once a dairyland area curving around the marina from Van Ness to the Presidio, might today be renamed Yuppie Hollow; the only milk found here today is in the coffee-houses along **Union Street**. The old Victorian buildings have been transformed into miniature shopping malls. Pedestrian malls between the buildings lead to courtyards lined with boutiques and barns filled with antiques. There are restaurants, bars and cafés in the nooks and crannies of the Victorian row. On Sunday the patios are filled with brunchers. In the evenings, the singles bars are patronized by trim and healthy looking pleasure seekers.

Around Union almost everything is slightly overpriced, in keeping with the atmosphere. Up Fillmore, toward California and Sacramento, there are reasonably priced bars of the same type.

CLEMENT STREET

For good Chinese food many San Franciscans prefer the Clement Street area to Chinatown. This new "restaurant row" of San Francisco is not located in one of the quaint downtown neighborhoods, but rather in the neighborhood of Richmond which is set apart from the more bustling downtown area. Once home to Russian-Jewish immigrants, it now has a large Chinese population. The neighborhood would be basically nondescript if not for the strip of great restaurants. On Geary, the main street parallel to the south, there is also an abundance of good new restaurants. A Saturday afternoon on Clement St. finds local neighborhood residents milling around, shopping at small shops, window shopping, or hanging out at the local watering holes. There is hardly a tourist in sight. Clement St. is easily accessible by public transportation. Check with *MUNI* for exact routes.

THE MISSION

The predominantly Mexican **Mission District**, south of Market and between 16th and 24th Sts., had a reputation for being run-down and dangerous. It is actually a very exciting, lively place to walk, but dress casually and do not carry flashy photo equipment.

There was a time when it was solidly Mexican, and filled with cheap *taqueras*. The *taqueras* are still here, the food cheap, delicious and filling, but they are complemented now by Peruvian, Bolivian, El Salvadoran and Nicaraguan restaurants, in addition

to the Arab and Asian restaurants on the periphery, and *McDonald's* and *Pioneer Chicken*. The Mission is filling with immigrants, many of them unofficial and uncounted, which have culturally been enriching this neighborhood. Meanwhile, there has also been an influx of little espresso joints and crowded bohemian cafés. Walk around this area, watching the people and taking in some of the bright and powerful political murals that pop up in unexpected places (the public mural is a well-developed Mexican art form). Some of the best Latin beat music in the city can be found in the Mission.

This is the place to buy a meal-in-a-burrito. It is impossible to eat a burrito elegantly as it is likely to explode on first bite. When you are finished, temples throbbing from the hot sauce, cool down with a *paletta*, a fresh fruit bar which is refreshing and cheap, available in exotic flavors like mango.

The San Francisco cable car, with the Alcatraz Island in the background

On Capp and 16th, one small block east of Mission, is the old, ornate **Victoria Theater**. A little way down, at 65 Capp, is the **Capp Street Project**, a unique art program in which an artist lives on the premises for a specific time, working on a large art project which will be open to the public.

Mission Dolores, the oldest building in the city, dates back to 1782. It was originally established at another site in 1776, as the sixth in Junipero Serra's chain of missions. Dolores St. and 16th St. Open 9am-4pm. Small admission charge. Tel. 621-8203.

CASTRO STREET

The strutting street-wise youths of the Mission make a sharp contrast to the men along Castro Street, the next neighborhood up the hill to the west. Castro Street is the center of a proud, strong and organized gay community. Strolling along and taking in all the color can be enjoyable, though the card stores are not for the easily embarrassed. The chic "fern bars" of the neighborhood each seem to cater to a particular type of gay clientele. The area is now extending to upper Market street as well. The neighborhhod is easily reached by *MUNI* Metro.

The gays of Castro have helped shape this part of the city physically, culturally and politically. Gay entrepreneurs have transformed some of the pre-earthquake Victorian buildings into boutiques, bookstores and bars. A number of gay Representatives have been elected to the state government. The **Gay Games** and **Gay Pride Day** attract spectators and participants of all ages and preferences.

The appearance of AIDS threatened to devastate this community. After the first wave of shocks, local gay organizations took assertive action in mobilizing public action to fight AIDS.

West and south of this area are **Twin Peaks** and **Mt. Davidson**, both of which offer expansive views of the city. Mt. Davidson is the highest point in the city, nearly 1,000ft. (340m) high. Visit Twin Peaks on a clear night, so as to enjoy the panoramic view.

HAIGHT-ASHBURY

In the 1960s, **Haight Street** and the surrounding Victorian neighborhood (of Haight-Ashbury) was filled with the electrifying excitement, color, vibes and drugs of the "new age", the hippie era. Some of rock's greatest and most drug-pumped musicians lived and played in the area. When George Harrison walked down the street, you would have thought it was the Second Coming; The Panhandle and Golden Gate park filled with youth for impromptu concerts, frisbee games and LSD sharing. The smell of pot was everywhere. The Victorian houses became crash pads, the stores took on new, garish fronts and sold the latest in drug paraphernalia. Underground newspapers heralded the new revolution. Psychedelic posters covered the walls. Streets were jammed with long-haired, blue-jeaned, beaded, broke and bloodshot youth.

A Victorian style neighborhood

Inevitably the crash came. Those turned on, burnt out. The pushers and exploiters moved in. Heroin became rampart. Jimi Hendrix, Janis Joplin and Jim Morrison were only the better-known of the many who drugged themselves to death. With the start of robberies, rapes, muggings and sordid premature deaths the "new age"

proved tarnished. Later the punks moved in with their dyed hair, shaved heads, chain and leather fashions and fashionable rage.

Now the Haight is on an upswing, while still keeping its funky and alternative character and a feel for its past. The street has a strip of reasonable and tasty eateries. It's a good place to stoke up on a solid breakfast before a day of walking through Golden Gate Park, or to warm up with a cappuccino and a burrito. Along the Haight are small unusual art galleries displaying everything from primeval African masks to post-modern grotesquery.

A sign in a hilly city

Within a compact area are various stores which, in different ways, echo the explosions of the sixties: a good old-fashioned "head shop", a radical bookstore, a fantasy bookstore, an oldies record store, several vintage clothing stores, a few organic veggie cafés, ethnic art and pop-art posters and a boutique of sexual gadgetry. For some authenticity, there are still groups of bizarre-looking people floating up and down the street. Some look incredibly young and others sadly old.

In the middle of the Haight is the *Red Victorian Moviehouse*, 1659 Haight, Tel. 863-3994. Next door you will find the bed and breakfast inn of the same name. This theater offers great old movies, including daily matinees, in a setting as pretty and entertaining as anything on screen, and the popcorn is free.

At *Haight Books*, 1682 Haight, the books are piled high and there are places to sit. A bright arched store front with gargoyles and other creatures marks *Play With It*, 1660 Haight. Inside is every kind of toy that anyone, young or old, could possibly want. There's a play table for children, and an artificial waterfall plunges from the gallery into the miniature boat pond.

The *Anarchist Collective Bookstore*, 1369 Haight, includes a library and reading area. Despite the heavy name, *Bones of Our Ancestors*, 622 Shrader, off Haight, sells fine silver work, gems and cut stones, crafted by a mellow-looking couple.

Bicycle rentals are available at *Avenue Cyclery* on Haight just up from Stanyon.

GOLDEN GATE PARK

The long, narrow, green strip that is Golden Gate Park, is criss-crossed with cycling paths and foot paths, and has small secluded spots for reading, relaxing or courting. There are wide fields, ponds with ducks and swans, several museums, bright gardens, and an open-air stage for weekend concerts. One could easily spend a day in the park, especially on a weekend when it is closed to traffic and all sorts of people gather and stroll through. Some of the weekend roller-skating here is almost ballet.

The area was covered with shifting sand dunes when acquired by San Francisco in 1852. Squatters claimed it as their own and backed that claim with armed guards. When the city proposed plans for a large municipal park, the idea was ridiculed. Yet the city administration – with tremendous fore-sight – persisted with the plan, battling shifting sands and shifting politicians. In 1887, John McLaren, a Scottish gardener, was appointed park superintendent at the age of 40 and, until his death at 96, he dedicated himself to shaping a beautiful, variegated landscape with thousands of species of plants from all around the world.

Ironically, the park which was once ridiculed, helped shape the city. The trolley lines, that were laid down from the east to make the park accessi-ble, defined areas for rows of houses and new neighborhoods. The park itself became a refugee center after the 1906 earthquake, and was home to some families for almost a year.

The great Golden Gate Bridge, leading to the Golden Gate Park

The park is bordered by Stanyon St. on the east,

the ocean on the west, Lincoln on the south and Fulton on the north.

Several bike and skate rental outlets can be found along Fulton. The narrow Panhandle extends east from Stanyon, skirting Haight-Ashbury.

Park headquarters, at Fell and Stanyon Sts. can provide maps and information. Open daily 6am-10pm. Tel. 666-7090.

The **Conservatory of Flowers** just west of headquarters, resembles an old Victorian palace which some wizard, with a sweep of his hand has turned into glass. Among the 7,000 plants are rare orchids that normally grow at elevations up to 5,000 feet in dense fog. The conservatory's mark of distinction is its ability to grow plants from high-altitude subtropical and cloud forests. Open daily. Admission charge.

Centered around the music concourse, which hosts free Sunday concerts at 1pm, are the park's main museums: The California Academy of Science, with the Steinhart Aquarium and Morrison Planetarium, and on the opposite side of the concourse, the de Young Art Museum and the Asian Art Museum.

The **Academy of Science** is the oldest scientific museum in the west. Open daily from 10am-5pm, until 7pm in summer. Admission charge, Tel. 750-7145. It presents a varied array of exhibits, depicting natural history, the physical sciences, the evolution of man and the diversity of primitive cultures.

The **M.H. de Young Museum** has a well-rounded selection spanning the history of western art from its Egyptian and Classic origins, through to modern European art. The American Galleries span the history of America as depicted through its art. Open Wed. 10am-8:45pm, Thurs.-Sun. 10am-5pm. Admission valid for the Asian Art Museum and Palace of the Legion of Honor on the same day. Tel. 863-3330.

The **Asian Art Museum** in a wing of the de Young, is internationally known for the scope of its collection of eastern art, which includes the

famous Avery Brundager collection. Open Wed.-Sun. 10am-5pm. Tel. 668-8921.

Near the two art museums is the **Japanese Tea Garden**, constructed in 1894. Open from 8am-6pm. Admission charge. Free before 9am and after 5pm. A brochure with a map and history of the garden is available at the ticket booth. The tea house is a pretty spot to relax. Open 10:30am-5:30pm.

The distinctive Japanese landscape was created by a wealthy Japanese gardener who had worked with nobility in Japan. He and his family lived in a house in the garden and sculptured the landscape around them, with the help of immigrant gardeners from Japan who worked on the grounds in exchange for room and board. However, ugly political reality penetrated even this delicately sculpted Japanese garden and the family was interned in temporary camps during WWII, along with many thousands of American Japanese. The "Japanese Tea Garden" became "The Oriental Tea Garden". Only several years after the war was the original name restored, but the original gardening family never regained its position. The garden today is an exotic little island of pagodas, fish ponds, curved wooden bridges and carved Japanese gates.

Exotic plants flourish in the **Strybing Arboretum and Botanical Gardens**, which contains a huge variety of plants from Chile, Australia, Southeast Asia, the Mediterranean and California. The **Garden of Fragrance**, designed for the visually impaired, displays plants chosen for their color, texture and fragrance.

Scattered throughout the park are 11 lakes, each with its own character. Rent a boat and row to Strawberry Hill in the middle of Stow Lake, where you'll find Rainbow Falls. For something completely American, there is the buffalo paddock. The park has riding stables toward the western end. For those who want to experience the Victorian atmosphere of the park, there are buggy rides, ranging from 10 to 90 minutes.

South of Golden Gate Park, near the corner of 19th Ave. and Sloat, is the **Stern Grove**, a beautiful natural amphitheatre surrounded by fir, eucalyptus and redwood trees, where a great series of free concerts is held every Sunday during the summer. For programs; Tel. 558-4728.

THE CITY'S COAST

Although San Francisco is a crowded city, the entire western edge of the city's peninsula is fringed with parks and recreational areas, from Fort Fenston in the south to the tip of the peninsula beneath the Golden Gate Bridge, and continuing east along Crissy Field and the Marina to Fort Mason. Most of these areas are joined, and together they comprise the **Golden Gate National Recreation Area** (GGNRA) administered by the National Park Service. Following the paths that link these areas together is an excellent way of getting to know San Francisco. This urban-natural area extends across the bridge into Marin County up to Point Reyes. At Fort Ferston it is possible to see the concrete remains of the bunkers and gun

emplacements designed to protect the Pacific Coast from Japanese invasion during World War II. It is a great place to watch or photograph hang gliders as they leap off the cliffs or soar above the beach and water. Opposite Ocean Beach, on Sloat St. near the Great Highway, is the **San Francisco Zoo**, which includes a children's zoo. Open daily 10am-5pm. Tel. 753-7083.

Ocean Beach extends north to the rocky headland on which the *Cliff House* is built. Since 1863 this restaurant has offered refreshment and gorgeous views. It is an extremely relaxing place to sit and sip some Irish coffee. Downstairs below the *Cliff House* is a platform affording a closer view of **Seal Rock**, covered with seals which are easily seen and heard. Located here is a National Park Service Visitor Center, Tel. 556-8642, with a small exhibit on the history of the area. Information is available on the trails which lead from here to the Golden Gate Bridge and beyond. Across from the Visitor Center is the **Musee Mechanique**, displaying old arcade games which test your strength and tell your fortune. The **Camera Obscura** gallery-museum takes the visitor inside a camera and allows a close view of Seal Rock.

Above the *Cliff House* is **Sutro Heights Park**, offering a view of Seal Rock and the coast. Down the slope to the north are the ruins of the gigantic Sutro Baths which served as a quiet country resort for many years until it burned down.

Just north of Sutro Heights, a trail leads down the tree-covered slopes to **Land's End**, a small protected cove in which you might think you're in another world, especially on a foggy day. There is no vehicle access and no swimming allowed, due to rough waves. Above these slopes in **Lincoln Park**, off California St. is the **California Palace of the Legion of Honor**, modeled after a French palace, and housing an art museum. The emphasis is largely on French art. Greeting visitors is Rodin's famous sculpture *The Thinker*, and inside the museum there are more of his sculptures. Open

Wed.-Sun. 10am-5pm. A single admission charge allows entrance to the **de Young Museum** and the **Asian Art Museum** as well. Tel. 750-3600.

From the museum, **El Camino Del Mar** follows the coast through shady groves, and offers beautiful views of the Golden Gate with ships sailing under the bridge. Nearby **China Beach** is one of the few swimming beaches in the city. Open 7am to dusk with changing rooms, showers, restrooms and a lifeguard. A little beyond it is **Baker's Beach**, offering nice views but no swimming. The coastal road here runs between parkland and the **Presidio**, the large military base that looks more like a country club.

Hiking trails through the western edge of the city lead to the Golden Gate Bridge. There is a parking area for cars, and buses 28, 29 and 76 stop here. The 76 continues into the national recreation area in the western part of the Marin Peninsula. One of the nicest ways to spend a free day is to take a bus to the bridge, walk across and hike on to Sausalito via the side road to the east, past Fort Baker. After refreshment and browsing in Sausalito, return by ferry to the city.

Fort Point, now a preserved historical site, is situated near the water directly beneath the Golden Gate Bridge, at the narrowest point of the strait between ocean and bay. Built before the Civil War, it was modeled after the many fortresses in the east which were in use during the war. Fort Point, however, never had occasion to test its invulnerability. The view of the bridge is unique. There is a museum, and guided tours are available. Open daily from 10am-5pm. Admission free. Tel. 556-1693.

To the east of Fort Point is **Crissy Field**, with a foot path and open beach. This brings a walker to the Marina, and the long green with its guided exercise path. Beyond that lies Fort Mason, which houses the GGNRA headquarters, Building 201, Tel. 556-0560.

San Francisco Bay

San Francisco Bay is not actually a bay, but an estuary, the transition zone between fresh and salty water. The 50-mile (80km) long estuary is made up of delicate ecosystems that weave together to form a unique biological and

ecological community which includes grey whales that migrate along its coast (every year one or two stray into the bay), marine organisms that are born here and migrate out to sea, and crustaceans and plankton in the inland marshes. Rivers fed by fresh water in the Sierras and the Cascades flow into the Great Central Valley, and then out into the San Francisco Bay.

Unfortunately, the bay has been somewhat spoilt by landfill and dumping of waste. Parts of the bay were filled to create additional land for residential and industrial development. Once the bay was edged by 300 square miles of delicate, biologically rich marshland, but today three-quarters of this area has been filled. Untreated waste water was poured steadily into the bay right up to the 1960s.

While the wastes increased, the natural flushing action that pushed them into the bay decreased. Most of the fresh water from the feeding rivers is diverted for Central Valley agriculture. This plays havoc with the delicately balanced ecosystems of the estuary.

In the mid-sixties, a citizen's organization spearheaded by a group of Berkeley women set out to oppose the developers and federal planners who had diverted water from and filled in the bay. The fight against many local cities and huge corporations seemed quixotically futile at first, but a groundswell of support arose from local residents, and after tough political battles a state commission was assigned to study and control future bay development.

This fight helped to stir up environmental battles and protests across the country over projects that in an earlier era would have been implemented without forethought. The commission has even helped the bay start to reclaim a little of its lost territory, by assuring that if an area is filled, a previously filled area will be broken open to the water.

But the ongoing struggle for control of the fate of the beautiful San Francisco Bay is endless. There are increased controls on landfill and dumping, and a vast increase in the amount of land set aside as parks and reserves, but freshwater, the lifeblood of the bay's ecosystems, is still siphoned off upriver.

There are several organizations, some educational and non-profit, others private, that provide "ecological" cruises. These examine and explain various ecological communities in the huge and variegated bay area. Some are seasonal, following the migration of the grey whales:

The Oceanic Society: Building 240, Fort Mason, Tel. 441-1104. Field trips in the marine environment, trips to the Farallon Islands, guided cruises to bay islands.

Canoe Trips West: 217 Redwood Highway, Greenbrae, 94906, Tel. 461-1750. Canoe trips, accompanied by naturalists, around the marshland, several times a year. Self-guided tours of the estuaries and lagoons, all year round.

Marine Ecological Institute: 811 Harbor Blvd., Redwood City, 94063, Tel. 364-2760. A four-hour "discovery voyage" in the southern bay. Also, "Bay Discovery Day".

Golden Gate Audubon Society: 2718 Telegraph Ave., Berkeley, 94705, Tel. 510-843-2222. Bay shoreline field trips, bird trips throughout northern California, spring birding cruises to the Farallons. Trips from Monterey for bird-watching and whale-watching.

AROUND SAN FRANCISCO

The Peninsula

South of San Francisco, the peninsula extends toward San Jose, the rich Santa Clara Valley and the Santa Cruz Mountains. The area is rapidly developing into one suburban mass.

Stanford University is the large and verdant centerpiece of Palo Alto. One of the finest and most prestigious universities in the country, it contrasts sharply with the active and sometimes stormy atmosphere at Berkeley. Around the university are some very good bookstores, plus some interesting shops, cafes, restaurants and cinemas. At the main entrance to Quadrangle and in Hoover Tower there are information booths. Campus information and free maps can be obtained, Tel. 415-723-2560 or 723-2053.

A free shuttle runs through the huge campus and student-guided tours are conducted during the school year and summer. Bicycles can be rented on campus and swimming, windsurfing and boating are available on the artificial lake. The university's two main sites to see are the **Stanford Linear Accelerator** and the **Museum of Art.** The mile-long research facilities of the accelerator can be viewed by pre-arranged tour, Tel. 415-926-3300. The Museum of Art includes ancient art as well as a Rodin collection.

The city of **San Jose**, with a population of 800,000, has grown without any apparent order. Gobbling up the surrounding rich farmland and small towns, it has spread and sprawled into a city larger than San Francisco. San Jose is the unchallenged center of the high-tech **Silicon Valley**.

You can visit the **Winchester Mystery House**, 525 S. Winchester Blvd., by Route 17 and I-280. In summer, 9am-8pm. Call to check on shorter hours in fall and winter. Admission charge, Tel. 408-247-2101. Firearms heiress Sarah Winchester tried to outwit the ghosts she knew were pursuing her, by making her house into a huge maze, with 160 rooms, and doors and stairways leading nowhere. The kitschy, commercial tour also leads nowhere, but the story is bizarre enough to lure in the unsuspecting.

The string of small towns, state parks and reserves along the San Mateo coast, on Highway 1, have thus far been spared the suburban expansion climbing the eastern slopes of the hills. There are coves, beaches and tidepools to explore. South of Half Moon Bay, San Gregorio Beach, with its shoreline caves, is especially beautiful. South of Pigeon Point is the **Ano Nuevo State Reserve** for the big lumbering elephant seals. This is one of the few areas where these animals can be approached closely. Five miles (8km) inland at **Butano State Park** there are redwood forests, laced with trails.

Two pleasant youth hostels are found at Montara Lighthouse Point, and further south at Pigeon Point. There are several state park campgrounds along the coast as well, at Half Moon Bay and Butano State Park.

Berkeley

There's a time when the operation of the machine becomes so odious, makes you so sick at heart, that you can't take part, you can't even tacitly take part. And you've got to put your bodies upon the gears and upon the wheels, upon the levers, upon all the apparatus, and you've got to make it stop.

Mario Savio, Free Speech Movement leader.
Berkeley, 1964.

Berkeley, a city of 100,000, east of the bay, has traditionally been a center of political and intellectual ferment. This intensified during the 1960s and 1970s when the city became one of the main centers of the Vietnam War protest movement. Citizen groups tackled rent control law, the police and the power utilities, as well as international issues. In the early 1970s, a coalition of radicals was elected to the city council, but somehow not much was accomplished and the coalition lost much of its momentum and original support.

It's to Berkeley's credit that it has retained its original charm and colorfulness from the turbulent sixties – unlike Santa Cruz which became commercialized or the crime-ridden Haight-Ashbury in nearby San Francisco. On arriving in town, drive to Telegraph Rd. (outside the campus entrance) with its colorful stalls, quaint shops and cafés, and absorb that special local liberal atmosphere that has disappeared totally from many urban centers on the West Coast.

HOW TO GET THERE

Berkeley is located off I-80 north of the Oakland Bay Bridge. The University Ave. exit is the main one and leads right to the university, but finding parking in the campus area is extremely difficult.

Berkeley is easily accessible from San Francisco by *BART*. A shuttle, named *Humphrey Go-BART*, runs from the main *BART* station at Shattuck to the university campus and university properties in the hills. The local bus system, *AC Transit*, also runs to San Francisco but is generally slower than *BART*. However it covers the Berkeley-Oakland region extensively. Bicycles are allowed on certain *BART* trains, and a bicycle affords an easy and excellent way to tour the campus. They are available for rental around the campus area. For information about special fares and discount tickets call BART's Office of Customer Service, Tel. 464-7133.

One central number serving as a transportation clearing house will refer you to any other transportation office you might need: Tel. 644-POOL.

ACCOMMODATION

Berkeley is not the ideal place to seek lodgings, which are either in the very high bracket of the hotel/motel chains, or dingy old hotels along Telegraph. Along University Ave. there are a few standard motels, none of them scintillating. On the bayshore near Route 80 there are some motor inns, and near the marina is the modern *Marina Marriott*, Tel. 548-7920, Res. 800-228-9290.

FOOD

There is considerably more choice in restaurants than there is in lodging in Berkeley. On Telegraph, restaurants rise and fall quickly, but there are a few standbys that have developed deservedly excellent reputations through generations of students. Shattuck Ave., a more staid shopping area, has seen a number of new restaurants open in the last few years. With competition tight for the student market, there are many good eating deals around.

Edy's: 2201 Shattuck Ave., in the heart of downtown, Tel. 843-3096. Carved wooden booths, old-time feeling. You almost expect to see ponytails and bobby socks. Good old-fashioned ice cream concoctions.

The Blue Nile: 2525 Telegraph Ave., Tel. 540-6777. Excellent Ethiopian food. If you really want to show your worldliness, scoop up your entree with injira bread and feed your companion.

Chez Panisse: 1517 Shattuck Ave, Tel. 548-5525. Classier than most of the local places. Known for mesquite-grilled entrees. Expensive.

Spengers Fish Grotto: 1919 4th St., Tel. 845-7771. Near the highway. A grotto it is, and an established, popular seafood place.

IMPORTANT PHONE NUMBERS
Area code: 510.
Berkeley Convention and Visitors Bureau: 1834 University Ave., Tel. 549-7040.

Visitors Hotline: Tel. 549-8710.
University of California Visitors Information Center: Student Union, in Sproul Plaza, Tel. 642-5215.
Council on International Educational Exchange (CIEE). Travel Center: 2511 Channing Way, Tel. 848-8604. A goldmine of information for member and student travelers.
Greyhound: Tel. 834-3070.
Amtrak: Tel. 982-2278. Station in Oakland.
B.A.R.T.: Tel. 465-BART.
AC Transit: Tel. 800-559-INFO.
Berkeley TRIP: for information about local transportation options, Tel. 644-7665.

What to See

Although much of the culture of Berkeley emanates from the university, the city has a vibrancy of its own, with lots of music clubs and coffee houses, and with innumerable political, spiritual, alternative and therapeutic groups announcing themselves from every pole and bill-board. In the hills to the east are the beautiful, ornate homes of the wealthy, the professionals and the prestigious professors. The campus area is dominated by thousands of students. In the flat-lands toward the bay, live minority groups, as well as artists and former university radicals who stayed in Berkeley.

The **Berkeley Campus** is the oldest of the nine University of California campuses. With a student body of over 30,000 (up from the original 191 in 1873), Berkeley is one of the most honored and prestigious universities in the world; its graduate school has been rated the best in the country, even better than Harvard's, and it is a public institution in which students do not pay high fees. Relations between the huge institution and its students and the surrounding community have periodically, however, been tense.

In the fall of 1964 the Free Speech Movement split the campus when the university administration attempted to restrict political activity on campus, especially the

dissemination of political information by former students and outsiders.

In an escalating game of nerves played out in Sproul Plaza, a former student was apprehended by the police for distributing pamphlets in the plaza; a police car called to take the arrested student away, suddenly found its passage blocked by thousands of students. For 36 hours the trapped police car, with the detainee inside, was turned into a platform for endless political speeches. As one confrontation sparked another, 3,000 students ended with a passive sit-in at Sproul Hall, the administration building; they were dragged out one by one by the police.

By the next summer, the growing discontent on campus focused on the Vietnam War. The tactics of civil disobedience used by students the previous fall were applied to military installations in the bay area. Throughout the sixties, the Berkeley campus sustained the strongest local anti-war movement in the nation. With political activity flourishing once more on campus and various groups exchanging ideas at Sproul Plaza, a whole flurry of spin-off causes appeared.

In 1969, the campus again exploded over a university-linked issue, centering around a tiny plot of land to be used for a new sports facility. The move would have entailed removing some homeless "street people" who had adopted the lot as their own. Suddenly "Peoples' Park" became a symbol of a basic clash of values, and the university was viewed as the personification of an impassive and dangerous power structure. There were mass rallies on campus and in the park, followed by a police sweep of the park. The days of passive sit-ins had gone. Violent clashes occurred on Telegraph Avenue and, finally, one spectator was killed and another was blinded by police gunfire.

By the spring of the following year, Berkeley was in the forefront of the nation-wide anti-war movement that disrupted the nation's colleges, as American forces bombed Cambodia. Governor Ronald Reagan called out the National Guard, and residents faced the incredible spectacle of tanks rumbling down Berkeley's streets. In Sproul Plaza, thousands of demonstrators were hemmed in by National Guardsmen wearing gas masks, while tear gas was dropped on the helpless victims.

Campus protests lost momentum after that but occasionally flared up over specific campus-oriented issues. In 1974 student and newspaper heiress Patty Hearst was kidnapped by a radical group called the Symbionese Liberation Army. In a bizarre twist of events, the abducted heiress became a gun-toting, bank-robbing gang member, spouting revolutionary rhetoric; it appeared that something had gone askew with the idealistic protests of a decade earlier.

In the late 1970s, there was a resurgence of traditional university concerns with fraternities, sports, and practical majors leading to immediate careers. In the 1980s issues such as Nicaragua and South Africa stirred a few of the students. In the summer of 1986, a long campaign by campus and local activists resulted in the university divesting itself of financial interests in South Africa.

The student political information tables in Sproul Plaza still stand where they caused turmoil 30 years ago, but they do not attract the same crowds. Students rush past, pause to listen to a guitarist, to buy a donut or felafel or to laugh at the evangelist on the corner of Bancroft and Telegraph.

At the **Student Union**, at Bancroft and Telegraph, you will find the Visitor Center. Open Mon.-Fri. 8am-5pm, Saturday 10am-6pm. Self-guided tour maps are available and guided tours are held on weekdays at 1pm. Upstairs, watch the chess games in the lounge, or mingle with the students downstairs in the *Bear's Lair Pub*. A bookstore, student art gallery, and box office, with a schedule of all campus events, are located here. The free newspaper, the *Daily Californian*, lists all events, concerts, etc., on and off campus.

Walk through Sproul Plaza to **Sather Gate** (which once marked the southern end of the campus), under which many protest marches flowed in the 1960s. The controversial bas relief sculptures of nude figures kept in storage for over 60 years, were finally installed in 1981.

While serving a huge urban university, the

campus has a quiet, almost rural, beauty to it. Near the northwest corner of campus is a peaceful euca-lyptus grove. Toward the other end of campus is the quaint and shady **Faculty Glen**, with an old log cabin at the top and a stream running at the bottom.

The structure in the center of the campus, resem-bling a set of gaping concrete jaws, is the **Moffitt Undergraduate Library**, and nearby, on the east is **Doe Library**, the main library, with its long, cathedral-like reference room. On entering Doe from the north side, to your immediate right is a gem, little known even to Berkeley students: a plush and polished reading room, in which you half expect to see Ralph Waldo Emerson puffing on a pipe by the fire.

The Campanile tower, one of Berkeley's symbols

Rather Tower, the **Campanile**, offers a panoramic view of the bay. Take the elevator to view the 61-bell carillon. The bells chime out a variety of melodies every weekday, in concerts given at 8am, noon and 6pm.

At Euclid and Hearst, on the north side of campus, away from the hubbub of Telegraph, is a block of stores, restau-rants, and cafés.

The university houses a number of museums on or adjacent to campus. A list of them with phone numbers is available at the Visitor Center.

Bancroft Library is located in North Hall, one of the two original structures of the university. The library contains the university's collection of rare books and Western Americana, in addition to temporary rotating exhibitions. The library holds the first gold nugget found in the California gold rush and the collected papers of Mark Twain.

The **Earth Sciences Building** houses the Museum of Paleontology, the **Museum of Geology**, and the **Seismographic Station**. The **Museum of Paleon-tology** has an extensive collection of artifacts made by Ishi, the last known survivor of the Yana Indians of California, who was found near Oroville and brought to San Francisco in 1911 by Berkeley anthropologists. The displays of his handiwork are sad reminders of the Indian cultures which disappeared during the 19th century. Open Mon.-Fri. 8am-5pm. Weekends 1pm-5pm. Admission free. Tel. 642-1821.

Across Bancroft Avenue, from Krober Hall, the **University Art Museum** includes 11 exhibition galleries, a sculpture garden, and permanent collections of Asian and Western art,

The Campanile's bells, which chime out a variety of melodies

video and film collections, and a collection of the paintings of Hans Hoffman. There is a bookstore and café-restaurant. Open Wend.-Sun. 11am-5pm, Thur. 11am-9pm. Admission charge. Tel. 642-0808.

Also housed in the museum is the **Pacific Film Archives** (entrance from Durant Ave.), with continuous programs ranging from the classic to the obscure.

Up in the hills behind the campus are the **Botanical Gardens**, and the Lawrence Hall of Science, accessible by *Humphrey Go-BART*. The **Lawrence Hall of Science** is a great place to experience the sense of wonder that science is all about. Viewers participate in many activities covering a wide range of the sciences. There are planetarium programs, films and lectures. Open daily 9am-4:45pm. Admission free. Tel. 642-3343.

Up the hill from the Science Hall lies green and rolling **Tilden Park**. The 30-acre Botanical Garden in **Strawberry Canyon** holds a tremendous variety of plants from several terrains. Open 10am-5pm daily. Admission free. In a compact area you can walk from desert to lush rain forest, and then enter a jungle created in a greenhouse. Tel. 562-PARK (Park Headquarters), 841-8732 (Botanical Garden).

The **Berkeley Rose Garden**, at Euclid Ave. and Eunice, shows unusual roses and has a beautiful view of the bay. The **Judas Magnes Museum** exhibits an extensive collection of Judaica. 2911 Russel St. Open Sun.-Thur., 10am-4pm. Tel. 849-3650.

On **Telegraph Avenue** there has been a distinct rise in the level of style and fashion of the stores as espresso places, new boutiques, and chain bookstores have opened.

However, some things along this perennial Berkeley strip remain unchanged; the street vendors selling crafts, the panhandlers, the cult missionaries, the great used bookstores and a few old hippies.

There is an interesting selection of bookstores on the stretch of **Bancroft Ave.**, bordering Telegraph and facing the campus. There is the *University Press Bookstore*, the huge *Campus Textbook Exchange*, a combination bookstore-café, a map center, and the *Wilderness Press*, an excellent source for books on the outdoors.

People still gather at **People's Park**, east of Telegraph between Haste and Dwight Way. Young people sleep under the trees or lounge on old discarded furniture with the stuffing popping out, backpacks, sleeping bags and ragged bundles piled up.

On the block of Telegraph between Haste and Dwight Way, some of the classic Berkeley hangouts still exist. On Dwight and Telegraph is *Shakespeare's Used Books*, next to the veritable *Café Mediterranean* (the *Med*) where customers have been discussing Kafka and announcing God for decades. Three other bookstores on the block are institutions: *Shambala Books*, where you can sit on wooden benches and browse through every kind of spiritual text you could hope to find in this incarnation; multi-leveled *Moe's Books*; and *Cody's*, a huge store with a wide selection in every major field and a café

Shattuck Avenue is the main shopping area of Berkeley. It adjoins with University to form the main corner. There are a sprinkling of good restaurants, but far more variety is packed into the lively area off Telegraph avenue.

Marin County

Marin County is located on the peninsula north of San Francisco, connected by the Golden Gate Bridge. It is a combination of small towns, affluent suburbs, beautiful hills, shady glens and rugged coast. The peninsula is served by both *MUNI* and *Golden Gate Transit*. The latter provides the only local transportation.

The Marin sector of the Golden Gate National Recreation Area (GGNRA) is wild, rugged cliffside country that gives a totally different perspective to San Francisco's skyline.

Near the hub of the city, yet removed from it, **Point Bonita** thrusts out into the Pacific far beyond the bridge, in the midst of a cold ocean wind and churning waves; You can both enjoy the feeling that you are totally alone in the world, and still have time afterwards to sip beer or coffee in a hip, fern-filled, polished and cozy Sausalito café.

HOW TO GET THERE

MUNI bus 76 starts from downtown San Francisco, crosses the Golden Gate Bridge and heads west to **Rodeo Beach** on the edge of the Pacific and out of the city. From here you can choose from a network of trails that will take you in any direction, including north, to the extensive trail system of Mt. Tamalpais State Park, Tel. 673-MUNI.

IMPORTANT PHONE NUMBERS

Area code: 415.
MUNI (bus service): Tel. 673-MUNI.
Golden Gate Transit (buses and ferries): Tel. 332-6600.
Blue and Gold Fleet (ferry service): Tel. 705-4444.
Red and white Fleet (ferry service): Tel. 546-2628.

What to See

For a beautiful, not too difficult hike, follow the **Bobcat Trail** up into the ridges, to the **Morning Sun Trail**, and then across the freeway to Sausalito and a ferry ride home. There is no better place in the bay area to watch the sunset than from a ferry, as the sun sinks behind the span and spires of the Golden Gate Bridge.

Tennessee Valley, accessible only by foot from the end of Tennessee Valley Road, is worth the hike of about two miles (3km). It is a lush narrow valley ending in a small beach, completely isolated from the urbanized world.

The Marin Headlands Visitor Center (Open 8:30am-5pm, Tel. 331-1540) sponsors a wide range of guided hikes, history programs, and workshops. Included in these are guided hikes to the isolated lighthouse at Point Bonito. Open 8:30am-5pm, Tel. 331-1540. The *Golden Gate Hostel* is situated near the southern cliffs of the headlands (see San Francisco, "Accommodations").

Located in Fort Cronkite on the Marin headlands is the **California Marine Mammal Center**, a non-profit organization dedicated to rescuing and rehabilitating injured and ailing marine mammals, mainly seals and sea lions, but occasionally

*San Francisco's
skyline from Sausalito*

dolphins and whales as well. It is open to visitors, but usually only to groups, so call first. Open 10am-4pm. Tel. 289-7325.

Sausalito, on the Bay side of the Marin peninsula, was once a small, isolated fishing village, connected to the city by ferry prior to the building of the Golden Gate Bridge. Backed by the Marin headlands and fronted by the wharves and bay, its rustic houses were dug into the steep hillsides. The writer Jack London once lived and worked here.

Sausalito has been elaborately decked out for tourists, its old buildings filled with quaint and pricey tourist shops. It is a pleasant place to stroll through, especially after a bracing walk across the Golden Gate Bridge or through the wild headlands. There are bars, restaurants and cafés; visitor information is available at the Sausalito Chamber of Commerce, 333 Caledonia St. Tel. 332-0505.

The **San Francisco Bay and Delta Model**, built and operated by the U.S. Army Corps of Engineers, is a hydraulic scale model which reproduces the tides, flow, currents and other forces at work in the bay region. 2100 Bridgeway. Open Tues.-Fri. 9am-4pm, Sat.-Sun. and holidays 10am-6pm. Tel. 332-3871.

Beyond the main Sausalito docks floats a separate world of houseboats. The imagination – not to mention the material – that go into these creations is amazing. There have periodically been quarrels between the houseboat dwellers and development authorities, but they are still afloat.

The *Golden Gate Ferry* makes the run to San Francisco's Embarcadero, and the *Red and White Fleet* ferry docks at Fisherman's Wharf.

East of Sausalito lies the peninsula of **Tiburon**, with the small port section at the southern end, across from Angel Island State Park. Less crowded than Sausalito, Tiburon is also a nice place to stroll and has what is reputedly the best selection of waterfront restaurants on the bay, with a wide range of cuisine and prices. They are lined up, literally, side by side, some with open decks. Tiny **Main Street** has the usual art shops, and you can enjoy some wine-tasting around the corner at Tiburon Vintners. Further on is **Ark Row**, consisting of turn-of-the-century boats which were beached and turned into a row of small shops.

The *Red and White Fleet* ferry from San Francisco serves both Angel Island and Tiburon, and the nearby *Angel Island Ferry* travels between the port and the island park. A fine day's excursion would be to explore Angel Island by foot or bike, then continue to Tiburon for a meal, and return to the city. From time to time, the ferry company sponsors a discount on the return trip, if you eat at one of several specific Tiburon restaurants.

Angel Island is a natural and historic preserve in the mouth of the bay, just south of Tiburon. Having served alternately as an Indian hunting ground for sea otters and seals, a whaling supply station and a cattle ranch and military base, Angel Island finally became the arrival point for immigration from the west. A flood of European immigrants expected after the opening of the Panama Canal never came, but waves of Asian immigrants arrived. Filipinos and Japanese were admitted, while Chinese were held in barracks, where their inscriptions of frustration can still be read today.

The island is closed to cars, but bicycles are allowed. There are paths for cycling, a beautiful five-mile (8km) loop trail, and a history and ecology museum. Campsites are available by reservation. Regular ferry service is available from both Tiburon and Fisherman's Wharf.

For ferry information from Tiburon, Tel. 435-2131; from Fisherman's Wharf, Tel. 546-2896; for general information, Tel. 897-0715.

Mt. Tamalpais State Park is a favorite with local

*At Muir Woods
National Monument*

hikers. It has dense forests and magnificent views; access to the popular Stinson Beach Park is by foot and car. The summit, "Mount Tam", accessible only on foot, is where the newest outdoor rage was born. People who formerly spent hundreds of dollars on fancy racing and touring bicycles can now spend hundreds of dollars on "mountain bikes", low, sturdy, wide, knobby-wheeled bicycles that can zoom up and down dirt paths, slopes and trails. A map of trails is available at the Pantoll Ranger Station on Panoramic Way, Tel. 388-2070. The map indicates bike-in camping spots (first-come-first-served basis). A trail following mountain ridges, creeks and redwood stands leads to the rustic *West Point Inn*, where coffee and granola snacks await. Rooms and cabins available from Tues.-Fri. Tel. 388-9955.

In a cool, moist canyon beneath the slopes of Mt. Tamalpais is the **Muir Woods National Monument** (Tel. 388-2595), the natural redwood grove that is closest to the San Francisco metropolitan area. The grove, saved from felling by its inaccessibility but forever threatened, was finally placed under federal protection and named after John Muir, the inspiration behind the modern conservation movement. Reached by a loop road off Route 1, Muir Woods makes a beautiful short walk in itself or serves as a pleasant stop on a longer hike among the extensive trail network in the area. The entrance gate is open from 8am to sunset. It is hard to believe that this primeval forest, so close to the city, has managed to survive. On weekends parking can be a problem.

Point Reyes

The Point Reyes National Seashore is a blending and meeting of several beautiful landscapes: green rolling pasture land, scrubby chaparral ridges, lush meadows and forest, expansive sand dunes, large tidepools, sea-sculpted caves, and jutting cliffs exposed to the full force of the Pacific. An extensive mesh of trails, suitable for both day hikes and overnight camping expeditions crisscross this terrain. Point Reyes is long enough and varied enough to impart a sense of space even on a crowded holiday. When you climb down to the lighthouse at Point Reyes itself or look out from any of the other promontories exposed to the salty wind and smells of the tumultuous Pacific, the rest of the world just seems to fade.

Highway 1, the coastal highway that reaches Point Reyes and continues north, runs right along the **San Andreas Fault** which continues into the Tomales Bay separating Point Reyes from the mainland. Two major plates of the earth's crust meet along this fracture, causing a large rift with large and small geographical faults. Reflecting the pressures and stresses deeper in the earth's core, this fault zone is an area of comparatively rapid topographic change and motion, which includes the "continental drift", the floating of the plates, that make up the earth's crust. This drift explains, for example, why rocks in this craggy coast match those of the Tehachapi mountains 300 miles (480km) to the south. From fold to fold and ridge to ridge the climate and vegetation change rapidly. Even the weather changes rapidly, not only from day to day but from hour to hour. These sharply contrasting ecological zones support a great variety of wildlife which feeds upon the myriad riches of this interzonal area.

Shifting winds, nutrient-rich cold water, and other climatic factors combine to create a marine ecosystem as varied and abundant as the one it meets on land. Whales and porpoises may pass south along the coast a few hundreds of yards away from grazing elk. The protected marine sanctuary, which encompasses the **Farallon Islands** as well as the Point Reyes beach, contains the largest breeding rookery for seabirds on the American Pacific coast. Hundreds of thousands of birds live and breed here.

The strong undertows at Point Reyes make swimming too dangerous, and it is forbidden. The Bear Valley Visitor Center, Tel. 663-1092, posts a schedule of programs. Camping sites are spread out in the southern half of the park and are all primitive. The *Point Reyes Hostel* is on Limantour Rd., off Route 1. During the summer a free shuttle bus runs from the seashore headquarters to **Limantour Beach**.

Educational boat trips sail for the Farallon Islands or follow whale migrations. The Oceanic Society Expeditions

(Tel. 441-1104) and the Whale Center (Tel. 703-0109), both offer trips.

Marine World/Africa U.S.A.

South of the Napa Valley, the I-80 brings you to the town of **Vallejo**, at the very western edge of the agricultural Central Valley. The wild-animal extravaganza, Marine World/Africa USA, was moved here in 1986 from its original location in Redwood City. It is part circus, part zoo, part reserve, part research facility and part open and innovative classroom. It is bright and exciting, having been planned with care. The theme park has an amazing variety of cats, snakes, exotic birds, elephants and primates, as well as whales, dolphins and sharks. Rare habitats have been creatively reproduced. There is always something going on, always a show, in addition to the displays that invite children and adults to learn while playing, or play while learning.

Exit off I-80 to Marine World Parkway and follow the signs. Special *Red and White Fleet* high-speed ferries now follow the San Pablo Bay to Marine World, from Pier 41 at Fisherman's Wharf in San Francisco. For details, Tel. 415-546-2700 or 800-229-2784 (CA), 800-229-2874 (U.S.). *Greyhound* also reaches Marine World.

Marine World/Africa U.S.A. is open daily in summer 9:30am-6:30pm. Open only Wed.-Sun. until 5pm the rest of the year. Tel. 707-643-ORCA for recording, Tel. 707-644-4000 for administration.

WINE COUNTRY

Napa Valley

California produces 90% of all the wines in the United States. The Napa Valley is the finest wine-making region in California, and the lush valley produces wines of international fame. The great climatic diversity within the state enables the nurturing of a surprising variety of wine grapes. The days are hot, the nights cool, and the air is filled with the smell of grapes during the harvest season.

The first grapevines were brought to the Napa Valley in the 1820s by Spanish missionaries to make wine for sacramental purposes. By the 1850s, vineyards had spread throughout the valley; a few decades later the reputation of the valley's wine spread to the East Coast. Disease and prohibition, from 1919-1930, crippled the industry. When wine production revived, during the '60s and '70s, Napa Valley surged into the forefront of the wine-producing regions of the world. Wine is the major theme of this valley and the main reason the highways are lined with cars on a summer weekend.

About 100 wineries grace this valley, most scattered along Route 29 between Napa in the south and Calistoga in the north. The more renowned ones provide a good starting point, but there are other smaller, more obscure wineries which are also worth exploring. Meeting vintners and poking around the small farms and wine cellars in the California countryside is part of the fun.

HOW TO GET THERE

It is difficult to negotiate the Napa Valley without a car, especially if you wish to visit some of the less accessible wineries. *Greyhound* service connects the towns along Route 29. Within the town of Napa itself there is a good bus system known as the *VINE*.

Those who can afford it should see the valley by taking the *Napa Valley Wine Train*. Refurbished Pullman cars travel through the valley, stopping for tours and wine tasting at Yountville, Rutherford and St. Helena. The tour also includes a wine seminar and an excellent meal in the dining-car. Details and reservations, Tel. 263-2111 or 800-427-2124.

Cycling is an excellent way to see this valley. Bicycles can be hired in Napa or Calistoga. The flat country backroads make for easy riding. The Napa Chamber of Commerce has maps with suggested routes.

ACCOMMODATION

The emphasis in Napa Valley is on

elegant country-style old hotels, or B&Bs. In Calistoga there is a concentration of spa hotels. These places are very relaxing, and some are stunning. They also tend to be a little over-priced, but have much more atmosphere than the standard motel or hotel.

Wine Country B&B Reservations: Tel. 257-7757.

Calistoga Inn: 1250 Lincoln Ave., Calistoga 94515, Tel. 942-4101. Comfortable rooms in a landmark building. Shared baths. Continental breakfast, and wine in each room. $55-$60.

Comfort Inn: 1865 Lincoln Ave., Calistoga, Tel. 942-9400, Res. 800-221-2222. Pool, spa, restaurant. $60-$125.

Sheraton Inn Napa Valley: 3425 Solano Ave., Napa, Tel. 253-7433. Pool, spa, lounge, kitchenettes, tennis. $80-$160.

Camping
Bothe-Napa Valley State Park: 3601 St. Helena Highway, Tel. 942-4575. Located 20 miles (32km) north of Napa, between St. Helena and Calistoga. About 50 sites, hiking trails. Can get crowded in summer. Between April and Oct., Tel. 942-4575, Res. 800-444-7275 (through *Mistix*).

Additional camping is available at the Fairgrounds in Calistoga, Tel. 942-5111, and the Fairgrounds in Napa, Tel. 226-2164. Private campgrounds by Lake Berryessa.

SOME NAPA VALLEY WINERIES
Full lists of valley wineries, with their specialties, tasting and tour hours, available from the local Visitor Centers and Chambers of Commerce.

Charles Krug Winery: 2800 Main St. (Hwy. 29), St. Helena, Tel. 963-5057. The oldest in the valley, owned by Mondavi family. Frequent tours, historical displays. Open 10am-4pm daily.

Robert Mondavi Winery: 7801 St. Helena Hwy., Oakville, Tel. 963-9611. Tours and tasting.

De Moor Winery: 7481 St. Helena Hwy, Oakville, Tel. 944-2565. Tasting room, self-guided tours. A small but renowned winery.

V. Sattul Winery: Corner Hwy. 29 at White Ln., 2 miles (3km) south of St. Helena east of highway, Tel. 963-7774. Tasting room, gourmet deli, picnic grounds. Consistent winner in major competitions. Wines sold exclusively from here.

Inglenook Napa Valley: 1991 St. Helena Hwy., Rutherford. Tel. 967-3359. Tours, tasting. Known for its Cabernet Sauvignon.

IMPORTANT PHONE NUMBERS
Area Code: 707.
Emergency: 911.
Napa Valley Conference and Visitors Bureau: 1310 Napa Town Center: Napa, Tel. 226-7459.
Calistoga Chamber of Commerce: 1458 Lincoln Ave., Calistoga, Tel. 942-6333.
General Transportation Info: Tel. 252-6222.
Napa City Bus: 1130 1st St., Tel. 255-7631.
Evans Airport Service: Tel. 255-1559. Daily service between Napa City and SFO. Reservations.
Greyhound: Napa, Tel. 226-1856; Yountville, Tel. 944-8377; Calistoga, Tel. 942-6021.
Napa Charter Lines: Tel. 224-2351.
Vin Tours: Tel. 546-9483 (small group tours).

What to See

St. Helena is the nucleus of the valley's wine making industry. Some of the best known California labels can be recognized on the visitor's map and roadside signs. Christian Bros., Beringer Bros and Charles Krug (the oldest operating valley winery) are located north of town. The architecture of these wineries can be as interesting as the wines. Some are like medieval castles or monasteries. The Beringer winery ages its wine in huge vats in a network of tunnels which were carved out of the adjacent hillside by Chinese workers. Near the town there are other smaller wineries.

The **Beaulieu Vineyards** at Rutherford have a beautiful tasting and display room. The well known **Inglenook Vineyards**, just north of Rutherford, runs a popular tour. The **Sterling Vineyard** has a beautiful view of the valley, and a tram for carrying visitors. 1111 Dunaweal Ln., Calistoga. Open 10:30am-4:30pm. Admission charge, Tel. 942-3344.

Many valley events and festivals revolve around wine; the **Grape Festival** and the **Harvest Festival** are held in August, and some of the hotels sponsor weekly wine-tastings.

Drive around the valley, and make stops to taste wine at assorted vintners. If you drive north to Calistoga along Highway 29, return to Napa by the pleasant Highway 128, skirting the slopes of the eastern hills. This route leads past Lake Berryessa where public land is interspersed with private

Napa Valley

resorts. Along the western shore are restaurants, boat ramps, campsites and picnic spots.

Wine Tasting Tips

It is easy to feel overwhelmed by the volume and variety of wines in the fertile northern valleys of California. How is the novice to distinguish between all the prize-winning wines.

There are a few general guidelines for evaluating wine. Proceed from white, to reds, to dessert wines, because the reds leave more tannins on the tongue and dull the taste. Check the wine for clearness or cloudiness, and a pleasing color. Swirl the wine to release its "nose": a combination of aroma (from the grape) and bouquet (from the wine-making process). When tasting, check for fruitiness, tartness, smoothness or hardness.

The Davis 20-point system, based on such qualities as clarity, color, scent, sweetness, acidity, body and flavor, can give you some standards for judgement. Literature is available from the various wine organizations listed, and the winery tour guides can advise you.

There are also guidelines for proper wine-tasting conduct. Raise the glass to the light and squint critically; sniff delicately; sip, purse the lips, roll the tongue, pause meaningfully and frown. Then come the words, spoken with a slow nod: "A marvellous spicy rush, but a fading finish... a lovely late afternoon wine with a tickly center." After the fourth or fifth glass, more expansive poesy is allowed: "As light as a sparrow's song... as rosy as a young girl's cheeks".

Wine tasting at a winery

It is also possible to visit local farms to taste and purchase apples, peaches, strawberries, walnuts, etc. The county publishes a guide to farms that welcome visitors. Write: Napa County Farm Trails, 4075 Solano Ave., Napa 94558, or inquire at the Napa visitors center. An open-air farmer's market is held Fridays at the Dansk Square parking lot, south of downtown St. Helena.

Calistoga, at the northern end of the valley, has retained the atmos-

*Wine Country –
a typical vineyard*

phere of an old western farmtown. The commercial section is really just one street, with old covered sidewalks. The old railroad station at the east end of town has been refurbished as a small mall, and the old railcars are the attractions. The local Chamber of Commerce is located here. In the middle of the block across the street is the old *Calistoga Inn*, a renovated B&B that served travelers in the last century.

The mineral springs in Calistoga has been attracting tourists for many years. One of California's major early figures, the flamboyant Sam Brennan, creator of San Francisco's first newspaper (which announced the gold rush to the world) first bought up the springs and pushed through a major plan to make the area a resort for city-dwellers. The springs were tapped, channeled and sealed off by elaborate spas and inns; the luxurious treatments include wallowing in thick black mud, whirlpool bath, steam room and blanket wrap.

Calistoga's **Old Faithful Geyser** shoots a plume of steam and water up to 60 feet (20m) high about every 40 minutes. Located about two miles (3km) north of Calistoga at 1299 Tubbs Lane. Open everyday, including holidays, 9am-5pm in winters, 9am-6pm in summers. Admission charge, Tel. 942-6463.

The **Petrified Forest**, at 4100 Petrified Rd., is a 1/4-mile trail with 10 exhibits of petrified redwood trees. Step back in time over 3 million years and walk the trail of the Petrified Redwood Giants. The site includes a museum and a picnic area. Open daily winter 10am-4:30pm; summer 10am-5:30pm. Admission charge, Tel. 942-6667.

Robert Louis Stevenson State Park is located on Mount St. Helena, five miles (8km) north of Calistoga on Highway 29. The famous Scottish writer lived there in 1880 with his new bride, in an old mining shack. Here he wrote *Silverado Squatters*, relating his experiences in the area. The forested mountain sides inspired the setting for *Treasure Island*. Open during daylight hours, the park has a hiking trail leading to the mountain summit, with vistas of the distant high peaks of the eastern ranges. The **Silverado Museum** in St. Helena features a collection of Stevenson memorabilia and manuscripts. 1490 Library Lane, St. Helena. Tues.-Sun. noon-4pm. Admission free, Tel. 963-3757.

Sonoma Valley

The crescent-shaped Sonoma Valley stretches north from the San Pablo Bay to Santa Rosa. The mountains to the east keep out the intensely dry heat that hits the Napa Valley, and the western mountains block the heaviest fogs, allowing only light fogs and cool moist breezes to penetrate.

In the early 19th century, Spanish, Russian and American interests collided in this fertile valley. Local expressions of larger diplomatic struggles were played out here, and Sonoma became the flashpoint for the rebellion of local American settlers against Mexican rule.

Sonoma was settled comparatively late. The **Mission San Francisco Solano**, the northernmost and last in the Franciscan mission network, was founded here in 1823, and by 1830, with 1,000 local Indians under its authority, it dominated the valley, but for a short time. The Mission is open daily from 10am to 5pm. Small admission charge, Tel. 938-1519.

In 1833, Captain Mariano Vallejo was sent by the Mexican government to contact Russian outposts and establish Mexican settlements, but the Franciscan mission thwarted his efforts. Returning four years later, Vallejo reduced the mission to the status of a parish church, freed the Indian workers and redistributed mission lands. Vallejo himself received a huge land grant and set up a lucrative agricultural empire. His far-reaching civil and military power shaped Sonoma's development. His adobe home on the plaza, La Casa Grande, drew visitors from around the world.

Amid increasing American desire for the rich lands of California, a group of 30-40 American frontiersmen captured the Sonoma settlement in June 1846 without resistance. They arrested Vallejo and imprisoned him. They raised a home-made flag of a bear, and this famous "Bear Flag Rebellion" made California an independent republic, until the United States took over a month later. The uprising was hardly the heroic enterprise lauded in California

history. The Americans, in fact, had been seeking a pretext to make their move and attacked the settlement when Vallejo was away. General Vallejo returned home to find his ranch stripped of livestock and other commodities by the self-proclaimed patriots.

Vallejo had the dignity to take an active role in American politics in California even after the regime he had been part of was toppled. He was a delegate to the state's constitutional convention and was elected to the State Senate. He even offered a tract of land for the building of a permanent capitol. Although his great holdings were steadily whittled away, he never became embittered and retained his dignity. He immersed himself in composing a five-volume history of Mexican California. When he died in 1890 at age 82, hundreds of people filled the little central plaza of Sonoma, then carried his body to the small cemetery above town.

ACCOMMODATION

The greatest concentration of hotels and motels is found in the Santa Rosa area, and at various points along U.S. 101. There are, however, a number of small inns scattered through the Sonoma countryside. For suggestions and information, contact: Lodging Reservation Service of Sonoma Valley: Tel. 800-5-SONOMA.

B&B Association of Sonoma Valley: 19455 Sonoma Hwy., Sonoma, 95476, Tel. 938-9513 or 800-969-4667.

Bed & Breakfast Inns of Sonoma: P.O. Box 125, Sonoma, 95476, Tel. 996-4667 or 800-284-6675.

Sonoma Mission Inn and Spa: 18140 Hwy. 12, Sonoma, 95476, Tel. 938-9000, Res. 800-862-4945. Pool, spa, restaurant, golf, tennis. Rate for double rooms: $110-$400.

Jack London Lodge: 13740 Arnold Dr., Glen Ellen, 95442. Pool, Tel. 938-8510. Rates for double: $55-$75.

FOOD

Sonoma Cheese Factory: 2 West Spain St., Tel. 996-1931. Watch how the cheese is produced by hand and sample the results. A deli as well, with a garden patio.

La Casa: 121 East Spain St., Tel. 996-3406. In a historic building; Mexican food reasonably priced.

Depot Hotel Restaurant: 241 1st St. West, Tel. 938-2980. The atmosphere is rural, the cuisine hearty.

IMPORTANT PHONE NUMBERS
Area Code: 707.

Sonoma Valley Visitors Bureau: 453 1st St. East, Sonoma, Tel. 996-1090.
Sonoma County Transit: Tel. 576-RIDE or 800-345-RIDE.
Golden Gate Transit: Tel. 544-1323.
Train Rides: Twenty minute steam or diesel train trips, Tel. 938-3912.
Bike Rentals: Sonoma Valley Cyclery, Tel. 935-3377; *Goodtime Bicycle Co.*, Tel. 938-0453.
Sonoma Airporter: Tel. 938-4246. Transportation to San Francisco Airport.

What to See

Old Sonoma, a shady, quiet and compact area, is still centered around the original small **plaza**, and one can pass a couple of hours strolling and exploring here. The verdant plaza holds the **Visitor Center**, where you can pick up a self-guiding tour explaining the old adobe buildings that stand scattered around you. There are several good and reasonably priced restaurants and delis around the plaza.

Many of the historical landmarks, and the **Sonoma State Historical Park**, are on Spain St. just north of the plaza. Here stands Vallejo's first home, with a small Indian exhibit in the rangers' building right next to the *Toscano Hotel*. In the *Toscano* itself, meticulously restored to its 1858 design, you'd expect to find Jack London or Mark Twain lounging in the lobby with their feet up.

The park includes the **Mission Complex**, Tel. 938-1519, near the corner of E. Spain and 1st St. Admission charge. The missionaries' quarters is the oldest building remaining in the complex. Exhibits depict the various stages of history in Sonoma. In the courtyard, demonstrations of crafts from earlier periods are given. Part of the original Bear Flag (most was destroyed by fire) is preserved in the mission.

Nearby is the *Blue Wing Inn*, reportedly built by Vallejo, which may have housed John Fremont, the explorer and officer who was instrumental in consolidating American rule in California.

The **Vasquez House**, set back on 1st St. east of the plaza, was transported by ship from the East at a cost of $64,000, by Joseph Hooker, an army officer who later achieved fame in the civil war. It now houses a library and tiny coffee shop. Open Wed.-Sun. 1pm-5pm, Tel. 938-0510.

The **Depot Museum**, behind Spain St., recreates an authentic old railroad station, down to the brakeman's lantern and ticket counter. Only the call for "All aboard" is missing. In Depot Park between 1st St. East and 1st St. West. Open Wed.-Sun. 1-4:30pm. Free admission, Tel. 938-1762.

One of the most interesting spots in the plaza area is the **Works**, which displays 3-dimensional contemporary art. 148 E. Napa St., Haye Art Center, Tel. 935-3132.

Sonoma Valley witnessed the earliest experiments in the state with vine cultivation and wine production, and there are wineries throughout the valley, as well as in the town.

The **Sebastiani Winery**, an easy stroll from the plaza along E. Spain St. (there is ample parking near the winery), is the largest and one of the best-known valley wineries. 389 E 4th St. Regular tours. Open 10am-5pm. Admission free, Tel. 938-5532. Some of its vineyards are 100 years old. The 20-minute tour is entertaining, well organized and offers more than just the usual drinking jokes. The oak casks and redwood tanks here, decorated with beautiful wood-carvings, emit intoxicating smells. There is also a museum of Indian artifacts.

The **Buena Vista Winery**, about a mile east of the town center, was founded in 1857, the first in California with stone cellars. 18000 Old Winery

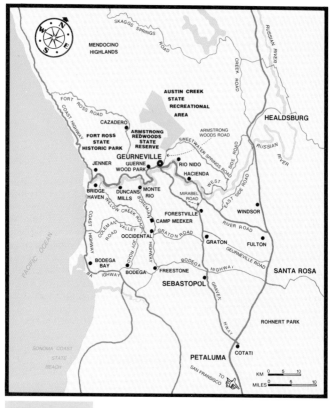

RUSSIAN RIVER

Rd. Open daily 10am-4:30pm, Tel. 938-1266 or 800-926-1266. Now a historical landmark, it is worth a visit for the limestone catacombs alone. There are picnic grounds and playground equipment made of barrels and casks. The winery also hosts performances, including Shakespearean plays.

The **Gundlach Bundschu Winery** is also one of the originals. The personnel are pleasant, the grounds pretty. There are regular tastings and self-guided tours. 2000 Denmark St. Open daily 11am-4:30pm, Tel. 938-5277.

The founding of the **Glen Ellen** winery, one of the better-known wineries in the area, can be traced back to General Vallejo's time when he owned the property. Jack London Village, Arnold Dr., Glen Ellen, Tel. 939-6200. Tasting from 10am-4pm. Tours by appointment, Tel. 996-1066.

Several companies offer tours which include visits to some of the wineries in the area:
Sonoma Wine Tours: tours for individuals or small groups, Tel. 546-9483.
Vin Tours: small group tours of Napa and Sonoma Counties, Tel. 546-9483.
Events: Tel. 996-1090.

Russian River and Sonoma Coast

The Sonoma Valley connects with the **Russian River Valley** region, which leads out to the Pacific. The hillsides and valleys carved by the Russian River and its tributaries are exceptionally fertile, covered by deposits of loam and shady soil. The warm summers, cool winters and fog drifting in from the Pacific along the Russian River Valley create a climate that is distinct from Napa's, yet still excellent for vine-growing. In autumn, the low hills gleam an unbelievable gold and the aromas of fermenting fruit fill the air. Towering redwoods grow here, and the coastline is rocky, and backed by cliffs.

The Russian River Valley has attracted small-time farmers, suburban developers and commuters, vintners, fishermen, back-to-the-land hippies and most recently urban gays who have set up resorts in some of the small towns.

HOW TO GET THERE

The best way to travel through this area is by car, but it is still possible to get around Sonoma county by bus. A number of municipal and regional bus companies connect all parts of the county; check schedules and coordinate times, to avoid long waits.

Golden Gate Transit (GGT) provides a daily service between Santa Rosa, Marin County cities and towns, and San Francisco, with stops at cities and towns in Sonoma County along U.S. 101. One bus route serves Sebastopol and Forestville, which during the weekday rush hours is used by business-attired commuters. Transfer between *GGT* and the other bus services in the county at the transit mall in downtown Santa Rosa.

Sonoma County Transit reaches all corners of the county, connecting with the *City Bus* (in Santa Rosa), the *GGT* network and the local networks of the small towns along the Russian River. Transfers within the same bus company are free. A transfer to another bus network allows a reduction in fare. You can pick up the bus schedules at city halls, libraries, Chambers of Commerce and some major businesses throughout the towns of Sonoma County. *Greyhound* also serves Sonoma County, with direct buses from San Francisco, eliminating the need to transfer.

ACCOMMODATION

The Russian River Valley is the perfect region to indulge yourself with a stay in a cosy rustic B&B, scattered throughout the valley's small towns, both inland and along the coast. Standard hotels and motels are found mostly along U.S.

The rocky Sonoma Coast is a seabirds' paradise

101 in the Santa Rosa vicinity. For information on local B&B inns, see "Accommodation in Sonoma Valley".

State park camping is available at **Bodega Dunes** and **Wright's Beach**, in addition to **Anderson Creek State Park**. For reservations contact *Mistix* (Tel. 444-7275), not the park. The County also operates several campgrounds. The **Doran Park** campgrounds is located at the southern end of Bodega Harbor, at the very tip of the narrow jetty separating the harbor from the ocean. For information and reservations for the county campgrounds, call Tel. 722-5602, Tel. 800-822-CAMP (CA), Tel. 800-824-CAMP (outside CA).

IMPORTANT PHONE NUMBERS

Area Code: 707.
Sonoma County Convention & Visitors Bureau: 5000 Roberts Lake Rd., Rohnert Park, Tel. 586-8100.
Russian River Chamber of Commerce: P.O. Box 331, Guerneville 95446, Tel. 869-9000.
Sonoma County Transit: Tel. 576-RIDE or 800-345-RIDE.
Golden Gate Transit: Tel. 544-1323.
Greyhound: Tel. 542-6400.
Mendocino Transit Authority: Tel. 576-RIDE. *MTA* runs a van down the coast into Sonoma County.
Santa Rosa Transit: Tel. 576-5306, or Tel. 576-5238.

What to See

Guerneville is the center of the Russian River resort area. During the summer it is crowded, and the cafés and restaurants tend to be a little more expensive than in some of the other towns. From near the main junction of the town, there is an easy walk down to the sandy bank of the river itself. The houses, which are a considerable distance from the shore, were flooded (and some were washed away) during the great floods of 1985 which ravaged the entire valley. Guerneville has become a popular resort for the gay community of San Francisco.

Just 2.5 miles (4km) north of Guerneville, off Highway 116, are the cool primeval redwood forests of the **Armstrong Redwoods State Reserve**, which adjoins the **Austin Creek State Recreation Area**. About twenty miles (32km) of hiking trails run through them, from the deep cool redwood-filled valleys to the scrubby peaks. Easy trails loop through the redwood grove which includes some of the tallest trees remaining in this region of California. Check local papers to see whether a play or concert is being presented at the reserve's 1,200-seat amphitheatre.

There is a drive-in campground at **Bullfrog Pond**, as well as primitive walk-in campgrounds further to the west. For information, contact the park's head office at 17000 Armstrong Woods Road, Guerneville, 95446, Tel. 869-2015 or Tel. 865-2391.

The **canoeing** is fantastic along the wide and gently meandering Russian River. Numerous rental companies will arrange to launch your canoe at one point and pick you up further downstream. The river is gentle most of the way and there are numerous landing beaches with road access. The information office at Guerneville will have some addresses. Discount coupons are available from local Chamber of Commerce offices.

The winery of **F. Korbel and Bros.**, operating since 1862, is located in an old, beautifully land-scaped complex; it is famous for its sparkling wines. The winery is located at 13250 River Road, Guerneville. Open daily, May-September. Tasting 9am-5pm; wineshop open 9am-5:30pm. Call for winter hours, Tel. 887-2294. In addition to a tasting room and winery tours every 45 minutes, there are free tours of its beautifully cultivated gardens.

For the annual jazz festival in August, **Russian River Jazz**, the audience gathers near the river to hear some of the biggest names in jazz. For such a predominantly rural county, there is surprisingly a

lot of theaters of varying approaches and degrees of professionalism. For general information on local and other artistic events and resources, peruse the local free weeklies, or contact the *Cultural Arts Council of Sonoma County*, Tel. 579-ARTS.

A loop drive into Russian River country makes a beautiful one or two-day excursion from San Francisco. From San Francisco, take U.S. 101 north to Santa Rosa, the most populous area of the Sonoma region. Take the 116 exit for Guerneville, which passes through **Sebastopol** and other small towns up to the Russian River. The highway follows the river to the sea, at **Jenner**. North of Jenner, the winding coastal road leads through increasingly rugged land with high overlooks over the ocean. To the south, the beautiful ocean-side cliffs continue. The coastal route back to the city, passes pretty **Bodega Bay** with its small fishing town and peaceful bayside seafood restaurants. Further south, it passes Point Reyes and the seaside parklands of Marin County. The wineries begin at **Healdsburg**, north of Santa Rosa on U.S. 101.

After driving up to Healdsburg, as you head north on 101, you'll pass the town of Cloverdale, which sponsors a knee-slapping, foot-stomping fiddle festival every year. Check the date if you plan to driving through the area, by calling the Cloverdale Historical Society, Tel. 894-2067. Follow the river course from Healdsburg or Cloverdale. The small roads which parallel the freeway and Russian River are lined with wineries. The road follows the river flowing west past the wineries, all the way to the ocean. Some of the old wineries still age their wines in the one hundred-year-old stone cellars, while others are more modern.

For a map which pinpoints and describes the various wineries, as well as events and general information, contact: Russian River Wine Road, P.O. Box 255, Geyserville, 94923, Tel. 800-253-8800.

Although Highway 116 is the main road leading from U.S. 101 to the ocean, you can alternately take some of the smaller roads south of the river, where you'll find some incredibly green, rolling countryside. Try to get to the town of **Occidental**. Barely two blocks long, it is known for its two excellent Italian restaurants, the *Union Hotel* and the *Negri* which stand facing each other like two feuding castles. Both pile on the pasta, salads, fresh sourdough bread, sauces, meats and cheeses. The *Union Hotel* rolls on Friday and Saturday nights with foot stompin' music; the bar has the atmosphere of a macho beer commercial. From Highway 116, take the Bohemian Highway south from Monte Rio to Occidental.

Just east of Jenner on Highway 116 is **Duncan Mills**, with a population officially listed at 20. An old resort, railroad depot and lumbertown, much of the original architecture has been restored, and today Duncan Mills is basically a walk-through museum of restored Victorian buildings, a railroad museum, manicured gardens and cultivated quaintness.

Highway 116 meets the Pacific Coastal Highway and the ocean near the small Jenner Visitor's Center, a small semi-open shelter with self guided exhibits and explanations of the animal life along this stretch of coast. The coastal highway here is like a winding roller coaster. Bluffs and promontories divide the shoreline into a series of small, disconnected, crescent-shaped beaches and coves. The climate is much cooler than even a few miles inland. In the winter, the whales migrating south frolic just off the coast where the ocean floor drops suddenly away. North of Jenner Junction, the Russian River meets the sea, meandering around sandbars that in spring are covered with seals mating and giving birth. Sharks occasionally drift into the inlet. The largest, caught a few years ago, weighed over a ton. For information, call Sonoma Coast State Beach headquarters at Bodega Bay, Tel. 875-3483.

North of Jenner on Highway 1, stands **Fort Ross State Historical Park**, the reconstruction of Russia's 19th century fort. Park and museum open daily, except holidays, 10am-4:30pm. Parking charge, Tel. 847-3286. It is easy to sense the isolation the soldiers must have felt in this southernmost exposed and remote outpost.

The Russians had been reaching south to hunt for sea otters and to grow wheat and crops for their Alaskan settlements, as well as to establish a foothold for further inland expansion. The Spanish were simultaneously reaching up from the south,

trying to solidify their hold on the colony which had technically already been in their possession for hundreds of years. The Americans, meanwhile, had been exploring overland as far west as the Pacific, and as far north as the mouth of the Columbia River. The local Indians had traditionally used the site seasonally to collect abalone. All this led to a clash of cultures and nationalities in microcosmic isolation. The Fort Ross Museum depicts the story clearly and vividly. The fur hats, leggings and embroidered leather bags in the replicated cabins are remarkably similar to the relics of an American frontier memorial. The architecture, however, is clearly Russian.

Bodega, south of Jenner, is the home of the county's fishing fleet, docked in Bodega Harbor. It is a small fishing village of less than 4,500 people. Small shacks and stands sell fresh seafood, clam chowder, smoked fish and deli items. From the restaurants at the harbor, one can watch the small fishing boats coming into dock laden with fish. The fish are hauled up in crates, swung over and dumped into the huge basins on the scales. The fishermen shovel ice over the silvery mounds of fish; they gut the fish caught by their passengers and toss the guts over the railing, while circling gulls swoop down and restaurant customers try to enjoy their seafood. There's nothing touristy about this place!

At Fort Ross State Historical Park

INLAND CALIFORNIA – NORTH

Traveling inland, away from the Pacific coast, you discover a different bit of country more suited to nature lovers. Vast green valleys, surrounded by the Sierra Nevada Mountains supersede the rambling, industrial urban areas and sun-drenched resort centers. Among the more beautiful spots are the San Joaquin Valley, the Sierra Nevada Mts. and Yosemite National Park, and of course, the Lake Tahoe gambling resort on the Nevada border.

Be aware that the heat and humidity in summer are often almost unbearable.

Sacramento

The city of Sacramento which boomed during the gold rush became the terminus for wagon trains, stagecoaches, steam paddlers, the *Pony Express*, the telegraph lines and, finally, the country's first transcontinental railroad. In fact, it was in Sacramento that the scheme for the railroad was born, the idea nurtured by a group of ambitious and imaginative businessmen, who were destined to play a major role in the shaping of the young state's growth and economy. Sacramento became a center for politics and was eventually made state capital.

Sacramento is situated on a main route connecting San Francisco to points east; it is also in the middle of a fertile agricultural valley, thereby making it a center for produce distribution. The city has never been famous, however, for its dynamism or culture.

Lately the city, with its population of about 400,000, has been stirring itself. The Capitol was renovated, the surrounding commercial area is being over-hauled. A new cultural life is developing. Sacramento now has a lively music and art scene. There are numerous art galleries, featuring some excellent local artists, and there are clubs and bars scattered around the downtown area playing jazz and other music.

HOW TO GET THERE

With two major inter-state high-ways intersecting at Sacramento, the city maintains its role as a major crossroads and distribution point. I-80 runs from San Francisco to the east coast, and I-5 runs from Mexico to Washington State. I-99, skirting the eastern edge of the San Joaquin Valley, also reaches Sacramento.

Sacramento's **Metro Airport** serves national as well as regional and state carriers. Sacramento is also a junction for major *Amtrak* lines, with trains running west to San Francisco, east over the Sierras, north to Seattle, and south through the length of the San Joaquin Valley. *Greyhound* has regular extensive service to Sacramento.

TRANSPORTATION

It is easy to maneuver through the city by car thanks to the logical grid of lettered and numbered streets. Several bus lines operate locally. *Regional Transit* buses serve most of the Sacramento area and its suburban satellites. The *Yolobus* line connects downtown, Old Sacramento and West Sacramento, as well as Davis and other surrounding towns. *Commuter Bus* lines cover the city. A downtown tram line, using renovated trolley cars travels along the K Street Mall between the Convention Center and Old Sacramento. The schedule is slightly reduced on weekends. Sacramento is pleasant for cycling, with its many parks, bicycle paths and flat terrain.

ACCOMMODATION
The two major freeways that pass through Sacramento are lined with hotels and motels; most major chains are represented.

In the heart of downtown there are some old, rather run-down and sleazy hotels. Along 16th St., in the area of the Governor's Mansion, a number of motels, ranging widely in price and facilities are clustered. In West Sacramento there are more motels, slightly lower in price,

about half a mile from Old Sacramento. For a listing of West Sacramento lodgings, call the West Sacramento Hotel/Motel Association, Tel. 372-9378, or Tel. 800-962-9800 (CA).

The most basic, standard motels here start at about $35. The hotel tax is quite steep here, about 10%.

There are few camping facilities in the immediate area. On U.S. 50 to the east, towards Placerville, is the Folsom Lake State Park with campgrounds, as well as recreational activities centered around the lake, Tel. 988-0205.

FOOD
California Café Bar and Grill: 1689 Arden Way, Suite 1058, Tel. 925-2233 (Arden Fair Center). Multi-cultural menu, fresh seasonal foods.

Tiffany's Bakery at LedenWolff Culinary Academy: 3300 Stockton Blvd., Tel. 456-7263. Full service bakery. Fresh breads, muffins, croissants, international pastries.

A serene ride in an Old Sacramento park

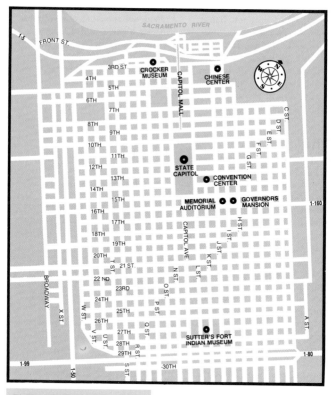

SACRAMENTO CITY CENTER

Café Dolce: 1200 K St., Tel. 442-2233 or 442-0670. Espresso bar, baked pastries, breakfast menu, salads, sandwiches, soups, burgers and daily specials, cold beer and wine.

California Pizza Kitchen: 1735 Arden Way, Tel. 568-0932 or 568-0957. A variety of pizzas, pastas, salads, soups and desserts.

Chevy's Mexican Restaurant: 1369 Garden Highway, Tel. 649-0390. Fajitas, fish, quail and homemade tortillas.

IMPORTANT PHONE NUMBERS
Area code: 916.

Sacramento Convention & Visitors Bureau: 1421 K St., Weekdays 8am-5pm, Tel. 264-7777.
Old Sacramento Visitors Center: 1104 Front St., 9am-5pm daily, Tel. 264-7777 (442-7644 weekends and holidays).
California Division of Tourism: 801 K St., Suite 1600, Mon.-Fri. 8am-5pm, Tel. 322-2882.
Visitor Information (weekends and holidays): Tel. 442-7644.
Sacramento Metropolitan Airport: Tel. 929-5411.
Davis Airporter Downtown Shuttle: Tel. 567-6682 or 800-927-RIDE. Transportation between the airport and downtown.
San Francisco Airport Bus:

Tel. 371-3090. Buses to San Francisco Airport.
Amtrak: 4th and I St., Tel. 444-9131 or 800-872-7245.
Greyhound: 1107 L St., Tel. 444-6800. At Capitol Park.
Yolo Bus-Commuter Lines: Tel. 756-BUSS.

Regional Transit: Tel. 321-BUSS.
Davis Medical Center Operator: Tel. 734-2455.
Emergencies: Tel. 911.
AAA (Emergency Road Service): Tel. 800-222-4357.
Road Conditions: Tel. 445-7623.
Weather: Tel. 646-2000.

What to See

The local **Convention and Visitors Bureau**, at 1421 K St., Tel. 264-7777, distributes thick glossy magazines and directories listing everything there is to do in Sacramento. A special *Discover Sacramento Switchboard* offers updates on art, entertainment and recreation activities. The state offices offer a tremendous range of resources, libraries and public information offices.

The **California Office of Tourism** is the best one-stop information source for the visitor. Every region in the state is covered. In addition to scanning the racks of tourist-oriented brochures, ask to see the office's publication list, for pamphlets and information sheets on a wide range of subjects concerning this multi-faceted state.

The main points of interest (with a couple of exceptions), are clustered around two areas: the State Capitol, and Old Sacramento.

OLD SACRAMENTO

Old Sacramento's six blocks combine authentic historical reconstruction with predictable tourist shops. In the 19th century this booming, new city on the bank of the Sacramento River was the western hub of the telegraph, stagecoach, *Pony Express* and the railroad. Old Sacramento is situated on Front St. near the river, just west of the Capitol. The Visitor Information Center provides pamphlets for a self-guided walking tour that passes a parade of old stores, warehouses, historical plaques, etc. Free walking tours are conducted on weekends, departing from the passenger depot near the California State Railroad Museum, at 10:30am and 1:30pm.

A street in Old Sacramento

The **California State Railroad Museum** is more than just a collection of locomotives. It aims to show how the railroads broke ground across the rugged countryside and revolutionized the country, illustrated by Buster Keaton's brilliant and hilarious film *The General* which is screened here. Museum admission includes the Central Pacific Passenger Depot, a reconstruction of the original depot that was once a bustling, thriving center. Steam train rides are available during the summer months from the depot to Miller Park. Located at I St. between Front and Second St. Open 10am-5pm. Admission charge, Tel. 552-5252 ext. 7245 or Tel. 445-7373 (office).

Next to the Railroad Museum is the **Huntington-Hopkins Hardware Store**, where the dream of a transcontinental railroad was discussed and launched. The second floor is the recreation of the Central Pacific's boardroom and library. Open 10am-5pm. Admission free. Tel. 323-7234.

A further reconstruction of the past can be seen at the Sacramento History Center on the corner of I and Fronts Sts. Here you can enter the world of the gold rush that swept the area, including an exhibition of some of the original utensils used by the gold diggers. Open from 10am-5pm. Admission charge. Tel. 264-7057.

The **Old Eagle Theater**, 925 Front St., constructed as a theater in 1849, screens a 15-minute film depicting the city's past. Admission charge, Tel. 446-6761.

The Capitol

Old Sacramento has become the unofficial center for a variety of Sacramento celebrations, such as Admission Day festivities in September, the Dixieland Jazz Festival on Memorial Day, and the Blues Festival in September. On these occasions, the streets and clubs spill over with crowds and music.

The Capitol Park is green and beautiful and the **Capitol** itself has been renovated. The adjacent downtown area is also in the midst of a facelift. The Capitol renovations include beautiful marble mosaic floors and crystal chandeliers, a touch of turn-of-the-century grandeur. The museum has exhibits on past governors, and a film details the restoration. Open daily at 9am-5pm, guided tours available. Tel. 324-0333.

Near the Capitol is the majestic **Crocker Museum**. 216 O St. Open Wed.-Sun. 10am-5pm, Thur. until 9pm. Small admission charge. Tel. 264-5423. The first art museum in the west, the building is a beautiful work in itself. The museum was founded by the railroad tycoon Edwin Bryant Crocker. He went to Europe on an art-buying spree with his wife and picked up the 18th and 19th century masterpieces that form the basis of the museum collection. He also commissioned works by American artists. The collection today includes contemporary pieces and works by Californian artists.

The Governor's Mansion

California's governors no longer hang their hats in the **Governor's Mansion**, with its oriental carpets, Italian marble fireplaces and French mirrors. The 15-room Victorian mansion is open to the public. 16th and H Sts. Open daily 10am-5pm. Small admission charge. Tel. 324-0539. Further north on 16th St., is the **California Almond Growers Visitor Center**. 1701 C St., Tel. 446-8439. Everything you've ever wanted to know about almonds, a major California export item, is explained through films, exhibits, and guided tours at specific times.

Sutters' Fort, the original settlement of Sacramento, was established in 1839, near the Sacramento River. Its history is presented through a self-guided audio tour. Behind the fort is the **State Indian Museum**. Open daily, 10am-5pm. Small admission required. Tel. 324-0971.

As if being the state capital wasn't enough, Sacramento claims the title of **"Camellia Capital of the World"**, and salutes the flowering shrub in March with two weeks of parades, exhibits, bicycle races, a beauty queen contest and the Camellia Ball.

To conclude your visit to Sacramento, you can board the *River City Queen* and sail down the

Sacramento River. Operative all year round, this is a refurbished steam boat which takes tourists on a two-hour trip, twice a day from 1200 Front St. It is a pleasant sail, as well as being inexpensive. The band on board plays tunes from a by-gone era. For reservations: Tel. 921-1111. During the summer season, an additional pleasure boat, *Matthew McKinley*, leaves from 1207 Front St., Tel. 552-2933 or 800-433-0263.

Davis

Just west of Sacramento on I-80 is the **Davis Campus of the University of California**. Established as an agricultural school, it became a general campus in 1959; it is still one of the leading agricultural research centers in the world in such disciplines as agronomy, nutrition, plant pathology, wine-making and veterinary medicine.

The campus has about 20,000 students (and it seems as if each one has at least three bicycles). The campus with its student-oriented community life form a separate entity, a sort of pastoral college town.

Along Putah Creek at the southern edge of campus is a lush, shady arboretum with a bicycle path, a redwood grove and picnic grounds. On campus visit the **Gorman Museum of Native American Art** in the Tecumseh Center. The **Silo**, a "modern" dairy barn in 1914, now housing offices and a snack bar, is the student crafts center. If you're into weeds, the botany department in Robbins Hall has one of the largest weed collections in the world. If you prefer golf, the department of horticulture

(near the Faculty Club) has a putting-green area for studying grass, on which visitors are welcome to try their skill. The **Memorial Union Building**, center of student life, has a coffee house, bookstore and other facilities.

Across from the Union is the terminal for *UNI-TRANS*, a student-owned and operated bus system, featuring a fleet of authentic London double-decker buses, which runs through most of the Davis area during the school year, and connects with the *Regional Transit* system running to Sacramento.

IMPORTANT PHONE NUMBERS
Area code: 916.
Memorial Union Information Desk: Tel. 752-2222.
Information Services: 129 Mark Hall, Tel. 752-0539. For maps for self-guided tours.
Campus Events and Information Office: 4th floor, Memorial Union, Tel. 752-1920.

Gold Country

Steamers and sailing-vessels came for some time as overcrowded with passengers as the passengers' brains were overcrowded with illusions.

Josiah Royce, California historian

In 1848, there were about 14,000 people in California (not including the Indian population). By 1852, the population reached about 200,000. Behind these seemingly dry numbers lay the convolutions and upheavals of the **California Gold Rush**.

When James Marshall discovered gold at Sutter's Mill, he and Sutter tried to keep the news quiet at first, but by late spring everybody in California was heading for the Sierra foothills. Other settlements were neglected; soldiers and sailors deserted to work in the mines.

Fantastic stories spread about fist-sized nuggets in the stream beds and gold dust on the pathways. "Authentic journals" reported walking through the foothills for three weeks and picking up lumps of gold worth $50,000.

It is true that some of the first golddiggers had tremendous strokes of luck when the richest sources were tapped and fortunes were made during that first wild summer of 1848. Some "enterprising" miners used Indians to work the mines while they raked in the profits.

By autumn, the news of quick and easy fortunes reached the east. Dreams of a wild, free life in a faraway world lured men from their routines and families. Eager, unskilled youths made easy prey for swindlers who sniffed fortunes in the pockets of men rather than in pockets of earth.

CALIFORNIA

To reach the "golden land" was no easy venture. Travelers crossed the western frontier by foot, horse or wagon – others circled Cape Horn by steamer, or disembarked at the Isthmus of Panama, and from there went by foot or horse across to the Pacific coast, where they boarded steamers heading north. Travelers by sea were exposed to tropical humidity, disease and corruption. The Pacific voyage was marked by storms and the chill fogs of the California coast. Often the navigation charts used were unreliable. Beyond that, however, lay the Golden Gate. The incredible beauty of the land must have been a most welcome sight after the arduous journey: the narrow, hilly peninsula, the immense bay opening up and the city of San Francisco – a collection of tents clinging to the hillsides, and ships crowding the wharves.

The miners expected to make their fortunes and then return home. Most never made that fortune. Some left, some stayed on and found other jobs. Some wandered from camp to camp. They had no interest in sinking roots and creating a community. They were concerned only with surviving from day to day, waiting until they struck their lode. The wages they made were spent on exorbitantly priced goods. A loaf of bread could cost as much as a dollar, a blanket $100. There are many stories of farm boys dragged into miserable lives of roaming the drinking and gambling camps.

Enterprising newcomers made greater fortunes supplying the needs of the miners than they could have made mining. Mines required lumber and miners demanded meat. Huge areas of pine forests were felled, and vast numbers of deer, elk, bear and other game were slaughtered. Loads of jerky and hides were exported through San Francisco. An immigrant tailor made a pair of strong canvas pants for miners, using metal rivets for the pockets to hold heavy tools; the new style caught on, and today Levis are a universal brand name.

Foreigners, especially the Chinese, were distrusted as miners, but were exploited as cheap labor in other fields. Local Indian tribes were exposed to disease and cruel treatment at the hands of the miners, leading to the extermination of many tribes.

The early miners sifted through stream beds with small pans resembling strainers. It was a lonely and exhausting job. With the advent of sluicing, mining became a major operation, often involving the diversion of rivers and combing of the sediments. The goldmining towns, originally ragged clusters of tents which sprang up wherever gold was found, became lines of wooden shacks and cloth houses along muddy streets. Councils were appointed to keep order. Justice for wrong-doers was swiftly decided by makeshift courts: flogging and banishment for some crimes, lynching for more serious ones.

About five hundred of these flimsy, transient mining camps sprang up between 1848 and 1860, originally in the deep ravines where the first finds were made, then on the gentler slopes as the search widened. More than half the towns disappeared completely and only a handful became permanent towns. The places still seen in the gold country today give one a glimpse of a world bursting with courage, determination and greed, and which irrevocably transformed California.

Gold country runs north and south along the Sierra foothills, from Nevada

City in the north to the area of Oakhurst in the south. It is beautiful country-side, with rounded hills, deep gorges and high cliffs. Highway 49 is the main route through the towns and sites of the gold country. The gold country is roughly divided into three sections: From Oakhurst to the Sonora-Columbia area in the south; from Columbia to Auburn in the central region; and from Auburn north, encompassing Grass Valley, Nevada City, then Oroville to the northwest and Downieville to the northeast.

Each town is lined with the same remodeled hotels, reconstructed plank side-walks, and old brick storefronts displaying postcards and chocolate chip cookies rather than dry goods and shovels. Despite the similarity of the towns, the region invites diversion. Following the backroads and small highways of the gold country affords an interesting and beautiful, if time consuming, approach to the parks of the Sierras.

Traveling through the gold country is difficult without a car. Travel by *Grey-hound* is possible, but can be time-consuming. Some towns have local bus systems.

I-80 slices through the hills towards Lake Tahoe and Reno, and passes Auburn close to the center of gold country. U.S. 50, heading east from Sacramento, reaches Placerville, the main center of gold country during the region's heyday. The road climbs east toward the southern end of Lake Tahoe.

Auburn

Auburn, on I-80, is the most easily accessible gold town. The town has an upper and lower part. The lower part has been historically preserved as **Old Town**, with restaurants and antique shops. The length of the town can be walked in 10 minutes, but a mini-bus, with stops along **Lincoln Avenue**, the main street, connects the two sections. Buses leave every 45 minutes. The Chamber of

Commerce provides a free guide to historic buildings.

In Old Town there is a square surrounded by sandwich bars, shops, bars and pizzerias under the gaze of a statue of a giant "forty-niner". The smell of Mexican food wafts from two restaurants. *Tio Pepe*, at the end of the square behind the red fire station, is spacious, with Mexican decor, and is moderately priced. A few doors down from the fire station is the *Café Delicais*, which is smaller, simpler, cheaper, and usually packed. The *Hong Kong Restaurant*, 958 Lincoln Way, up the hill from Old Town, is the best deal in town and maybe in all the hills; Chinese lunch buffet at a bargain price.

IMPORTANT PHONE NUMBERS
Area code: 916.
Chamber of Commerce: 601 Lincoln Way,
Tel. 885-5616.
Placer County Transit:
Tel. 885-BUSS.

Nevada City

Nevada City has preserved its Victorian architecture and the atmosphere of a real town, with more than one street to peruse. Somehow, Nevada City has established itself as the hip center of the

Mother Lode. Its preserved "western" appearance has made it often the choice setting for movies and ads. San Francisco artists often retreat here. The annual **Music of the Mountains Festival** at the end of June draws big name musicians. Restaurants are diverse, elegant, organic, trendy and expensive. A lively music scene offers everything from folk to blues to classical guitar.

The Chamber of Commerce can provide a self-guided walking tour. Although none of the buildings are particularly interesting in themselves, together they paint a general picture of how a thriving gold rush town must have appeared.

The *National Hotel*, on Broad St., is a historical landmark. Mark Twain stayed here. Today it operates a dining room and saloon. The hand painted wallpaper, the old overstuffed furniture, and the polished banisters give the hotel an authentic feel. Tel. 265-4551.

The *Nevada Theater*, just up the street, is the oldest in the U.S., and the place where famous 19th century entertainer Lotta Crabtree made her debut. She grew up in Grass Valley and was taken under the wing of Lola Montez, an early European dance sensation already past her prime. At the age of eight, Lotta was dancing for small local functions. After her debut in Nevada City, she toured the mining towns for years, often in grueling one-night stands, until she finally moved on to San Francisco, and then to New York, where she earned international fame and made a tremendous fortune. Tel. 265-5040.

On Spring street, the **American Victorian Museum**, houses Victorian memorabilia and knick-knacks, as well as an excellent radio station (KVMR, 89.5 FM) and a lively bar. The museum also holds events during the famous, turn-of-the-century style 4th of July celebrations.

ACCOMMODATION
Nevada City has a number of quaint B&B inns, but you'll have to pay for the charm. Motels are found in Grass Valley and near the highway.

IMPORTANT PHONE NUMBERS
Area Code: 916.
Chamber of Commerce: 132 Main St.,
Tel. 265-2692 or 800-655-6569.
Greyhound: Spring and S. Pine Sts.,
Tel. 272-9091.
Gold Country Stage: Tel. 265-1411.

Around Nevada City

Grass Valley is located on Highway 49 just a few miles south of Nevada City. Its **Empire Mine State Historic Park** gives a clear picture of the workings of a major mine. One-and-a-half miles north of Highway 20, on Empire St. Open daily 9am-6pm until Labor Day, 9am-5pm until March 31st. Nominal admission. Tel. 273-8522. This was one of the largest and richest hard rock mines in the Mother Lode, and the first electrified mine. The

museum has beautiful gardens and mine buildings and interesting equipment. There are daily tours and audio-visual programs.

Heading north toward Yuba Pass, Highway 49 cuts through some rugged country. The town of **Downieville**, hugging both shores of the Yuba River, still preserves the old architecture and narrow winding streets of the early town. This town was once jammed with miners, and holds the dubious distinction of being the only gold rush town where a woman was hanged. Juanita, a Mexican dance hall girl who stabbed a miner, claimed that she had acted in self-defence; although she was with child, she was nevertheless hanged from hastily-built gallows.

A turn east at Tyler-Foote Crossing road will lead to **Malakoff Diggins State Historic Park**. Here, the world's largest hydraulic mine blasted away half a mountain and left behind a huge ugly pit, a monument to human disregard for nature. Nature, however, smoothed over the scars and shaped and polished the jagged cliffs into beautiful formations. Hiking trails abound, and there is a state campground at North Bloomfield, the deserted boom town that is now part of the park. Tel. 265-2740.

Georgetown

Off the section of Highway 49 between Auburn and Coloma, Highway 193 heads in the direction of Georgetown and makes a loop back to the main road. This route is off the beaten track. Some of the scenery is stupendous, along a winding road that dips into deep sharp-cliffed gorges.

Georgetown itself extends for only about two blocks, along one wide street. There are no special sites here. The town, however, in its unadorned simplicity, is authentic and peaceful. The area has many cycling routes and hiking trails, and the nearby American River offers white water rafting. Founded by a group of sailors, Georgetown was situated near one of the richest lodes. By 1853, about $2 million worth of gold was found in the area. When the gold diminished, the town managed to remain stable and even boasted on opera house.

In this tiny place there are two hotels worth mentioning: *The Georgetown Hotel* on Main street dates back to 1896. Each room has different decor, often with beautiful antique furniture. There are no private baths, but the claw-footed bathtub traveled around Cape Horn, if that's any solace. Downstairs, the bar is a local hangout, with live music at night. Tel. 916-333-4373.

Across Main St. and up a block or so is the *American River Inn*, a restored 1853 inn (the original one burnt down and was reconstructed at the turn of the century). The price includes full breakfast and use of the pool, sauna and bicycles. Tel. 333-4499.

Coloma

Coloma, on Highway 49 north of Placerville, is the place where James Marshall first found gold. The area, then called **Sutter's Mill**, was on the south fork of the American River. By the summer of 1848, 2,000 miners were camped on the river banks, and a year later 10,000 were mining here. Coloma was the natural hub of the gold country until the digging center finally shifted away and the town declined.

Today, most of the small town lies within the

Renovated old houses in Sutter's Creek

Marshall Gold Discovery State Historical Park. The park includes some old stone buildings, a Chinese store, and a cabin where Marshall lived after he discovered gold. At the river bank is a plaque marking the spot where he supposedly made his first discovery, and nearby stands an exact replica of Sutter's Mill. Across the road is the small and excellent park museum outlining the history before and after the discovery. Open daily 10am-5pm. Admission charge. Tel. 622-3470.

On the hill behind the old town is a tall bronze statue of James Marshall, in a heroic pose. From the museum, you can drive your car to the monument or take a one-mile round-trip hike by way of the Marshall cabin. The town swells with visitors around January 24th, the anniversary of the discovery of gold, when the event is re-enacted.

Placerville

Placerville, at the junction of Highways 49 and 50, replaced Coloma as the center of gold country. It became a stop for covered wagons after the Sierra crossing, a supply center for the mining camps, a staging point for expeditions to the Nevada silver mines, and a station on the *Pony Express* line. It also became known as Hangtown, after proving to be an efficient lynching center. Those days are vividly recalled by the dummy hanging from the second-floor of a building on Main street.

Placerville also seems to have inspired early Californian capitalism. Railroad magnates Leland Stanford and Mark Hopkins both worked here as small-time merchants. John Studebaker, the auto industrialist, once worked here as a wheelwright, and meat packer Philip Armour worked as a butcher.

Today, U.S. Highway 50 runs along a scenic, rugged route to the Sierras, South Lake Tahoe and Nevada, and Placerville provides a pleasant resting spot. There are reasonable and varied restaurants in the small old town center.

There are many B&B inns in the area, combining history and old-time Victorian luxury. The Chamber of Commerce has a complete list. There are also reasonable, if nondescript, motels on the outskirts of town. Most campgrounds in the immediate area are private. About seven miles (11km) to the east on U.S. 50 is the El Dorado National Forest Information Center which can provide a list of nearby campgrounds, some primitive, some more fully equipped, with varying prices. Information on camping in the wilderness areas near South Lake Tahoe is also available.

From far and wide, travelers come to *Poor Red's* in El Dorado for a plate of its famous ribs. Several miles south of Placerville, on Main St.

The **Gold Bug Park and Mine**, located on Bedford St., just east of Highway 49, is a pretty city park with miles of hiking trails and a real mine. Tel. 626-5056. There is a beautiful whitewater rafting stretch on the South Fork of the American River from Chili Bar near Placerville, west of Folsom Reservoir. One and two-day trips are offered on this stretch of river, by various rafting outlets. A list is available from the Chamber of Commerce.

The Placerville area is fruit growing and wine country. Visitors can stop in on any number of farms along a route mapped out by the local growers' cooperative. It is a nice way to get a look at the countryside outside the towns and tourist services, and to enjoy apple pie, apple butter and apple wine. Maps of the apple farms and wineries which are open for visits and tasting are available from the local Chamber of Commerce.

A rugged scenery along the way to Lake Tahoe

In June, there is a professional rodeo and the arrival of the annual U.S. 50 wagon train following the route of the old wagon trains from Carson City, over the Sierra Nevada to Placerville.

IMPORTANT PHONE NUMBERS
Area Code: 916.
Chamber of Commerce: 542 Main St.,
Tel. 621-5885 or 800-457-6279.
Greyhound: 1750 Broadway,
Tel. 626-1010.
El Dorado County Chamber of Commerce:
542 Main St., Placerville, Tel. 621-5885
or 800-457-6279.

Calaveras County

Calaveras County, toward the southern end of the gold country, had two tremendous strokes of fortune: it was situated on one of the richest areas of gold deposits, and it was named in Mark Twain's famous story, "The Celebrated Jumping Frog of Calaveras County". The gold has long since diminished, but the second resource is still proving lucrative.

Twain spent some time at the main hotel in **Angel's Camp** listening to the tales of the miners. His name has become associated with almost everything in the town, and frogs have become the town's symbol. They are painted on the sidewalks, and every year a jumping frog contest is held on the 3rd weekend in May, in which the human owners of frogs end up hopping around more than the amphibious contestants. Frogs are available for rent for those who don't bring their own.

At the northern end of town is the local **historical museum**, which is not really worth visiting, but the counter of the museum serves as a Visitor Center where you can obtain a map with a self-guided walking or driving tour of the Angel's Camp area.

Head northeast up Route 4 for some nice surprises. First there is **Moaning Cavern**, near Vallecito. Although it has been hyped up, it is interesting and it really does moan. If stairways bore you, try rappelling down 180ft. (61m) by rope (extra fee). Be aware, however, that 13,000 years ago some didn't make it and human bones have been found at the bottom. Continue along Route 4 to **Murphys**, a cute, tree lined, one-street town. At the *Murphys Hotel* you can see the Ulysses S. Grant Presidential

Suite, and the room where Mark Twain stayed.

About 16 miles (25km) further is **Calaveras Big Trees State Park** (Tel. 795-2334), the only spot outside Yosemite or Sequoia National Park where you'll find sequoias. There is a North Grove and a South Grove, with the North Grove at the park entrance and the southern about nine miles (14km) away. A mile-long trail loops through the northern grove, and a self-guided trail map is available. This park is very family oriented. The Visitor Center, which is open 10am-5pm daily, offers slide shows, nature exhibits, and schedules of guided walks and campfire programs. Bears can also be seen in the park. Reservations needed for most weekends. P.O. Box 120, Arnold, CA.. 95223, or through *Mistix*. Tel. 800-444-7275.

Calaveras Big Trees State Park is the only spot outside the Yosemite and Sequoia National Parks where sequoia trees are found

The town of **San Andreas** was established by Mexicans in 1849, but they were elbowed out by the Americans, and then the Chinese came. reworking the diggings abandoned by their less patient predecessors.

Only a few of the gold rush buildings remain today. There is a beautiful old courthouse, which houses the Chamber of Commerce, a museum with an interesting collection of artifacts, and the local historical society. It is worth walking around here and showing some curiosity about the region; the staff will reward you with warmth and some unusual local legends.

The cemetery on the western outskirts of town has stones bearing some chilling and pithy epitaphs. Black Bart, the notorious stagecoach robber, was caught, tried and convicted in San Andreas, and purportedly slept in the jail behind the courthouse. Black Bart was quite a character. Failing to find

gold legally, he worked as a clerk for a stagecoach company and studied the schedules, routes and drivers until the stagelines became easy prey. Meanwhile, he moved to San Francisco with his newly acquired wealth where he became a prominent businessman who hobnobbed with the powerful. When his finances declined, he changed outfits and robbed another stagecoach; always polite and gentle, he left behind a few lines of poetry.

IMPORTANT PHONE NUMBERS
Area Code: 209.
Calaveras Lodging and Visitors Association: 1211 S. Main St., P.O. Box 637, Angels Camp, Tel. 736-0049 or 800-225-3764.

Southern Mother Lode
Columbia State Historic Park has a strange existence. It is a tourist attraction, a state park, and a reconstructed town of days gone by when people sold sarsaparilla and penny candy; at the same time it is also a real modern town, complete with courthouse. Even though you know that the guy in the old-fashioned costume does not usually dress like that, and that the blacksmith plies his trade largely for the benefit of tourist, the town gives an unparalleled feeling for the past. Maps and guides can be obtained at the Visitors Center, Tel. 532-5064.

If you want gas, drugstores, cheap motels and other symbols of modernity, go to Sonora. Further west, off Highway 49, is Jamestown, an attractive antique looking town with brightly painted two-story frame buildings. Ride the steam-powered trains at the Railtown 1897 State Historic Park. Fifth Ave., off Highway 49/108, Tel. 984-4936.

You can also try your luck at gold digging by joining one of the teams that leaves Jamestown, headed by geologists and other gold diggers. This special tour does not ensure your discovering gold, however you will enjoy a unique experience. The length of these expeditions range from a day to a fortnight. For further details: Tel. 209-984-4653.

ACCOMMODATION
Best Western Sonora Oaks: 19551 Hess, Sonora, Tel. 533-4400, Res. 800-532-1944. Pool, spa, restaurant, lounge. $70-$120.

Sonora Townhouse Motel: 350 S. Washington St., Tel. 532-3633, Res. 800-251-1538. Pool, spa, kitchenettes. $50-$100.

IMPORTANT PHONE NUMBERS
Area Code: 209.
Tuolumne County Visitors Bureau: 55 W. Stockton Rd., Sonora, Tel. 533-4420 or 800-446-1333.
Greyhound: 260 E. Nonoway, Sonora, Tel. 532-1356.

Lake Tahoe

Lake Tahoe straddles two states and two worlds. Nevada lies along the eastern shore, and California on the western. Also to the west and southwest there are high rugged mountains, snow covered even in the summer. Among these mountains is **Desolation Wilderness**, a beautiful area set aside for hikers, where no vehicles are allowed. This is a real wilderness, a hiker's challenge and paradise. Yet within viewing distance of these peaks are the ski lifts, and the strip of motels and restaurants, and the flashing lights of the casinos of Stateline, the tiny resort on the Nevada border, literally across the street from California.

Tahoe itself is truly a jewel in the wilderness, pristine and immense, 22 miles (35km) long and 12 miles (19km) across. The lake was formed by the faulting and uplifting of the Sierra Nevada block, dammed up later by lava, and sculpted and gouged by glaciers. The waters of the lake are incredibly blue, due to the great depth (averaging 1,000ft./340m), purity of the water, and clarity of the atmosphere. The water is clear enough to see down to 120ft. (40m).

Lake Tahoe – deep-blue waters surrounded by green mountains

In 1859, with the discovery of silver at Comstock Lode in northern Nevada, loggers clear-cut the surrounding forests, hauled them over the eastern crests, and floated them by flume to the mining communities. Vast areas of woodland were slashed and razed, but, amazingly, the forests regenerated themselves.

Another onslaught against the ecologically delicate lake came about a century later when the natural beauty of the predominantly private shoreline was spoilt by the building of resorts. Waste was dumped into the lake, seriously damaging this mountain gem. Steps were rapidly taken to save the land that remained, and to limit continuing development.

Today, the area abounds with places to explore. Tahoe is a magnet for hikers, boaters, canoeists, revelers, skiers or gamblers. It is one of the prime vacation spots in the country. Recently, it has turned into a year-round resort, with extensive skiing facilities drawing the crowds in the winter.

The quietest period is early fall, when it is too cold and rainy for boating, swimming and most hiking, and too early for the fresh snows. Prices fluctuate not only between seasons, but during the week as well. Even during the off-season, the resort fills up on weekends, because it is so accessible and convenient to major urban centers. The endless row of hotels at South Lake Tahoe is packed over weekends, even in autumn; but during the week in the off-season, Tahoe is a vacationer's dream. Visitors can choose among the motels, with rooms that might cost less than $35 per night to luxury resort facilities. For meals, the casinos on the Nevada border offer great bargains similar to those in Reno and Las Vegas, though more limited. Great buffets are served for a few dollars and up.

HOW TO GET THERE

The two main approaches to Lake Tahoe from the California side both stem from Sacramento. U.S. 50 heads east through Placerville, and up through the Sierra foothills along an old covered-wagon trail, toward the lower end of Tahoe. The road is wide, but not a super highway. It is mind boggling to imagine covered wagons crossing this serpentine pass. I-80 climbs up to Truckee, north of Lake Tahoe, and over Donner Pass.

The **Lake Tahoe Airport**, located, near South Lake Tahoe, is served by *Trans World Express*. Shuttles run from Reno's airport, with its national carriers to Tahoe's resorts.

The *Amtrak* station at Truckee is on the *California Zephyr* line between San Francisco and Chicago. No tickets are sold at that station; make reservations, board the train, and pay the conductor. *Greyhound* also serves Truckee.

Tahoe Area Regional Transit runs buses between Incline Village in Nevada at the northest end of the lake, to Tahoma about halfway down the western shore. Buses also run between Tahoma and South Lake Tahoe. At the southern end of the lake, a bus serves key recreation sites between the town of South Lake Tahoe and the Forest Service Visitor Center at the southwestern tip.

Although the western shore of Lake Tahoe can be quite hilly, the area around South Lake Tahoe is beautiful for bicycle riding. It is a popular means of local transportation and rentals are readily available.

Several companies operate commercial boat cruises, combining travel and pleasure. They sail between the north and south shores of the lake, hit the casinos, and also dock near the ski resorts. The local Chamber of Commerce can provide company names and addresses.

ACCOMMODATION

The hotels and motels are lined up almost side by side all along U.S. 50 through South Lake Tahoe. At Stateline on the Nevada side are the casino-hotels. During the week visitors have their choice, but during weekends, even during the off-season of early fall, all these lodgings may be jammed, and prices are higher too.

Generally, the lodgings tend to be cheaper further away from the border casinos. The various casinos offer free shuttle service to the motels on the California side.

One of the lodges is *Tahoe Sands Inn*, located 5 miles (8km) from the airport and includes a pool, spa, restaurant and lounge. Rates begin at $43 per night for a double. P.O. Box 18692/3600 U.S. 50, South Lake Tahoe 96151, Tel. 544-3476, Res. 800-237-8882.

Also at South Lake Tahoe, there is a thriving business in condominium time sharing. These arrangements sometimes work out more economically than resorts. Most time sharing units have some sort of kitchen facilities, and can often be divided among two or more parties. For information, call *Security Timeshare Marketing*: Tel. 544-5611.

There are about seven state parks in the Tahoe region. The ones on the rim of the lake can be crowded through the summer. Parks further away, such as **Donner Memorial State Park** (Tel. 587-3841) or **Grover Hot Springs** (Tel. 694-2248 or 525-7232) are usually less crowded. Both are set in beautiful scenery. The central state park office for the area has details on the parks.

The huge **El Dorado National Forest**, bordering Lake Tahoe on the west, has numerous campsites, ranging in price. On Route 89 north of Truckee, there are less crowded campgrounds along the road.

FOOD

The best eating in South Lake Tahoe is found in the casinos of Stateline. Although the choice is more limited than at the major resorts, there are excellent buffets here. All-you-can-eat breakfasts, lunches, and sumptuous prime-rib buffets at attractive prices, but there are lines during prime hours.

IMPORTANT PHONE NUMBERS

Area Code: 916.
Lake Tahoe Visitors Authority: P.O. Box 16299, South Lake Tahoe, CA 96151, Tel. 544-5050 or 800-AT-TAHOE.
North Lake Tahoe Chamber of Commerce: 245 N. Lake Blvd., P.O. Box 884, Tahoe City, CA 96145, Tel. 581-6900.
Truckee-Donner Chamber of Commerce and Visitors Center: 12036 Donner Pass Rd., P.O. Box 2757, Truckee, CA 96160, Tel. 587-2757 or 800-548-8388.
National Weather Service: Tel. 447-6941.
Desolation Wilderness Area, U.S. Forest Service: 870 Emerald Bay Rd., Ste., 1, South Lake Tahoe, Tel. 573-2600.
Eldorado National Forest: 3070 Camino Heights Dr., Camino, Tel. 644-6048.
Tahoe National Forest: 22830 Foresthill Rd., Foresthill, Tel. 367-2224.
California State Parks: Tel. 653-6995.
Nevada State Parks: Tel. 687-4370 or 687-4384.
Coast Guard: Tel. 583-4433.
Greyhound: 1099 Park Ave., Tel. 544-2241 (South Lake Tahoe); Tel. 587-3882 (Truckee).
Tahoe Area Rapid Transit: Tel. 583-2371.
South Tahoe Area Ground Express (STAGE): Tel. 573-2080.
Road conditions: North Lake Tahoe – Tel. 546-5253; South Lake Tahoe – 542-4636.

What to See

Emerald Bay, towards the southern end of Highway 89, is stunning when first glimpsed from the road. It is a popular spot for overlooks and walks down the cliffside to the shore. Trails lead along the beautiful rock shoreline, down from the **Emerald Bay Overlook** (closed when icy) to **Vikingsholm**, a reproduction of a Norse fortress, which is open for guided tours during the summer June-Sept. 10am-4pm. Small admission. Tel. 914-541-3030. Both parks have camping facilities, but campgrounds are continually crowded during the summer.

Across the road from Emerald Bay is a parking area for the short, steep hike to the footbridge above the cataracts of **Eagle Falls**. If the snow has cleared, you can continue on the same trail about one mile to **Eagle Lake**.

The Forest Service and State Parks operate tours

throughout the baronial estates that graced the southern lakeshore at the turn of the century. The **Valhalia Estate** and **Baldwin Log Cabin** host concerts, ranging from chamber music to bluegrass, in the summer. Check with the Forest Service Visitor Center for schedules. Tel. 367-2224.

Lake Tahoe has a tremendous concentration of ski resorts, including the famous **Squaw Valley**, site of the 1960 winter Olympics. Between them, the resorts provide a variety of runs, as well as several hundred miles of cross country trails. Most of the ski resorts are clustered along the western shore of the lake. Several of them offer shuttle connections to hotels and resort areas. In February, the annual winter carnival of **Snowfest** fills the lakeshore resorts with concerts, dances, theater, parades and skiing exhibitions. Tel. 583-7625.

The aerial tram ride at the **Heavenly Ski Resort**, south of Stateline, off U.S. 50, climbs to an elevation exceeding 8,000ft. (2,720m), offering a breathtaking view of Lake Tahoe and the Sierra Nevada. There is also a restaurant at the top with great views, a wonderful place for late Sunday brunch. Tel. 541-1330.

To sail on Lake Tahoe, you must either hire a boat or join an organized sail on the pleasure boat the *Tahoe Queen*, which sails several times a day during the summer, on a two-hour route. You can also board the boat for a dinner-dance in the evening. The boat also sets sail during winter and spring, though at greater intervals. Boarding is at Sky Run Marina, at the Stateline casinos. The scenery viewed on this tour is much more spectacular than anything seen through the boat's glass bottom. Admission charge. For details and reservations: Tel. 916-541-3364 or 800-23-TAHOE, ext. 856.

A little further south of the lake is the **Grover Hot Springs State Park**, surrounded by hiking trails and abruptly rising peaks, and containing two deliciously hot pools. Camping is available 3 miles

Yachts on Lake Tahoe

(5km) west of Markleeville, which is on Route E1. From Lake Tahoe, take Route 89 south to Route 88, skirt east to Woodford, and then south on E1 for the turnoff to the park at Markleeville. Admission charge. For information regarding opening hours, call Tel. 694-2248 or 800-444-PARK.

The **Desolation Wilderness**, looming west of the South Lake Tahoe region spans both slopes of the Sierra Nevada. It embraces 10,000ft. (3,400m) high peaks, glacial valleys and over 100 lakes, and draws enough hikers and campers to necessitate the rationing of camping permits. The adjacent **Mokelumne Wilderness** is smaller, less crowded, and still rugged. Check with the Forest Service Visitor Center for maps, details and weather conditions in both areas.

Truckee is a small mountain town right off I-80, spruced up for tourists but not overdone. With its original buildings and wooden sidewalks, it maintains the ambience of an old frontier town. There are a few nice restaurants and cafés. The information center is located in the train station, on the southern end of the main street just beyond the traffic light (Tel. 587-2757 or 800-548-8388). Just north of I-80, off the Truckee exit, is a Forest Service Information Center, with details on camping and hiking throughout the immense **El Dorado National Forest**. It covers all the territory along the western shore of Tahoe and further west into the Sierra peaks, including the stunning Desolation Wilderness, and stretches down into the foothills.

At **Donner Lake**, just west of Truckee, the famous Donner party encamped during a terrible Sierra winter in 1846. Their story is one of poor judgement, misfortune, heroic struggle and grim survival. A group of almost 90 people headed west in the summer of 1846 in wagons, under the leadership of two brothers, George and Jacob Donner. By the time they reached the vicinity of Reno, in October, the party was already fraught with tension and bickering due to a serious mistake in routing. They had lost wagons and much cattle. After receiving some relief from one of their members who had crossed the pass earlier to Sacramento, they rested for a week and began the climb over the Sierras. The delay was a fatal mistake, for the snows fell early and heavily. The party was trapped near the lake, huddled in makeshift cabins and brush tepees, while the land lay buried under 22 feet of snow. A party of 15 hiked west on improvised snowshoes to seek help; Only seven of them lived, reduced to cannibalism to survive. A relief party reached those who stayed behind at the lake only in February. The survivors had eaten oxhide and bones, and there were more signs of cannibalism. The last survivors were saved only in April. 42 of the 89 members died before reaching their destination.

The picturesque Lake Tahoe area

The cannibalism caused much controversy, and even accusations of murder in one case. A museum at **Donner Memorial State Park**, at the southeast corner of Donner Lake, presents the tragic story. Open 10am-6pm daily. Nominal admission fee.

Donner Lake can provide a pleasant alternative to lodging around Lake Tahoe, especially during the summer. The accommodations at Donner Lake tend to be less expensive than at Tahoe, and the facilities of the lake itself less crowded. Cabins are available with both weekly and nightly rates.

Toward Reno

California shares much of its long eastern border with Nevada. In the north, the border runs right through the Sierra Nevada and splits Lake Tahoe down the middle. There are ski resorts on both sides, protected wilderness tracts on the Californian side, and casinos on the Nevada side, literally a few steps across the stateline in some cases. If you are driving to California along I-80, the main cross-country route, Reno makes a convenient and popular stop. It is often used as an entertaining stopover point heading to or from California. Reno is the commercial and cultural center of northern Nevada's vast territory. At the eastern base of the Sierras, it is at the starting point for one of the main passes over the crests, in pioneer days as well as today. Besides the lure of its casinos, Reno has cheap food and lodging which make it a logical resting point before crossing the mountains, or even a base for side trips into the Sierras.

The casinos are the big attraction in Reno. At night, sitting on its high, open plateau beneath the shadowy mountains, Reno resembles an electric Emerald City; downtown the waves of lights lose their dazzle. Reno, which calls itself "The Biggest Little City in the World" has neither the glamour and excitement of Las Vegas, nor the rustic charm of one of the small mountain casino resorts.

Reno is served by *Greyhound*. The *Chicago-San Francisco Amtrak* line runs right through the city. Regional and national carriers use Reno's airport.

The intersection at Virginia and 2nd St. forms the center of the casino area. Many of the casinos are housed in the large and blazing downtown hotels, as in Las Vegas. These include *Harrah's, MGM Grand Hotel, The Sahara Reno, Circus Circus, Mapes* and others. There are restaurants, coffee shops, bars and casinos open all night long.

Reno, like Las Vegas, has an abundance of inexpensive lodgings and

fantastic dining deals. As long as you keep the gambling impulse under control, this is a penny-pincher's paradise. Even during the summer season, good rooms can often be found at attractive prices. There are plenty of blazing motel signs along the central strip, and spread out along the roads connecting to I-80. Many of the motels offer coupons, distributed by the casinos and redeemable for cash, free cocktails, turns on the slot machine, etc.

IMPORTANT PHONE NUMBERS
Area Code: 702.
Commission on Tourism: Capitol Complex, Carson City, 89710, Tel. 800-NEVADA-8. Brochures and information on the entire state available upon request by mail.
Reno/Tahoe Gaming Academy: An initiation into the mysteries of the gambling games, and tours of the casinos, Tel. 348-7403.
Reno International Jazz Festival: Held in April and often featuring big names in jazz, Tel. 786-5409.

YOSEMITE

In 1851, Indians used to raid the White settlements in the central valley and then disappear into the Sierra Mountains. A force led by Major James Savage followed their trail through the foothills into the high mountains; they suddenly came upon an immense valley carved from rock that stunned him with its beauty and grandeur. Yosemite had amazingly remained undiscovered by White explorers until then, and was never the same again. The almost magical valley, with its sheer granite cliffs, high falls and sculpted domes, immediately attracted people, some overwhelmed by its beauty, and others wanting to exploit and "improve" it. Although the boundaries of the park are secure today, the debate over its future continues as the valley fills up every summer with campers and trailers, resembling an L.A. suburb that has been transplanted into the wilderness.

Just a decade after its discovery, the need was recognized to preserve the wonders of this ice-carved valley, and in 1864 Yosemite became the nation's first state park, kicking off California's direct involvement with the protection of its natural areas. The protection however, was far from perfect, and in 1890 the area was placed under federal jurisdiction, guarded by the U.S. army. The army dealt with law-breakers forcefully. When stockmen allowed their sheep to continually strip the hillsides of vegetation, with the excuse that they could not control their flocks, the army drove the sheep out and released them, and the stockmen suddenly discovered new ways of controlling their sheep.

It was John Muir, a Scottish immigrant, who spearheaded the fledgling conservation movement. He also founded and headed the Sierra Club, and especially fought for the protection of Yosemite. As a young man, he wandered through America on foot and stopped when he reached the Sierras. He knew Yosemite Park intimately, and collected an enormous amount of data about the area. Geologists doubted that glaciers had formed Yosemite Valley,

At the Yosemite Park – a frozen lake in the High Sierra

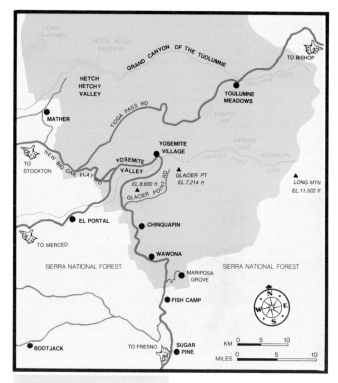

YOSEMITE NATIONAL PARK

but Muir discovered glaciers in the area, as well as the scars of ancient glaciers. He often explored the rim of the valley overnight carrying no more than a notebook, a tin cup and some tea.

Muir began to write of the Sierras, with great eloquence and literary style that captured the public's attention. He purposefully and incessantly used his pen to prod the public into political action to protect Yosemite and other wilderness areas in the Sierras. He became a powerful force with contacts in high places, and personally led President Theodore Roosevelt through the back country of Yosemite, the two men camping out in four-foot snow drifts. Muir convinced Roosevelt that large tracts of forest land should be protected from foresters. Under Muir's leadership, the fledgling Sierra Club became a forceful voice for preservation; it is now one of the most powerful groups in the entire American environmental protection movement.

Ironically, Muir's greatest political defeat also involved Yosemite. North of Yosemite Valley, and clearly within the park boundaries, was the **Hetch Hetchy Valley**, second only to Yosemite in the beauty of its sculpted canyon. The city of San Francisco decided to build a dam here, even though for a slightly greater investment it could have been built elsewhere.

The battle reached the Roosevelt Administration and Congress. The President supported the plan to build the dam within the boundaries of the park, despite Muir's objections. The hard-fought battle tore apart the conservation movement, pitting those who wanted to manage resources with planned and multiple uses against those who wanted to preserve the area exactly as it was (a rift that continues today within California and across the country). The battle dragged on for twelve years, until Congress finally approved the dam's construction, and building commenced in 1913. Muir, crushed by the defeat and the loss of the canyon, died a year later. But the battle over Hetch Hetchy made a powerful impact and contributed directly to the founding of the National Park Service in 1916, which ensured the creation of the park and helped formalize their boundaries.

HOW TO GET THERE

Yosemite National Park is located in the Sierras, east of the Monterey Bay area, across the San Joaquin Valley and beyond the foothills. No major freeway leads to it. Route 99, running north-south along the eastern edge of the valley, is the closest freeway to the west, and the point from which several local highways split off for Yosemite. There is no easy way to travel the length of the Sierras without leaving them and following the foothills or even returning to the flat central valley itself. Even in the foothills, only small winding roads zigzag along the length of the hills.

Highway 120 leads from Manteca in the northwest to the northern entrance to the park. Highway 41 comes from Fresno in the southwest, skirting the region of the Mariposa Grove, and Highway 140 goes directly east from Merced to the Yosemite Valley. This is the main entrance to the park. Highway 120 (closed in winter), to the north of the Yosemite Valley continues east into the high country of the Sierras, where the peaks are the most rugged. This beautiful road passes through Tuolumne Meadows, the junction and center for backpackers tackling some of the lovely high country trails; it continues to the steep Tioga Pass and down to I-395. As can be seen on the map, from Yosemite south-

wards to Sequoia National Park, this is the only highway that traverses the sharply ridged spine of the Sierras.

Public transportation to Yosemite is non-existent. The private bus company, the *Yosemite Transportation System (YTS)* (Tel. 373-4171), makes connections with commercial bus terminals in Lee Vining, Fresno and Merced, and with the *Amtrak* stations in Merced and Fresno. Fast one-day tours are also available from San Francisco, but don't blink or you'll miss something.

Hitchhiking within the park is quite acceptable. People who might not normally assist hitchers are willing to do so here, as it is clear that many hikers are making their way to trailheads at the beginning or end of a hike.

When Yosemite Valley is congested, a car can be as much of a liability as in an urban downtown, but you can take advantage of the *Valley Shuttle*. Leave your car at the campground, or in the Curry Village parking lot. Some of the buses are double-deckers, which are a novelty if you haven't been to England. Some areas are open only to shuttles or to bicycles, which can be rented. There are some beautiful rides on the valley floor; the path to Mirror Lake is a particularly recommended.

ACCOMMODATION

With very few exceptions, all eating and lodging concessions are run by the *Yosemite Park and Curry Company*. Reservations for private accommodations are made through one central office: *Yosemite Park and Curry Co.*, Yosemite National Park, 95389, Tel. 252-4848.

The greatest number and variety of lodgings are concentrated in the valley, but each of the regional centers of the park also provides private lodging. Tuolumne Meadows has tent-top cabins, a central dining lodge and drive-in and walk-in campgrounds. White Wolf, on the same road, has cabins and tents. Both facilities are open only in the summer. Wawona has lodges and the old *Wawona Hotel*.

Reservations for all Curry accommodations are essential in summer and are recommended all year round. A deposit of one day's rent must be paid in advance.

The *Ahwahnee Hotel* in the valley is a massive edifice of stone and timber, the kind of place where you want to sit by a roaring fire with a glass of sherry while recounting your tale of survival in a blizzard. Rooms cost around $200 per night; there are also two-story cottages. *Yosemite Lodge* is a more standard hotel with moderate to high-moderate prices. *Curry Village* is a sub-division with canvas roofs. The concrete-and-canvas Housekeeping

Camp units have double beds and wood burning stoves and cost slightly more than the Curry Village tents. Open in the summer only.

The Upper River, Lower River, North Pines, Lower Pines, and Upper Pines campgrounds are all drive-in areas at the east end of the valley. Reservations are required in advance for summer spots, but occasionally you can find someone willing to share a space, for partial fee payment. These sites are like parking lots covered in pine needles.

Do not, however, consider snoozing in your car along a dirt road or putting your sleeping bag down somewhere in the valley, because you will probably be caught and fined.

Two walk-in campgrounds in the valley often have space until late in the day, but don't rely on it during high summer season. Backpacker's Camp is located just behind the North Pines Campground, near Mirror Lake. Toward the western end of the valley is Sunnyside, used primarily by climbers, who tend to keep themselves apart. A few nights spent listening to them and you'll either be determined to scale El Capitan or equally determined never to climb a ladder again.

Motels, lodges and private campgrounds are also found in the small towns on the fringe of the park: in Lee Vining east of Tioga Pass, El Portal along Route 140, and Oakhurst along Route 41. Backcountry camping is free along the numerous mountain trails, but a wilderness permit is required. Even for backcountry hiking, reservations are recommended because the trails have quotas, and certain quotas fill up fast. Apply for a permit at the Yosemite Valley Visitor Center or at a ranger station; you may be asked for an approximate itinerary. Bear-proof lockers are available at some campgrounds.

There are drive-in campgrounds, heavily frequented by trailers, along the main highways throughout the park. Some on the outer periphery may have spots available early in the day as people leave. During the summer, it is wise to make reservations for these spots too. Two campgrounds in Yosemite Valley and one in Wawona remain open the year round.

The trail ascending the steep Half Dome

ACTIVITIES, SERVICES, GENERAL INFORMATION

The *Yosemite Guide*, a free newspaper, is your key to current park information. It contains a current

A sequoia tree at the Mariposa Grove

listing of all interpretive programs, facilities and services, general information, and feature articles. The guide is available at entrance stations, ranger stations, and visitor centers. Current road, weather and camping information is available by telephone. Consult the Yosemite Guide for numbers.

Special information for disabled visitors, and wheelchair-emblem placards for vehicles for special driving privileges are available on request at entrance and information stations.

Printed information in Spanish, Japanese, German, and French is also available on request.

The *Yosemite Road Guide* is a descriptive booklet keyed to numbered posts along park roads. It can be purchased at most information stations and gift shops in the park.

Numerous publications about the park are available at outlets throughout the park or by writing to Yosemite Natural History Association, Box 545, Yosemite National Park, 95389.

Every Visitor Center and some of the ranger stations conduct local campfire evenings, general and specialized walks such as early morning bird-watching and late night star gazing.

The park can be divided into three basic parts: the gently sloping west, with its groves of sequoia trees; Yosemite Valley, which is both the most beautiful and the most overcrowded, and the spectacular, jagged peaks of the high country, with Tuolumne Meadows as the central base. Within these areas is a remarkable range of terrain and animal life.

IMPORTANT PHONE NUMBERS
Area code: 209.
Tuolumne County Visitors Bureau: 55 W. Stockton Rd., P.O. Box 4020, Sonora, 95370, Tel. 533-4420 or 800-446-1333.
Yosemite National Park: Tel. 372-0264 or 800-452-1111.
Yosemite Concession Services Corporation: Curry Village, Yosemite National Park, Tel. 252-4848.
Yosemite Valley Campgrounds: Tel. 372-8502, Res. 800-365-2267.
Tuolumne Meadows Campgrounds: Tel. 372-4025, Res. 800-365-2267.
Yosemite Cross-Country Badger Pass Ski Area: Yosemite National Park, Tel. 372-1244.

Western Area

There are three groves of sequoia in Yosemite. **Tuolumne** and **Merced Groves** are located just inside the entrance along Highway 120. Near the southeast entrance off Highway 41, is the **Mariposa Grove**, which is the largest, and the one where there are free trams that circle through the grove accompanied by guides. Among the trees here is the Grizzly Giant, about 2,700 years old. A tunnel cut through another one of the trees, as a novelty, caused damage to the shallow root network over the years; a heavy snowfall finally toppled the tree. There are gentle trails, a small museum in a cabin, and plenty of opportunities to approach the trees directly.

Along Highway 41 on the way to the Yosemite Valley, **Wawona** is a business and service center offering related programs in the evening, as well as a restored historical village where frontier crafts are practiced and demonstrated; Stagecoach rides are offered. Gasoline is also available. The old, rambling building just south of the junction is *Wawona Hotel*, built in 1875 and still operating today. Food and lodging are available at the *Wawona*.

The one and only turnoff for the **Glacier Point Overlook** is also on Route 41, at Chiquapin Junction; it's a detour well worth taking. On the way to Glacier Point is the **Badger Pass Ski Area** (the road beyond this point is closed during the winter), Tel. 372-1244. From the edge of a sheer rock cliff dropping 3,200ft. (1,088m) to the valley floor, the view from Glacier Point is vast and fantastic; From this perspective, the glacial cut through the valley walls is clearly visible. Backing it all are the snow-covered peaks of the high Sierra. Bus tours from the valley floor reach this point. The Panoramic Trail is a beautiful trail of several miles from this point to the Yosemite Valley floor. The eight-mile (13km) trail offers a pleasant and not very strenuous hike.

Leave your car in the valley, hitch a ride up to Glacier Point, and then start hiking downhill. This will bring you to the top of Nevada Falls, and then past Vernal Falls. The descent past misty and verdant

A view of the valley and the Yosemite Falls from the Glacier Point Overlook

Vernal Falls leads to the valley floor, where a shuttle bus will take you back to your car.

The Valley

From naturalist John Muir to photographer Ansel Adams, artists, writers, and nature-lovers have been enchanted by Yosemite Valley. This glacier-carved canyon along the Merced River, with its sheer granite walls and bulging outcroppings, its sculpted domes and waterfalls plunging from hanging valleys, is one of the great natural wonders of the world. Over two million visitors visit Yosemite a year, and many of them never realize that the seven-mile (11km) valley is but a small sliver of the 1,200-square mile park.

Half Dome and **El Capitan** are probably the two best-known monoliths along the valley floor. Master mountain climbers try their skills on the sheer cliff of El Capitan. Half Dome can be reached by good hikers via the easier rear route; the last section of the hike is accomplished with the aid of cables embedded in the rock. There are incredible views from the top which is wider than its seems from below. The waterfalls are strongest around May when swollen with melted snow. The greatest of the waterfalls is **Yosemite Falls**, plunging over two falls, down 2,400ft. (816m). The other major falls are **Ribbon**, **Bridalveil**, **Nevada** and **Vernal Falls**. Vernal Falls and Nevada Falls are accessible from the Happy Isles Nature Center at the far eastern end of the valley, along the

The Yosemite Valley

steep, slippery Mist Trail. At the top, trails head towards Half Dome, Tuolumne Meadows and Glacier Point.

The valley can be a depressing place. It became so overdeveloped by the 1970s that the Park Service began to impose restrictions. The rows of trailers in the campgrounds, with two antennas and blasting radios, seem incongruous with the surroundings, and many of the stores and tourist facilities seem inappropriate to the character of the park. In recent years, the Park Service has closed down some tennis courts, redirected traffic, and introduced a campground reservation system for the valley; but with two million visitors a year, the valley can get awfully crowded.

Nevertheless, you should not miss the opportunity to explore the valley; there is an enormous amount to discover, especially in the huge park area beyond the lip of the valley.

The enormous El Capitan cliff

The valley is the center of everything in the park. Here you can rent horses, take climbing lessons or sit on the porch of the luxurious but rustic *Ahawanee Hotel*. Immerse yourself in spring's wildflowers in the mosaic of meadow and woodlands in the west.

Yosemite Valley has a comprehensive system of guided programs, and every visitor center in the park conducts its own programs too.

The Valley Visitor Center, located just west of Yosemite Village, provides an interesting introduction to the natural and human history of the valley and park. The **Indian Cultural Museum**, and the **Indian Village**, behind the Visitor Center, commemorate the local Indians who dwelled in this valley for thousands of years, hunting game and collecting acorns. At the eastern end of the valley, accessible by shuttle, is the **Happy Isles Nature Center**, named for the tiny islands formed by the confluence of the Merced River and Illouette Creek. Several heavily-wooded acres provide exhibits and information on the park's features; the

A general view of the High Sierra around Tuolumne Meadows

ranger on duty can answer questions. This is also the starting point (or end point) for the trail to Vernal Falls, Half Dome and Glacier Point.

Tuolumne Meadows

Tuolumne Meadows is the center for Yosemite's high country, and a base for motorists, day-hikers and overnight trekkers. The alpine meadows, the lakes and granite slopes in this area form some of the most stunning scenery in the High Sierra, and it is easily accessible from Tuolumne by even a short hike.

Tuolumne Meadows, the largest sub-alpine meadow in the Sierras, teems with wildflowers and wildlife in early summer. To the east, on Route 120 is the eastern entrance to the park, beyond Tioga Pass, which is about 10,000ft. (3,400m) high. Tuolumne Meadows is a hub for a network of short and long trails following the High Sierra watershed and penetrating into some of the wildest sections of Yosemite. The famous **Pacific Crest Trail** (called the John Muir Trail at this section) passes through here, and many hikers use this as a starting or endpoint for hiking one section of this trail. Ambitious and experienced hikers can follow the trail south all the way into the Sequoia National Park; there is a beautiful overnight hike from here to Yosemite Valley. Another beautiful route for good hikers follows the Tuolumne River into the appropriately named Grand Canyon of the Tuolumne, where horses can be hired.

One of the best times to visit Tuolumne, and the whole park, is early fall, before the November snowstorms. The aspens, willows, pines and other deciduous trees create a stunning autumnal collage. The guided activities are reduced after Labor Day, but there is still enough to keep the eager visitor busy, with the additional bonus of no crowds. Lodging, camping and motels in Lee Vining are more available.

The Eastern Slope

East of the high bulwark of the Sierras is a vast area of arid plateaus, twisted volcanic formations, and islands of forest and greenery. The main route along the eastern slope is I-395. No road crosses the spine of the Sierras south of the Tioga Pass in Yosemite to the separate, other-worldly eastern terrain. About 30 miles (app. 50km) north of the Tioga Pass, off I-395 to the east, is **Bodie**, one of the remnants of the little-known gold rush on the eastern slope of the Sierras. Once boasting a population of 12,000, 65 saloons, and an average of one murder a day, Bodie is now a genuine ghost town, preserved by the state park system in its state of natural decay. Pick up a visitors brochure at the ranger's house on Green St.

IMPORTANT PHONE NUMBERS

Area code: 619.

Mono Lake Chamber of Commerce: Hwy. 395 at Third St., P.O. Box 29, Lee Vining, Tel. 647-6595.

Lee Vining Chamber of Commerce: Hwy. 395 and Main St., P.O. Box 130, Lee Vining, Tel. 647-6629.

Mammoth Lakes Visitors Bureau: 3399 Main St., P.O. Box 48, Mammoth Lakes, 93546, Tel. 934-2712 or 800-367-6572.

Mammoth Mountain Bike Park/Adventure Challenge Course: One Minaret Rd., Mammoth Lakes, Tel. 934-0606 or 800-228-4947.

Due east of Lee Vining is **Mono Lake**, haunting and moon-like. The lava-strewn islands are the only remaining signs of ancient volcanic explosions from the depths of the lake. The tufa spires add to the strange appearance. It is possible to canoe on the lake, among the spires, and to take ranger-guided walks through this unusual landscape. The remnant of an ancient inland sea, Lake Mono has no outlet. The beaches around the lake are covered in eroded pumice. These lava-strewn islands constitute the state's largest rookery for California's gulls.

Mono Lake – strange geological formations

For years, state environmentalists and local groups have battled L.A., which has been diverting water from four of the five streams that feed the lake since 1941. This water, together with water from the Owens Valley, south of the lake, is diverted to Los Angeles by aqueduct, supplying most of the city's water supply. The level of the lake was lowered over the years by this diversion process, threatening the lake's brine shrimp colony and the California gulls that feed on them.

Mono Lake is managed by the Bureau of Land Management. Information on the lake and on tours can be obtained from the Lee Vining Information Center on I-395, as well as at the Bakersfield District Headquarters of the Bureau of Land Management: 800 Truxton, Room 302, Bakersfield, 93301, Tel. 805-861-4191.

Half-an-hour's drive south of this unearthly feature are the very earthly pleasures of **Mammoth Mountain**, a popular ski resort in alpine woods style, which is one of the largest in the country. In addition to the downhill ski slopes, there is an extensive network of cross-country trails, and hiking trails leading into the high country's **John Muir Wilderness**. The ski season is unusually long, lasting occasionally to the Fourth of July.

For information on Mammoth's ski conditions, call the 24-hour Snowline: Tel. 619-934-6166. Mammoth has a wide range of accommodations and restaurants. For the Visitors Bureau, call Tel. 619-934-2712 or 800-367-6572. The ranger station's Visitor Center, Tel. 714-924-1094 (24-hour recording) or 924-5500, can give details on camping grounds in the area.

Mammoth is located on Route 203, the gateway to some of the **Inyo National Forests**, scenic forested backcountry. Campgrounds open in late April or early May and stay open after Labor Day, until the first snows. As is true of most popular resorts, the prices here are a bit higher than in the periphery. For information call Tel. 619-873-2400.

Devil's Postpile National Monument also lies on Route 203. The 60-foot (20m) columns, resembling a giant pipe organ, were created 900,000 years ago as molten lava poured from the earth's crust. At Rainbow Falls, the San Joaquin River plunges 140ft. (48m) over lava ledges. **Oh! Ridge** provides a spectacular view of June Lake, as well as something just as rare in these parts: a campground that is not always full. In the summer, a shuttlebus operates from Minaret Summit to the monument. P.O. Box 501, Mammoth Lakes 93546, Tel. 209-565-3341 (winter), 209-934-2289 (summer).

The scrubby bristlecone pines, the oldest organisms in the world, grow in the bare, exposed terrain of the White Mountains. The sequoias are mere babes in the woods compared to the gnarled and grizzled bristlecones, which are more than 4,000 years old. The oldest, the 4,700 year-old Methuselah Tree, was already ancient at the beginning of the common era. Some of the fallen trees date back an incredible 9,000 years. The bristlecone pine forest is reached by taking U.S. 395 to Bigpine, about 15 miles (25km) south of Independence. Head east on Route 168 for 13 miles (20km), to Westgard Pass, then 10 miles (16km) north on White Mountain Rd. Contact the Inyo County Park Department for information: Tel. 619-878-2411. No gas, water, or commercial services are available in the forest itself. Evening ranger programs are held. There is an information station in the forest.

THE NORTH COAST:
MENDOCINO AND THE REDWOOD COUNTRY

The Mendocino Coast

The question periodically arises, even in the state legislature, regarding the northern section of California secession of the state. The joke hints that this part is different from the rest of the state, more attuned in geography, resources, climate, society and mentality to Oregon and the Pacific Northwest. There is hardly no Spanish influence: no missions, Spanish names, red-tile roofs or white-washed adobe. The tiny coastal villages seem to have been transplanted from New England, where many of the early settlements' founders originated.

This is the land of lumber. There are endless acres of towering trees, especially redwoods, but Douglas fir and others as well. Since the days of the earliest White settlements, the lumber industry dominated the region's economy, followed by fishing, ranching and other activities. The lumbermen rapidly cleared the slopes, suddenly threatening the two thousand year old redwoods with extinction. But the lumber industry itself has since fallen on hard times; the vast network of lumber operations and mill towns has shrunken over the years. The coast is dotted with the debris of an earlier age; barren stump-studded slopes, abandoned installations and mill towns.

Except for the quaint village of Mendocino, and the line of redwood parks to the north, there are few famous tourist sights in this neck of the woods. However, if you are a beach-stroller, bluff-climber, tide pool prober or light-house-lover, a hunter of driftwood, taster of wine, and fanatic for New

Fog blankets the Mendocino coastline

England you will find this area fascinating. The pace is slow, easy and relaxing.

Fog blankets the Mendocino coastline in summer, and storms pound it in winter. During the tourist season, from Memorial Day to Labor Day, the nights can be cool and damp. The fog is not constant, but when it drifts in, it can drip down your neck and wet your clothes.

In June, you'll witness the colorful explosion of azaleas and rhododendrons. October may surprise you with balmy days. But winter, stretching to April or even May, is a world of grey sea along grey cliffs, with foghorns bleating through grey fogs under grey clouds.

HOW TO GET THERE

By car, head north from San Francisco, inland along U.S. 101 or on Highway 1 along the coast. U.S. 101 is faster but bypasses the coastal rollercoaster road of Highway 1. Several roads connect the two parallel highways, offering the opportunity to see the beautiful diversity of this countryside, while still making good time.

Greyhound runs along U.S. 101, serving Ukiah and Willits, operating a line from Eureka as well, north toward Arcata and south toward Fort Bragg. A regular bus route between Fort Brag and Santa Rosa stops at Mendocino. The *Mendocino Transit Authority (MTA)* operates a coastal van between Eureka and Sonoma, stopping at junctions with links to the transportation networks of Sonoma County.

IMPORTANT PHONE NUMBERS

Area code: 707.
Chambers of Commerce:
Fort Bragg-Mendocino Coast: 332

N. Main St., Font Bragg, Tel. 961-6300 or 800-726-2780.
Ukiah: (serving Mendocino as well) 2112 Broadway, Eureka, Tel. 442-3738 or 800-356-6381.
Eureka/Humboldt County Convention and Visitors Bureau: 1034 Second St., Eureka, Tel. 443-5097 or 800-338-7352 (CA), 800-346-3482 (USA).
Mendocino Transit Authority: 241 Plant Rd., Ukiah, Tel. 462-1422.
Redwood National Park Information Center: P.O. Box 7, Orick 95555, Tel. 488-3461.
State Parks:
Mendocino/Fort Bragg area: Tel. 937-5804.
Prairie Creek Headquarters: Tel. 488-2171.

What to See

Heading up U.S. 101 brings you to Mendocino's well-known wine country. Valleys, ridges and mountains divide the region into a patchwork of "microclimates", creating individuality and variety

among the valleys, and great diversity among the grapes and wines produced there.

There are several cluster of wineries. The southern inland valley around Hopland, on U.S. 101, is fringed by vineyards. There are wineries at either end of town, with tasting rooms. For those with a more proletarian palate, try the **Mendocino Brewing Company.**

Further north, in the deep valley surrounding Ukiah, are more wineries, as well as restaurants and motels. For an especially lovely diversion off U.S. 101, turn northwest on Highway 128, just north of Cloverdale. This two-lane country road glides through the green and golden hills of the Anderson Valley, towards the coast. The wineries are scattered between Booneville and Navarro, interspersed with picnic areas stores along the way to pick up picnic fixings.

Driving north up Highway 1, the first town along the Mendocino coast is **Gualala**, an old lumbertown transformed to a more tourist-oriented center. The non-profit Gualala Arts organization presents the "Art in the Redwoods" festival in August. Store fronts in **The Gallery** center proffer some fine craftwork, paintings and sculpture. North of Gualala, the coastal road undulates past jutting cliffs, headland, coves, islands, slivers of beach, salt marshes and rare, fragile patches of giant dunes. Take your time here to relax and take in the scenery.

Don't miss a visit to the historic old and elegant **Miland Hotel** on Highway 1, north of Gualala, built at the beginning of this century.

About 4 miles (6.5km) north of Gualala is **Anchor Bay,** with restaurants and Bed & Breakfast accommodations. Protected on the north and south by jutting land masses, the coast here is sunny when the rest of the earth disappears in fog. Ten miles (16km) further north is **Point Arena**, with its lighthouse dominating the nearby bluff which can be climbed. Open 11am-2:30pm daily. Admission charge, Tel. 882-2777.

Mendocino, the muted jewel of this coast, began with the inauspicious name of Meiggsville. In the

19th century Harry Meiggs came seeking a wrecked cargo of Chinese silk. He ended up founding the area's first sawmill. Although Meiggs headed on to establish a rail system through the Andes, the logging industry remained and prospered. Meiggsville became Mendocino, a logger's town of saloons, hotels and brothels, all built in the gabled and turreted style of an old New England village. Today, it appears much the same, minus the brothels.

Be sure to take the self-guided walking map in the beautiful restored **Kelley House Museum**, 45007 Albion St., Tel. 937-5791, and wander around the lovely streets.

It is a quiet isolated village of artists, artisans, fishermen and small tourist oriented shops, which has maintained its dignity and charm.

The stark headland cliffs just beyond town which form Mendocino Headlands State Park are breathtaking. A walk along the cliffs on a foggy day, followed by a soak in one of the local hot tub establishments and a drink in a wood-paneled bar, makes for a beautiful day.

The Visitor Center for Mendocino Headlands State Park, at the Ford House on Main St., provides maps and information. Open Thurs.-Fri. noon-5:30pm, Sat.-Sun. 10am-5:30pm, Tel. 937-5804.

The **Mendocino Art Center** is the town's cultural and artistic center. 45200 Little Lake St. Open daily 10am-5pm, Tel. 937-5818. The influx of artists and the locally run art educational programs give the town a cosmopolitan touch; The center supports an art gallery which is open all week, and a Sunday afternoon concert series.

Considering the kind of small town resort it is, Mendocino's food and lodging are reasonably priced.

Russian Gulch State Park, Tel. 937-5804, lies just north of Mendocino, with its carved and pockmarked headland. It is a pleasant hike up Russian Gulch Creek to the waterfall. Further to the north, **Van Damme State**

Park (Tel. 937-5804) is known for its forest of waist high pygmy conifers. The trees, stunted by poor soil, manage to hang on. Admission charge.

Fort Bragg is a dirty industrial lumbertown of about 5,000, which stands out in contrast with the greenery around it. It has reliable, reasonably priced standard motels, as well as a few nice B&B lodges. Fort Bragg and Eureka have plenty of cheap eateries, as do some of the smaller mill towns along the coastal route. On Fort Bragg's North Harbor Dr., several seafood restaurants offer reasonably priced delicious meals, serving the morning's catch, hauled to Noyo Harbor by the local fleet.

South of Fort Bragg, the **Mendocino Coast Botanical Garden** encompasses 14 acres of dazzlingly colorfull shady glades. 18220 N. Hwy. 1, Fort Bragg. Open 9am-4pm, Nov.-Feb.; 9am-5pm Mar.-Oct., Tel. 964-4352. Route 20 itself provides a scenic and direct connection between the coastal road and 101, Fort Bragg and Willits. There's hardly a town to be seen, only endlessly stretching forests, with some camping spots. Here, the logging trucks on the road may slow you down on the narrow winding road.

An interesting option is to take the Skunk Train (so named for the smell of the early engines), along a 100-year old rail route, hewn through the mountains to haul lumber. An open-air car allows you to take in the wind and scenery. The 7-hour round trip from Fort Bragg includes an hour stop in Willits. A shorter ride chugs to the old logging town of Northspur. The depot is on Laurel south of Main St., Tel. 964-6371.

Redwood Country

I see that you're a logger, and not just a common bum, 'cause nobody but a logger stirs his coffee with his thumb.

American Folk Song

North of Fort Bragg, Route 1 veers inland at Rockport and joins Route 101 at Legget. North of Legget along the highway begin the parks of towering redwoods.

Today's redwood groves represent less than 10% of the vast acres that once flourished on the California coast. Of those surviving, slightly more than

50% are protected; the greatest concentration of these trees, including some of the tallest, grow along this section of the coast. They are of tremendous girth, towering well over 300 feet (120m; the length of an American football field), and sometimes grow so closely together that their hefty trunks appear to form a solid wall, generating shade, fog, and lush luminous greenery. In some areas the line between the protected forest and the shorn unprotected earth is starkly obvious, with the scarred, denuded land extending literally to the edge of protected groves.

ACCOMMODATION

The Mendocino area contains many B&Bs, some built in a distinctly New England style. Prices range from moderate to expensive, and facilities from rustic to luxurious. This is really the land of B&Bs. They fit in perfectly with the tone of the countryside, whereas regular motels spoil the country atmosphere.

There are some motels around, however. They can be found in Fort Bragg and Eureka. In the Eureka area, the average motel price is lower than in more southern parts.

Mendocino Hotel & Garden Cottages: 45080 Main St., Mendocino, Tel. 937-0511, Res. 800-548-0513. A well-known hotel in a beautiful setting, with rooms and cottages ranging from $50-$230, singles and doubles.

Benbow Inn: 445 Lake Benbow Dr., just south of Garberville, Tel. 923-2124, Res. 800-355-3301. Has remained a pocket of rustic elegance for many years. Expensive, but it may be just right for a special occasion.

Camping

From the Mendocino area north to the Oregon border, state parks with camping facilities are plentiful along the beaches and in the region of the major redwood groves. Many have drive-in campgrounds, while others have more primitive walk-in campgrounds, and campgrounds primarily for hikers and cyclists.

In the Mendocino area, *Russian Gulch State Park*, Tel. 937-5804, is particularly beautiful. *MacKerricher State Park*, 3 miles (5km) miles north of Fort Bragg, is popular, Tel. 937-5804. State parks in the vicinity of Avenue of the Giants tend to fillup quickly.

For State park information in the Mendocino/Fort Bragg region, call Tel. 937-5804. For state park camping information in the Redwood National Park area, call the office in Crick: Tel. 488-2171.

A youth hostel run by the AYH is located in Klamath, *Redwood National Park Hostel*, 14480 Hwy 101, Tel. 482-8265.

FOOD

Brannon's Whale Watch: 45040 Main St. Entered through an old whale-watching tower, this spot is popular for lunch and breakfast. The upstairs view will make you want to linger over another cup of coffee.

The Cheese Shop: Little Lake and Lansing, Mendocino. The atmosphere many be rural but the selection is fit for a gourmet; you can find everything needed for a picnic on the headlands.

Seagull Inn Cellar Bar: Lansing and Ukiah St., Mendocino. The beautiful bar is actually upstairs. Locals and visitors drink and listen to the live music.

Cap'n Flint's: 32250 North Harbor Dr., Noyo Harbor, Fort Bragg. A popular local seafood restaurant. Reasonably priced.

Samoa Cookhouse: 445 West Washington St., Eureka. This was a genuine lumbercamp cookhouse. The dinners are filling enough.

What to See

Coming from the south, **Richardson Grove State Park**, Tel. 247-3318, is the first redwood park, about eight miles (13km) south of Garberville. One of the smaller ones, it nevertheless has some stunning groves. It is very popular, and its three campgrounds are often full in the summer. The information center has regular ranger programs and guided hikes.

North of Garberville is the **Humboldt Redwoods State Park**. The largest redwood park in the region, it links together several separate groves, including the famous **Avenue of the Giants**, along which most visitors to the park pass. From the south, the route begins about six miles (10km) north of Garberville. This 33-mile (53km) stretch of road parallels Route 101 and the south fork of the Eel River. It passes through lush and misty pockets carpeted with ferns and moss; the endless walls of redwoods on either side cast everything in deep, cool shadow. **Rockefeller** and **Founder's Grove** are the best known groves. They encompass some of the tallest of the redwoods. There is a pleasant nature trail at Founder's Grove. The Visitors Center offers an explanation of the natural history of these groves, and also schedules campfire programs and guided hikes from July to Labor Day. For information on park activities, call Tel. 946-2409.

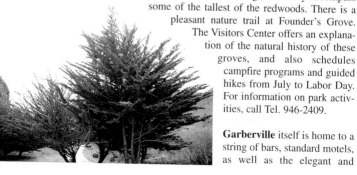

Garberville itself is home to a string of bars, standard motels, as well as the elegant and expensive *Benbow Inn*, which in its heyday gave shelter to such luminaries as Herbert Hoover and Spencer Tracy.

Garberville is also the reputed center for the local marijuana industry. This is no small honor, for marijuana has become one of California's biggest cash crops, though the travel brochures don't mention this. These coastal hills and valleys form the center of the high country.

In the 60s and 70s, when thousands of young emigrants from the urban mainstream headed for the hills seeking a simpler, home-spun way of life, they brought their smoking habits with them. Garden plots of home-grown marijuana crops turned into a cottage industry; sophisticated techniques and experimentation improved the quality and potency of the product. Markets were developed in the cities, especially as the American government squeezed or threatened to squeeze the Mexican sources. Marijuana fields proliferated in the isolated hills and valleys. Local authorities even distributed instructions for hikers who stumble upon a marijuana plot during a stroll. They launched raids

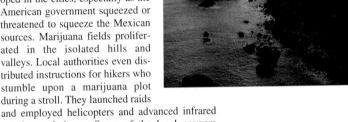

and employed helicopters and advanced infrared spotting techniques. Some of the local growers who have been transformed from rebels into hip entrepreneurs guard their investments with armed sentries and watchdogs.

Parallel to the stretch of redwood parks, the coast extends toward **Cape Mendocino**. No roads run along the length of this rough coastline, but various inland roads reach the coast. The towns in this region known as **"The Lost Coast"** were once thriving fishing, lumber and mining communities, but were bypassed when the highways and the port at Eureka were planned.

From South Fork on U.S. 101, take Mattele Rd. west toward **Petrolia**, for a worthwhile excursion. The area which is not frequented by crowds is pristine and primitive. The road skirts the **Kings Range National Conservation Area** (primitive campgrounds, with no registration needed), then passes through Petrolia, and later hugs the headlands. There are stretches of black beach, where

one can enjoy silence and solitude. Further along is the little doll-house town of **Ferndale**. The restaurants here are reasonably priced, the shops unusual, and the home-made candies delicious. The **Ferndale Museum** at Shaw and 3rd gives a vivid glimpse of North Coast history. Open Wed.-Sat. 11am-4pm, Sun. 1pm-4pm; Jun.-Sep. Tues.-Sat. Small admission, Tel. 786-4466.

Eureka, situated on Humboldt Bay, is a typical lumbertown, from its trucks to its smokestacks to the lumberjack breakfast specials. The industrial rumbling and dirt contrasts sharply with the intricate old rambling Victorian buildings which bear witness to the old lumber kingdoms.

The prime example of this opulent style from the past is the **Carson Mansion** at 2nd and M St., near the refurbished business district. Nearby is the **Clarke Museum** with an exquisite marble exterior and collections portraying local Indian and pioneer culture. 240 East St. Open Tues.-Sat. noon-4pm. Donation required, Tel. 443-1947.

Fort Humboldt sits on a hill, overlooking the bay. The museum and logging exhibits give a feel for the rough and simple lifestyle of a typical 'jack. Located at 3431 Fort Ave. off U.S. 101. Open daily 9am-5pm. Admission free, Tel. 445-6567.

Arcata, 10 miles (16km) to the north, home of **Humboldt State University**, has a few fancy cafés and restaurants. The university's National History Museum, on 1315 G St., exhibits dinosaurs and other fossils, butterflies and shells. Open Tues.-Sat. 10am-4pm. Donation recommended. Tel. 826-4479.

The unique annual Arcata-to-Ferndale **Kinetic Sculpture Race** in April stipulates that all entries must be amphibious and human-powered.

The **Redwood National Park** merges with three state parks – Jedediah Smith, Prairie Creek and Del Norte – to form a contiguous 30-mile (48km) strip of protected redwood land, between Crick and Crescent City. In most areas the park parallels U.S. 101 on both sides of the road, and the drive through is beautiful in itself. The parks include a shoreline of beautiful duned beaches, rocky coves and bluffs. There are pull-offs and parking areas which afford access to paths for strolling and to various groves. The **Tall Tree** grove can be reached by an 8-mile (13km) hike or by shuttlebus in the summer from the **Redwood National Park Information Center**, located one mile south of Orick on U.S. 101, Tel. 488-3461. Sections of the park clearly show how real and immediate the threat to the redwoods is; the earth has been stripped right up to the park border.

The trails in the park make good day trip routes or sites for single overnights, but are not so suitable for extensive backpacking. There are nature trails at the Lady Bird Johnson Grove and Lagoon Creek; one trail near the Prairie Creek headquarters is suitable for both sighted and blind people. Prairie Creek, closer to the ocean than some of the other parks, is especially luxuriant in ferns, lichens, moss and other plant ground cover. In **Jedediah Smith**, canoes and kayaks glide along the Smith River in summer.

The **Prairie Creek Headquarters** on U.S. 101 in Crick has exhibits and information. Open daily 8am-5pm, until 8pm in summer, Tel. 488-2171.

SHASTA AND LASSEN

The northern border region of California is rugged, isolated and stunning. It is a different world up here. The mountain scenery is as gorgeous and overwhelming as in the Sierras though geomorphologically quite different, and here there are no crowds. Enormous amounts of snow fall on the foothills of the Cascade Range, which extends all the way up to Washington. Valleys of fertile volcanic soil are filled with flowers in spring. There are high, semi-arid plateaus, black twisted volcanic formations, and bubbling sulfuric pools. The long Central Valley, which extends southwards as far as Bakersfield, reaches its northern limit around Red Bluff and Redding at the southernmost peaks of the Cascades.

To the north and west of Lake Tahoe, the Sierra Nevada mountains seem to merge with the Cascades, but in fact they are two distinct ranges. The peaks of the Cascades in California – Mt. Shasta, Mt. Lassen and the others - were shaped by volcanic action, and the formation of this mountain landscape is by no means complete. Frozen lava flows in the north are only 500 years old, and in the Lassen area, there was volcanic activity as recently as 1915.

Some quaint old mining and logging towns have been spruced up a bit for tourists. The 1849 gold rush extended this far north, and in fact there were several major finds here. The main attractions in California's far north are the wonderful natural formations, and the recreational opportunities which they afford. The main recreation areas are Whiskeytown-Shasta-Trinity National Recreation Area, Mt. Lassen Volcanic National Park and Lava Beds National Monument. Surrounding each of these protected areas are huge tracts of national forest land.

IMPORTANT PHONE NUMBERS
Area code: 916.
Mt. Shasta Visitors Bureau: 300 Pine St., Mount Shasta, Tel. 926-4865 or 800-926-4865.
Lassen County Chamber of

Commerce: 84 N. Lassen St., P.O. Box 338, Susanville, 96130, Tel. 257-4323.
Mount Shasta Ski Park: 104 Siskiyou, Mount Shasta, Tel. 926-8610.

I-5 is the main traffic artery penetrating the northern mountains, coming from the Central Valley and continuing into the central valley of Oregon. In the Lassen-Shasta area, along the I-5 route are the two main towns in the region; **Red Bluff** and **Redding**. Red Bluff is indeed located on a red bluff above the Sacramento River. Between these two towns, a traveler can find most of the basic necessary amenities. There are good reasonably priced restaurants as well as the usual fast-food stands, and several basic reasonably priced motels. For forays into the backwoods, stock up in advance on necessities – the range of items is broader and prices lower than in the national parks or small mountain towns.

The rodeo round up at Red Bluff

A popular circular route passes through both the Mt. Lassen and Mt. Shasta regions. Follow I-5 north beyond Redding and through the national recreation area, to the town of **Mt. Shasta**, which is situated at the foothills of the massive mountain of the same name. The town is small, with some motels, restaurants and grocery stores, and serves as a re-entry point for serious climbers and backpackers who roam the national forest which includes Mt. Shasta (the mountain, not the town), or the peak itself (this is only for experienced climbers). From this point, Route 89 heads east, and then curves south toward Mt. Lassen. Several small towns are connected by this highway. South of Lassen's national park, Route 36 turns west toward Red Bluff and I-5. A glance at the map will show that, in addition to this basic loop, there are numerous other options in the region.

The **Whiskeytown-Shasta-Trinity National Recreation Area**, north and west of Redding, is made up of three separate, unconnected units (thus the three-part name). At the center of each area is an artificial lake, created by the damming and channeling of waters for the benefit of Central Valley agriculture. Although the natural water courses were modified, and reservoirs were created in dry valleys, the surrounding areas were protected and reserved for public use. The lakes created by the Central Valley Water Project (launched as a federal work project during the Depression), filled the various dips and folds of the valleys and formed long, winding shorelines filled with coves and peaceful backwaters. For information on the entire area call the Visitor Information Center, Tel. 246-5154.

The lakes, especially in the Whiskeytown and Shasta sections, draw armadas of sailboats, powerboats, windsurfers and waterskiers. On **Shasta Lake**, huge houseboats can be rented and navigated at slow speeds along the various byways of the long lake, Tel. 275-5555 or 800-4-SHASTA. The **Shasta Dam** itself, at the confluence of the Sacramento, Pit and McCloud rivers, is one of the world's largest, and the centerpin of the Central Valley project. Free tours are given from 9am-4pm daily in the summer, Tel. 275-4463.

In the northwestern area of the Trinity section of the recreation area, is the **Salmon-Trinity Alps Wild Area**, an uncrowded and beautiful hiking region.

The Trinity Alps embrace more than 55 lakes, mountain ridges and deep canyons between the Trinity River and Salmon River. Permits are required for backcountry campers. Before hiking in this isolated wilderness, be sure to check conditions by calling forest service headquarters in Weaverville, Tel. 623-2121.

The volcanic forces over the ages have given the Lassen terrain an appearance and feel all its own. The park is dominated by **Mt. Lassen**, a plugged volcanic peak. From 1914, eruptions occurred intermittently for seven years and it exhibits a variety of volcanic formations. Extensive trails wander among hot pools, volcanic peaks and lush valleys enriched by volcanic soil.

Many of the main attractions near the main road are accessible by car or on foot from the main road. The park's two Visitor Information Centers are located near the northwest entrance, at **Manzanita Lake** and at the southwest entrance near **Sulphur Works**. The main park road, **Route 89**, arcs around the base of Mt. Lassen itself. The central portion of this highway is closed in winter due to the heavy snows, which can fall as early as October, lasting into late spring.

The main route to the park follows I-5 north to Red Bluff, and then Route 36 heading east. This road passes park headquarters at **Mineral**, Tel. 595-4444. Train service is available to Red Bluff. *Greyhound* runs to Mineral. It is advisable to stock up on groceries in Red Bluff or Redding rather than in the park.

Sulphur Works is not a factory but a thermal area of steam vents, irides-cent hot pools and bubbling mudpots. It can be reached by a two-mile (3km) self-guided trail. The **Bumpass Hell** self-guiding trail leads to the largest concentration of hot springs in the park. The round trip is about 2.5 miles (4km). The trail to the summit of Mt. Lassen is about 2.5 miles in one direction, but do not be misled by the short length of the trail. It is a tough climb along switchbacks to the 10,457ft. (3,555m) high peak. Take your time, and bring a sweater and hiking shoes appropriate for snow, even in summer. The view from the top is breath-taking.

Many trails head to the east of the park, which has almost no regular roads. There is a variety of loop-hikes which go past strings of alpine lakes. A segment of the Pacific Crest Trail crosses the park.

There are several main camping areas in the Lassen Park. Those near the road are, of course, the most crowded. The walk-in campground at Sulphur Works is near the hot pools and away from the crowds. Outside the park to the north is a vast expanse of forest service territory, with developed sites as well as plenty of dirt roads and places for camping. At the towns of Red Bluff and Redding on I-5 a wide array of accommodation are avail-able at reasonable prices. Basic, simple motel rooms are available for $40 per night and some-times less.

Lava Beds National Monument, located just below the Oregon border in the northeastern portion of California, is known for its strange lava forma-tions, and for the short but dramatic Modoc Indian War of 1872-73.

The sharp craggy landscape is the result of 5 million years of volcanic activity which has continued right up to very recent times. The youngest cinder cones are only 1,000 years old.

The rich volcanic soil supports a complex plant and animal community. For centuries the Modoc Indians hunted in the valleys and mountains, and used the reeds in Tule Lake to fashion their homes and boats.

The Modocs were connected with other Indian bands that lived in the Klamath Basin, which extends into Oregon. As settlers moved into the region, the American government attempted to relocate the native Americans together on a reservation, including tribes that had been age-old enemies. The Modocs wanted a reservation on their own land, and over a period of years began deserting their assigned reservation, until an army expedition was dispatched in 1872. Under the leadership of a chief named Captain Jack, 52 Indian rebels dug into the natural fortress of the lava beds and caves, and held off over 1,000 soldiers for five months. The Indian force was gradually whittled down or captured, until Captain Jack finally surrendered. He was hanged, along with three other leaders, and what was left of his band was taken to a reservation in Oklahoma.

The main approach to the park is from Route 39 to the east. The monument is about 30 miles (48km) south of the town of Tulelake, and 58 miles (92km) from Klamath Falls in Oregon. Public transportation reaches Klamath Falls, where cars can be rented.

A single road runs the length of the park, in a crescent from the northeast to the southeast corner. There is an information kiosk near the northeast entrance, but the main information center is near the southeast entrance, Tel. 667-2282. Admission charge.

Black lava flows and various lava formations can be seen throughout the park. Much of the monument is inaccessible by auto, and more than half is designated wilderness area. Ranging in elevation from 4,000 to 5,700 feet (1,360m to 1,940m), the monument is exposed to cold weather and snow during all seasons.

The park's sites divide roughly into two parts. In the north are historical reminders of the heroic but futile Modoc War, including **Captain Jack's Stronghold** with a self-guided trail through it. The monument's best known features, the innumerable lava tubes and caves, are concentrated mainly in the south, near the visitor center.

The visitor center presents exhibits on the Modoc Indians. Adjacent **Mushpot Cave** – the only one which is illuminated – offers explanations on the geology of the area; A film is screened four times daily. Other caves can be explored by flashlight. Flashlights can be borrowed from the visitor center. Guidebooks to the caves are on sale, and plastic helmets can be rented. The **Cave Loop Road**, dotted with caves, begins at the visitor center and is the most accessible and popular area for some easy amateur spelunking.

Daily guided walks, cave trips and campfire programs are available in the summer. During the winter, deer wander into the area in large numbers, and observing them is a popular activity. Situated on the Pacific Flyway, the monument is a fantastic place to observe the migrations of ducks and geese during the spring and fall. They fly by the millions over this territory, often stopping here to rest.

The main campground is located at **Indian Well**, near the visitor center. Off-the-road camping is allowed in the **Modoc National Forest**, Tel. 667-2246. Free sites are found at the forest service campground of Howard's Gulch, 30 miles (48km) south on Route 139. Reasonably priced standard motels are found in Tulelake.

The snowy Mt. Shasta

INDEX

INDEX

QUESTIONNAIRE

In our efforts to keep up with the pace and pulse of California, we kindly ask your cooperation in sharing with us any information which you may have as well as your comments. We would greatly appreciate your completing and returning the following questionnaire. Feel free to add additional pages.

Our many thanks!

To: Inbal Travel Information (1983) Ltd.
18 Hayetzira St.
Ramat Gan 52521
Israel

Name: _____

Address: _____

Occupation: _____

Date of visit: _____

Purpose of trip (vacation, business, etc.): _____

Comments/Information: _____

_____

_____

_____

_____

_____

_____

INBAL Travel Information Ltd.
P.O.B 1870 Ramat Gan
ISRAEL 52117